TOURO COLLEGE LIBRARY
Midtown

WITHDRAWN

D1058563

Costs and Consequences of Placing Children in Care

Child Welfare Outcomes
Series Editor: Harriet Ward, Centre for Child and Family Research, Loughborough University
The Child Welfare Outcomes series draws on current research and policy debates to help social work managers and policy makers understand and improve outcomes of services for children and young people in need. Taking an evidence-based approach, these books include children's own experiences as well as analysis of costs and effectiveness in their assessment of interventions, and provide guidance on how to develop more effective policy, practice and training.

also in the series

Young People's Transitions from Care to Adulthood
International Research and Practice
Edited by Mike Stein and Emily R. Munro
ISBN 978 1 84310 610 4

Babies and Young Children in Care
Life Pathways, Decision-making and Practice
Harriet Ward, Emily R. Munro and Chris Dearden
ISBN 978 1 84310 272 4

Safeguarding and Promoting the Well-being of Children,
Families and Communities
Edited by Jane Scott and Harriet Ward
Foreword by Maria Eagle MP
ISBN 978 1 84310 141 3

of related interest

The Pursuit of Permanence
A Study of the English Child Care System
Ian Sinclair, Claire Baker, Jenny Lee and Ian Gibbs
ISBN 978 1 84310 595 4

Costs and Outcomes in Children's Social Care
Messages from Research
Jennifer Beecham and Ian Sinclair
Foreword by Parmjit Dhanda MP, Parliamentary Under Secretary of State for Children,
Young People and Families
ISBN 978 1 84310 496 4

Residential Child Care
Prospects and Challenges
Edited by Andrew Kendrick
ISBN 978 1 84310 526 8
Research Highlights in Social Work series

Managing Children's Homes
Developing Effective Leadership in Small Organisations
Leslie Hicks, Ian Gibbs, Helen Weatherly and Sarah Byford
ISBN 978 1 84310 542 8
Costs and Effectiveness of Services for Children in Need series

Costs and Consequences of Placing Children in Care

Harriet Ward, Lisa Holmes and Jean Soper

TOURO COLLEGE LIBRARY
Midtown

WITHDRAWN

Jessica Kingsley Publishers
London and Philadelphia

MT

First published in 2008
by Jessica Kingsley Publishers
116 Pentonville Road
London N1 9JB, UK
and
400 Market Street, Suite 400
Philadelphia, PA 19106, USA

www.jkp.com

Copyright © Harriet Ward, Lisa Holmes and Jean Soper 2008

All rights reserved. No part of this publication may be reproduced in any material form (including photocopying or storing it in any medium by electronic means and whether or not transiently or incidentally to some other use of this publication) without the written permission of the copyright owner except in accordance with the provisions of the Copyright, Designs and Patents Act 1988 or under the terms of a licence issued by the Copyright Licensing Agency Ltd, Saffron House, 6-10 Kirby Street, London EC1N 8TS UK. Applications for the copyright owner's written permission to reproduce any part of this publication should be addressed to the publisher.

Warning: The doing of an unauthorised act in relation to a copyright work may result in both a civil claim for damages and criminal prosecution.

Library of Congress Cataloging in Publication Data
Costs and consequences of placing children in care / Harriet Ward ... [et al.].
    p. cm.
Includes bibliographical references.
    ISBN 978-1-84310-273-1 (hb : alk. paper) 1. Child care--Economic aspects--Great Britain. 2.
Child care services--Great Britain. 3. Children--Institutional care--Great Britain. I. Ward, Harriet, 1948-
    HQ778.7.G7C67 2008
    338.4'33627120941--dc22

                                            2008004451

British Library Cataloguing in Publication Data
A CIP catalogue record for this book is available from the British Library

ISBN 978 1 84310 273 1

Printed and bound in Great Britain by
Athenaeum Press, Gateshead, Tyne and Wear

7/28/09

Contents

List of Tables

List of Figures

Preface

The Costs and Consequences of Placing Children in Care aims to contribute to the current debate on how effective policies and practices can be introduced to improve outcomes for looked after children. While it focuses on children who are placed in the care of local authorities, its messages are important to the development of services for all children in need.

This book is the fourth volume in the *Child Welfare Outcomes* series, edited by Harriet Ward and produced by Jessica Kingsley Publishers. Earlier volumes have covered the development of services to safeguard and promote the wellbeing of children, families and communities, experiences of babies and very young children in care, and international messages concerning transitions to adulthood of care leavers. The series draws from original research and current debates to help social work managers and policy makers to understand and improve the outcomes of services for children in need. *The Costs and Consequences of Placing Children in Care* focuses on a theme that has only relatively recently begun to receive attention: how far improved understanding of the costs and effectiveness of services can lead to better decisions about the deployment of resources necessary to promote children's wellbeing.

This book describes a research and development initiative that began with a study designed to devise a methodology for calculating the costs incurred when children are looked after by local authorities and exploring relationships between costs and outcome. However it became evident that both the methodology for costing children's pathways through care and the computer application developed to perform the cost calculations had a potential value that went beyond the original study. Both are now being extended to cover a wider group of children and a broader range of services. The software application has also been developed from a research instrument into a practical tool to support planning and decision-making in children's services at both individual and strategic levels. As the Cost Calculator for Children's Services, it is now being implemented in a number of local authorities. This book covers the rationale for constructing the Cost Calculator for Children's Services and the empirical research that has informed its development.

However it should be emphasized that this book is not about cutting costs or reducing services, but about ensuring that resources are optimally used to the advantage of the children and young people they are intended to support. At the heart of the book are the children and young people who entered the care of the six local authorities participating in our initial study and whose experiences formed the basis for our calculations. The case studies given in Chapter 5 provide vivid illustrations of the extent of their needs and the costs in delivering services necessary to promote their wellbeing. Identifying where and how resources are spent to good effect, and where they could be better deployed, is a key element in the current national initiative to promote better outcomes for these young people.

The year 2008 is important for the development of child welfare policy in England and Wales. A new White Paper, focusing on looked after children: *Care Matters: Time for Change* (Department for Education and Skills 2007a), was published as we were editing the final chapters of this book, and a new Bill is being presented to Parliament as we go to press. By the time this book is published, new legislation will have reached the statute book. The Children and Young Person's Act 2008 will seek to ensure that children and young people who enter the care system receive high quality care and support and that they are able to share the same aspirations as those who live in supportive family homes. The research and development programme that we describe in this book aims to provide child welfare agencies with some of the evidence and tools they need to implement this legislation.

This is a complex book and it could not have been produced without the help of a large number of people. The research has been supported by grants from the Department of Health, the Department for Education and Skills (now Children, Schools and Families) and the Economic and Social Research Council (ESRC), as well as receiving funding from a number of local authorities. We are grateful for their support, and particularly for the advice and assistance given by Carolyn Davies and Richard Bartholomew at the Department for Children, Schools and Families. The programme of research has also benefited from the generous support of our advisory group, whom we also wish to thank: Jennifer Beecham, Sarah Byford, Helen Chambers, Peter Clark, Jonathan Corbett, Isabella Craig, Elaine Dibben, Jenny Gray, Helen Jones, David Quinton, John Rowlands, Marjorie Smith, Shiraleen Thomas, Caroline Thomas, Steve Walker and Katy Young.

The book would never have been completed without the editorial assistance of Emma Batchelor, whose calm support and expert attention to detail have been invaluable. Richard Olsen did some of the data collection and qualitative analysis and wrote the penultimate draft of Chapter Seven; he was a valued member of the original team and we are particularly grateful for his contribution. We would also like to thank Alison Wynn, who managed the research database and performed some of the statistical calculations and Jenny Blackmore, Rosemary Chapman, Don Nicholson, Mary Ryan and Jo Tunnard who collected data and conducted some of the interviews. Programming the intricate cost calculator model is a complex task. The code and the reports that it generates were initially formulated by Andrew Soper; the Unit Cost Database was originally designed by Mike Gatehouse; both are now very ably being developed as the Cost Calculator for Children's Services by Gill Lewis and Jessica Wang at Vantage Training Limited; many thanks to all these people for their expert assistance and advice.

We particularly wish to thank the six local authorities that participated in the original study that forms much of the focus of this book, the pilot authority which helped identify data collection and methodological issues, and the 17 others that have subsequently contributed to developing the cost calculator model further. Most important of all are the children and young people whose experiences are the core subject of this book; particular thanks to those who agreed to be interviewed. We hope that the findings help to improve and strengthen the services that support them.

Authors' Note on Cost Comparisons

The unit costs given in this book have been calculated at different times for what has become an extensive research programme that began in 2000 and is still ongoing. In order to facilitate comparisons we have, wherever appropriate, shown costs inflated to the most up to date prices available (2006–7) at going to press. Where costs have been inflated, this has been done by using Personal Social Services Research Unit (PSSRU) pay and prices inflators to 2005–6 (the latest year for which they are available) and the Treasury GDP deflator estimate to 2006–7. The inflation over the period was estimated at 25.8 per cent.

Many of the tables in this book show costs calculated from data collected from a sample of 478 children who were looked after by six local authorities over a 20-month timeframe. For various reasons explained in Chapter 2, there were different numbers of children selected for the sample from each authority. In order to facilitate comparisons we have frequently shown annual costs estimated for 100 children. Such calculations have been complicated by large numbers of children (177) who left the care of the authorities during the period, and by substantial variations in the percentage of leavers in each authority (ranging from 25% to 48%). Children who left the care of the authorities tended to be those who cost less while they were looked after than those who stayed; therefore estimating costs either by artificially extending the last placements of leavers to the end of the study, or by excluding leavers from the calculations would have produced a skewed picture.

We have therefore estimated annual costs for 100 children by dividing each cost by the number of placement days to which it relates (giving costs per day for the process) and then multiplying by the number of days for which 100 children would be looked after in a full year (36,500 days).

Chapter 1

Introduction

Introduction

How much does it cost to place a child in the care of a local authority? According to the most recent published data, the average gross weekly expenditure in 2006–7 for looking after a child in foster or residential care in England was £753 (The Information Centre for Health and Social Care 2007), or just over £39,000 per year: over 45 per cent more than the cost of sending a child to Eton. Are these costs accurate, and if so, why are they so high? Why are there substantial variations in costs both between and within local authorities, and how far do these relate to differences in children's needs? Most importantly, do higher costs reflect better services, and better outcomes for children? How, in other words, can we count the costs of care and accommodation, both in terms of expenditure to the local authority and value to the child, his or her family and the wider society?

There are a number of reasons why these questions have become increasingly pertinent over the last few years. First, a wide body of research has now demonstrated that outcomes for children looked after away from home can be less than satisfactory (Department for Education and Skills 2007a). Although some do well, we now know that many of those who spend long periods in care or accommodation achieve a poor standard of education (Jackson 2001; Social Exclusion Unit 2003). They may also become socially isolated (Bullock, Little and Millham 1993; Stein and Munro 2008). Their health may be indifferent or poor, and emotional or behavioural difficulties may deteriorate during the period in which they are looked after (Butler and Payne 1997; McCann *et al.* 1996; Ward 2002). Moreover, a number of inquiries and research studies have demonstrated that children who are looked after for their own protection sometimes continue to be abused in care or accommodation (Department of Health 1995a; Utting 1997; Waterhouse 2000). Questions are continually raised concerning the capacity of the state to take on the role of the corporate parent (Bullock *et al.* 2006).

Findings that seem to demonstrate disappointing outcomes for children who are placed in care or accommodation are compounded by information concerning the high costs of providing such a service. The numbers of children entering care each year in England have decreased by at least 25 per cent since 1996; most recent figures suggest that they have now fallen to 23,700 (Department for Children, Schools and Families 2007a). However this decline in numbers has been accompanied by a rise in costs per child, as those who are looked after stay for longer periods and/or are offered increasingly costly placements (Department for Education and Skills 2006).

Particular concerns have been expressed about the widespread use of agency placements, which are often more costly than those provided 'in house', although as yet providing little evidence of better outcomes (see Ayres 1997); however research suggests that when the exceptional needs of the children concerned, and the services provided to meet those needs, are taken into account, the disparities in costs are less extensive (Sellick and Howell 2004; Sellick 2006).

Although the above may represent a gloomy picture of a failing service, this is not necessarily an accurate interpretation. We do not know to what extent poor outcomes for this very vulnerable group of children are inevitable, given the extent of deprivation that they may have experienced prior to being looked after; indeed, we do not know whether these children would have experienced substantially worse outcomes had they remained at home. We are, however, beginning to gather evidence that shows that a high proportion of this group have physical or learning disabilities, poor physical health and/or emotional and behavioural disorders, and poor educational experiences at the point of entry to care or accommodation, all of which might go some way to explaining their relatively poor outcomes at exit (see Sempik, Ward and Darker 2008; Darker, Ward and Caulfield 2008; Meltzer *et al.* 2003). Such evidence goes some way to explain the high cost of the service; it also demonstrates that, if their life chances are to be improved, many of these children will require extensive compensatory care, provided by a range of agencies working in co-ordination with one another. The study that forms the focus of this book is one of several which have found it difficult to identify how far looked after children benefit from the help of professionals other than social workers, such as mental health practitioners or specialist teachers, simply because access to their services is rarely routinely recorded on social work case files (Gatehouse, Statham and Ward 2004; Cleaver *et al.* 2007a).

We know that effective early interventions are important if long-term distress and dependency on services in adulthood is to be avoided. However, shortages of resources and concerns about adverse outcomes have meant that agencies have tended to raise the threshold at which children are placed in care or accommodation. Consequently, those children who now become looked after are likely to be amongst the most needy and difficult to engage with, and the resulting concentration of extremely vulnerable children within the system may well have contributed to the increasing costs of the service. It is estimated that a very much higher proportion of young people in residential units have identifiable psychiatric disorders than those living in the community (Meltzer *et al.* 2003). There is also some evidence to suggest that attempts to hold together untenable family situations so that children wait longer before they are placed away from home, or are returned prematurely and quickly readmitted, have exacerbated the difficulties with which these children have to contend (Packman and Hall 1998; Sinclair, Wilson and Gibbs 2001; Ward, Munro and Dearden 2006). One question posed by this book is whether, by deferring admission to care until young people display behaviours that can only be managed, if at all, by extremely costly placements, local authorities spend more and to less effect than they would have done by placing earlier.

The costs and outcomes research initiative

The programme of research and development work described in this book began as part of a national research initiative, funded by the Department of Health (and later the Department for Education and Skills) in order to gather better research evidence about both the costs and the outcomes of services for children in need at a time when concerns were being expressed about spiralling costs and the pressures on limited resources. Fourteen studies were commissioned (see Beecham and Sinclair 2007). Our initial study, on the costs and consequences of placing children in care or accommodation, was intended to complement others in the series, and for this reason there were some fairly strict parameters.

At any one time there are about 385,000 children in receipt of social care services in England; the majority are supported within their own families, and only a very small proportion, just under 60,000, are placed away from home (Department for Education and Skills 2006; Department for Children, Schools and Families 2007a). Our study was restricted to tracing and exploring the relationship between costs, experiences and outcomes for children and young people in this latter group, during the period that they are placed in care or accommodation. Most of these children will have received extensive interventions from children's social care before they become looked after: they will have been the subject of initial and core assessments, they and their families are likely to have received a variety of family support services aimed at addressing their needs within the community, and some of these will continue after they return home. Other studies in the programme explored the costs and consequences of providing such services (see Carpenter *et al.* 2003; Cleaver, Walker and Meadows 2004; McCrone *et al.* 2005; Barlow *et al.* 2007) and therefore this issue was considered outside the remit of our original study.

Still other researchers in the initiative considered experiences similar to those of the children and young people in our study, but from different perspectives; thus Hicks and colleagues (2007) explored the relationship between cost and outcome in children's residential units, Berridge and colleagues (2002) evaluated the costs and consequences of placing children with special needs in residential schools, Biehal (2005) considered the costs and effectiveness of adolescent support teams, and Selwyn and colleagues (2006) explored the relationship between experiences, costs and outcome for children late placed for adoption. Since the completion of the Costs and Outcomes Research Initiative, we have continued to extend our conceptual framework and practical model for calculating costs and exploring their relationship to outcome; our current research and development programme has greatly benefited from these other studies, and been able to incorporate and build upon some of their findings (see Chapter 9).

Costs and consequences of local authority care

The first chapters of this book describe the research study on the costs and consequences of local authority care that was part of the Costs and Outcomes Research Initiative. In order to better understand these costs and their relationship to outcomes, we undertook a series of linked pieces of work. First we examined published data that provided a context for developing a better understanding of variations in both levels of need and service provision for looked after children in six local authorities (Chapter 2). We then worked with staff in these authorities to develop unit costs for a series of social work processes such as admission to care, maintaining placements and care planning, that would allow us to calculate and compare the costs to social care of children's pathways through care or accommodation (Chapter 3).

Using data from a sample of 478 children looked after over a 20-month period in the participating authorities, we calculated the costs of care pathways, and explored those factors within both the children's characteristics and the service responses that contributed to variations (Chapters 4 and 5). Recorded information from management information systems and case files, and qualitative data gathered through interviews with a sub-sample of children, were then used to explore further the relationship between need, cost and outcome as shown by basic indicators of wellbeing (Chapter 6) and the views of service users (Chapter 7).

The later chapters in this book show how the methodology for costing pathways through care or accommodation has been used as a basis for developing a computer application that links costs to social care processes over different timeframes for children with different levels of need. It was first used as a research tool to calculate the costs to social services of care episodes for the 478 children in the sample. Since then it has been developed, piloted and made available as a software application for use by social care agencies. The Cost Calculator for Children's Services (CCfCS) can be used by any agency wishing to gain a better understanding of costs and their relationship to outcomes when children are placed in care or accommodation (Chapter 8). The programme of research and development work that has grown out of our original study (see Chapter 9) demonstrates how we have begun to extend the cost calculator model to cover a wider group of children accessing different packages of services from a range of agencies. As services become more integrated following implementation of the Children Act 2004, it has become increasingly important to develop a costing model that can reflect the complex activities undertaken by a range of practitioners in response to need.

'Top-down' or 'bottom-up'

Routinely published data on the costs of personal social services are usually calculated using a 'top-down' approach, in which relevant expenditure is assembled and divided by units of activity, such as the number of days of residential care provided (see Holmes, Beecham and Ward forthcoming). Such calculations do not distinguish the numerous variations in costs engendered by the very different needs of the population served, the wide range of services necessary to meet those needs, and local circumstances and practices. By contrast, a 'bottom-up' approach separately itemizes the activities involved in supporting each individual child and calculates their costs. Children's characteristics can be identified so that the costs of the particular services they receive can be compared with their needs. Aggregate costs for different groups of children can then be calculated. The children can be classified in different ways, for example according to their needs, the type of services they receive or the outcomes they achieve. The approach also facilitates the exploration of cost pathways over time, and this both increases understanding of cost fluctuations and improves the prediction of future costs. A 'bottom-up' approach, therefore, provides a much more detailed picture and also offers the potential to explore how costs relate to outcomes.

The first attempts to use a 'bottom-up' approach in calculating unit costs of children's personal social services in England were the four Children in Need Censuses undertaken between 2000 and 2005 (Department of Health 2001a, 2002a; Department for Education and Skills 2004, 2006). These were surveys of activity and expenditure reported by social services in respect of children in need in a typical week; the data were collected at the level of individual children receiving services during the designated time period and were used to calculate the number of children in need, and the average weekly costs to social services both of children looked after away from home, and of those receiving support fron children's social services in their families or independently.

In the programme of work described in this book, we adopted a similar, 'bottom-up' approach. This approach made it possible to consider how different child, service and authority-related factors impact on costs over specific time periods (see Chapters 3 and 4), how children showing different profiles of need follow different cost pathways (see Chapters 4, 5 and 6), and whether it is possible to identify relationships between the value of services and children's experiences or outcomes (see Chapter 7). It also provided a solid foundation upon which we developed a practical model that allows costs to be aggregated over specific time periods and that produces reports that calculate costs by children's needs, by type of placement or by outcomes (see Chapter 8). In addition, the approach made it possible for us to extend further both our conceptual framework and the model to include wider groups of children receiving different packages of services (see Chapter 9).

Accuracy of unit costs

Our original study showed that it was possible to calculate the costs of providing care or accommodation to the 478 sample children throughout the period under scrutiny. Difficulties in implementing the methodology meant that some of the data were limited and the accuracy of the actual sums involved could probably be improved upon. For instance, costs were derived through focused discussions concerning activity held with over 140 staff in the six participating authorities (see Chapter 3); however this was an exploratory exercise for all the authorities concerned. Work currently being undertaken to extend the costing methodology to other groups of children (see Chapter 9) now requires more precise recording of the time spent on activities related to individual cases from a range of practitioners, with the aim of testing out and improving on the quality of these data.

Notwithstanding this caveat, we are still able to offer a robust methodology for developing costs and linking them to social care processes. Using the same methodology to calculate costs for six authorities has made it possible to compare their similarities and differences. Even if better data, collected in the subsequent research and development studies, or through implementation of the model in other authorities, produce different cost calculations, the underlying conceptual framework and the fundamental messages are unlikely to change. Developing unit costs is an iterative process; as the same methodology is used for larger numbers of cases, the average unit cost is likely to become increasingly robust.

Availability of data necessary to implement the cost calculator model

Successful implementation of the cost calculator model requires data on a limited number of variables concerning children's characteristics or needs, together with the dates of social work processes, and the types of care placements (see Chapter 8). Providing the necessary information as a matter of routine was considered ambitious when the cost calculator software application was first piloted in 2005, as much of the necessary data was then held on paper based files (see Ward, Holmes and Soper 2005). However implementation has become significantly less problematic following improvements in local authority electronic management information systems. Both the pilot and the subsequent implementation programme of the cost calculator model have shown that data items are most likely to be available if they are also required for national returns. As far as possible the data list is therefore built around the SSDA903 return on children looked after by local authorities (Department for Children, Schools and Families 2007a). Items that were demonstrably hard to access in the pilot, such as evidence of disability or emotional or behavioural difficulties, are shortly to be added to this return.

The implementation of the Integrated Children's System (ICS) in 2006 has also increased the potential for making successful use of the cost calculator model. The methodology for calculating the costs of social work processes was specifically designed with the ICS in mind. Both follow the Process Model for children's social services (Department of Health 2003a). It should eventually be possible to link the ICS processes of assessment, planning, intervention and review to the relevant unit costs so that costs can be automatically calculated as social workers and other practitioners record case management information. Doing so should improve transparency and make it easier to identify how resources can most effectively be deployed to improve outcomes initially for looked after children and eventually for all children in need.

Conclusion

Our original study on the costs and consequences of local authority care was able to trace how differences between authorities in both the needs of their care population and the patterns of response can substantially affect the costs of service provision for both individual children and groups at any one time and over a particular period. Variations in costs relate specifically to policies and practices within authorities; the supply and use of different placement types; and certain attributes of the children concerned. The impact of different groups of children with different configurations of need moving through the care system may be a major reason for fluctuations in costs over time.

This study provides both a conceptual framework and the tools for calculating the costs of social care interventions on a routine basis, and eventually linking these to the quality of the services received by children with different configurations of need, as well as to data about welfare outcomes. Both the conceptual model and its practical application are being developed further in subsequent studies. A major research and development programme to extend the model to cover case management processes and social care services to all children in need is currently under way. Other studies are also exploring how health, mental health and education services can be costed in a similar manner and added to the model (see Chapter 9). Socio-legal and youth justice services might be added at a later date. Our ultimate objective is to develop robust unit costs for a range of services for vulnerable children and the procedures that support them. These will then be used to develop the capacity of the cost calculator model so that it is eventually possible for agencies to compare the full cost to the public purse incurred over time by children with different levels of need, and to explore how these relate to outcomes.

Summary of the key points from Chapter 1

- Over the last few years it has become increasingly important to discover how far the costs of placing children in the care of local authorities are reflected in improved life chances. The body of research that now identifies poor outcomes for looked after children and the rising costs of the service make this question particularly pertinent.

- There are concerns that admission to care or accommodation is sometimes deferred until children display behaviours that can only be managed, if at all, by extremely costly placements, and that such policies are neither cost-effective to the authorities nor beneficial to the young people concerned.

- The first chapters of this book describe a research study that explored the costs of placing children in local authority care over a 20-month period. The study was successful in tracing how differences between authorities in both the needs of their care population and the patterns of service response could substantially affect the cost of provision both for individual children and for groups.

- Later chapters explain how the methodology for calculating the costs of care episodes and linking costs to outcomes has been developed into a computer application implemented as a practice and management tool in a number of local authorities.

- The original study is now part of a wider programme of research and development that is extending both the conceptual framework and the practical computer application to cover all children in need and to reflect the range of services they receive. The ultimate objective is to make it possible for agencies to compare the full costs to the public purse incurred over time by children with different levels of need and explore how costs relate to outcomes.

Chapter 2

Identifying Local Authorities and Children for Exploring the Costs of Care

Introduction

The programme of research and development work discussed in this book began with an empirical research study, using real data about children who were, or who had very recently been, looked after by six local authorities. The purpose was to explore those factors underlying the social care costs that arise when children are looked after by the local authority, in order to reach a better understanding of the relationship between costs and outcomes. The computer application that we constructed to calculate the costs for the original research study was then developed as a practical tool and piloted in a seventh local authority (see Chapter 8). After further modifications to take account of the messages from the pilot, it was launched as the Cost Calculator for Children's Services. At the time of writing, the Cost Calculator is being implemented by 17 English local authorities; the ongoing programme to extend it to include a larger group of children and a wider range of services continues to be underpinned by the findings from a formal empirical research programme that aims to: identify those processes that necessarily underpin the delivery of services for children and families; develop appropriate unit costs for them; understand those factors that engender variations; and explore what child-level data are necessary to model relationships between needs, services, costs and welfare outcomes (Chapter 9).

This chapter describes how we selected a sample of looked after children that would allow us to explore how costs accrue over time and why these might vary both within a care population and between populations looked after by different authorities. It shows how we began to identify data that might be relevant to the costs of care and that would inform the development of the first version of the Cost Calculator, an issue explored in greater detail in Chapter 3. It discusses how we identified the six local authorities from which the original sample was selected and considers what factors were most likely to contribute to the costs of the care they provided. The reasons for selecting the authority that subsequently piloted the Cost Calculator and the construction and development of the model itself are described later, in Chapter 8.

The local authorities

Selection

Local authorities in England and Wales are required to complete annual returns showing the average costs per week of placing children in foster care and residential units. Among the reasons for funding the whole Costs and Effectiveness Research Initiative were Treasury concerns at the wide variations between local authorities in the costs of such services as shown on the annual returns (Department of Health 1998; 2000a). For the financial year in which we were collecting the first tranche of data for the sample of children whose experiences formed the basis for our original calculations (2000–1), the national returns indicated that the gross weekly cost of placing a child in foster care ranged from £133 in Bolton to £578 in the City of London, while for those placed in residential units maintained by local authorities, the gross weekly cost ranged from £603 in Nottingham to £3213 in Peterborough (Department of Health 2001b). That extensive variance still persists is shown in the most recent national figures (2005–6) which indicate that the gross average weekly cost of foster care ranges from £224 (Somerset) to £753 (Wokingham) and that of residential care from £1202 (Bromley) to £4038 (Harrow) (The Information Centre for Health and Social Care 2007). Some of this considerable variance is very probably due to differences in the way in which unit costs are calculated, and one of the reasons for developing the Cost Calculator for Children's Services has been to introduce both greater transparency and more uniformity into the elements which form part of such calculations. The Unit Cost Database which forms an intrinsic part of the Cost Calculator has been developed specifically for that purpose (see Chapter 3 below).

Regional differences in salaries and in the prices of items that are purchased are another factor. Recognizing this, the initial research study ensured that two London boroughs were included in the sample and that their costs were calculated separately from those of the out-of-London authorities. In addition, the Unit Cost database tool has been designed to allow local authorities that are calculating their own unit costs to input their own salaries and other financial data.

However differences in the methodology for calculating unit costs and in regional prices are only likely to explain *some* of the variance. Our hypothesis was that there were also likely to be other local differences in the costs of care pathways, probably reflecting either different profiles of need in the care population, different patterns of service response to cost-related needs, or more likely a mixture of both. In order to increase the likelihood that the experiences of children in the sample would shed some light on why variations occurred, for this, initial, study we decided to approach three pairs of local authorities, matched for similarities in the extent of deprivation as shown by routinely collected indicators, and for differences in their published costs of foster and residential care. Every effort was made to recruit two shire counties with relatively low needs, two unitary authorities with average needs, and two London boroughs with high need populations. Within each matched pair there would be one authority with high and one with low placement costs. Because it was necessary to ensure that the selected authorities had sufficient children in a range of accommodation in order to make it possible to compare different placement types, only those that had at least 30 children placed in residential care were eligible for selection.

The project was linked to a complementary study, funded by the National Assembly for Wales (Gatehouse and Ward 2003; Gatehouse, Statham and Ward 2004) and so one Welsh authority was included in the selection. While the inclusion of this authority proved invaluable in many ways, not all the English published data on need and costs were collected in Wales at the time, and so the matching process could only partially be operated for its pair – an English unitary authority.

We also encountered a number of other difficulties in matching authorities. While the first authorities selected fitted the blueprint on paper, not all agreed to participate. As the second or third best match was invited to join the study, the similarities and differences between the authorities were less apparent. In particular, several London boroughs declined the invitation to participate on the very real grounds that they were short-staffed and under-resourced, and the matching process had virtually to be abandoned in the attempt to find recruits. The two that were eventually selected showed substantial similarities in the extent of need, but less difference than we would have liked in the relative costs of placements.

Evidence of need within the paired authorities

Local authority care is one of the most expensive services offered to children and families. The costs are influenced by a number of interrelated factors which determine both the proportionate numbers of children in any local authority who need to be looked after and the range of services available. Factors such as parental mental health problems, substance abuse, domestic violence, teenage pregnancy and homelessness may inhibit parental capacity and/or increase the risk of social exclusion, thereby creating external pressures on the demand for children's social care (Cleaver, Unell and Aldgate 1999; Bradshaw *et al.* 2004; Cleaver *et al.* 2007b). However although data that show the prevalence of many of these factors are now available at local level (www.neighbour-hood.statistics.gov.uk/dissemination), at the time the authorities were selected this was not the case. Evidence of need was therefore deduced from a number of socio-economic indicators that have been shown to relate to the demand for children's social care (Carr-Hill *et al.* 1997; Bebbington and Miles 1989), though in themselves they rarely appear as precipitating factors. We were able to find data for all six authorities on the prevalence of the following: population density, lone-parent families with dependent children, overcrowding, children in receipt of income support, minority ethnic groups.

As Table 2.1 shows, in spite of the difficulties experienced in selecting authorities, the three pairs were reasonably matched for evidence of need. The prevalence of these deprivation factors was higher than the national average in the two London boroughs, and lower than average in the two shire counties; the two unitary authorities had a higher than average incidence of lone-parent families, but a lower than average incidence of overcrowding and families from minority ethnic groups. However, population density and families on income support were high in Unitary 1, but low in Unitary 2.

As anticipated, the socio-economic data corresponded with evidence of demand for support from social services. As Table 2.2 demonstrates, while the authorities all showed a similar age structure, with between 22 per cent and 24 per cent of their populations aged 0–17, there were substantial similarities within the pairs and differences between the authority types in the proportions identified as 'children in need' and therefore receiving support from children's social care. For instance, the two London boroughs, which had above average evidence of need on all the recognized indicators, were providing social care support to about 24 children and young people in every thousand. Similarly, the two shire counties, which had below average evidence of need, were providing social care support to a substantially smaller proportion of their child population (15–17 per thousand). However, Unitary 1, which had shown less evidence of need, was providing support to a similar proportion of its population as the high need authorities.

The relationship between evidence of need and demand for services was more forcibly demonstrated by the marked differences between the authority types in the proportionate numbers of children looked after. The two high need London boroughs placed almost three times as high a proportion of their child population in care as the low need shire counties. Unitary 1 also stood out as having a high rate of children in care, twice that of Unitary 2, and closer to the London boroughs than the shire counties. Robust family support services that can offer effective, and preferably early, interventions are likely to reduce the demand for care. Two

Table 2.1: Summarizing socio-economic factors influencing demand for services by local authority

| | Authority | | | | | |
	London 1	London 2	Shire 1	Shire 2	Unitary 1	Unitary 2
Authority type	Inner London borough	Inner London borough	Shire	Shire	Unitary	Unitary
Population density[a]	✓	✓	✗	✗	✓	✗
Lone-parent[b]	✓	✓	✗	✗	✓	✓*
Over-crowding[b]	✓	✓	✗	✗	✗	✗
Claiming income support[a]	✓	✓	✗	✗	✓	✗
Minority ethnic groups[b]	✓	✓	✗	✗	✗	✗

Key:

✓ Indicates that prevalence of particular factor is higher in the authority than the national average (England and Wales).

✗ Indicates that prevalence of particular factor is equal to or lower in the authority than the national average (England and Wales).

* Equivalent to national average of Wales.

a Data source: Census 2001 (Office for National Statistics 2003).

b Key Indicators Graphical System, 2002 (Department of Health 2002c).

authorities (London 2 and Shire 1) spent about 10 per cent more of their budget on those children in need who were not looked after than did the others. However as Table 2.2 demonstrates, London 2 still had the highest proportion of children looked after, and only in Shire 1 did a high spend on family support services appear to correspond with a lower rate of admission to care.

Table 2.2: Demand for services by local authority

	Authority					
	London 1	*London 2*	*Shire 1*	*Shire 2*	*Unitary 1*	*Unitary 2*
Population[a]	248,900	244,900	552,700	734,600	158,000	114,100
Percentage of population aged 0–17	24	24	23	22	23	23
Number of children in need receiving a service per 1000 of 0–17 population[b]	24	25	15	17	25	Not available
Children looked after per 10,000 aged under 18[c]	122	140	41	55	98	49[d]
Percentage expenditure on children in need who were not looked after[e]	20	31	33	23	20	–

Key:

a Census 2001 rounded to preserve anonymity of local authorities (Office for National Statistics 2003).

b Children in Need Census 2001 (Department of Health 2002a).

c Children Looked After statistics, year ending 31 March 2001 (Department of Health 2002d).

d Personal Social Services Statistics Wales, year ending 31 March 2001 (Local Government Data Unit Wales 2003).

e Key Indicators Graphical System, year ending 31 March 2001 (The Information Centre for Health and Social Care 2007).

– Data not available.

Differences in costs between paired authorities

Subtracting each of the percentage expenditure figures shown in Table 2.2 from 100 gives the percentage expenditure on looked after children in each authority. There was much less variation in these figures than in the proportion of children in need who were looked after, implying that there could be considerable variations between authorities in expenditure per looked after child. For example, London 2 looked after 56 per cent of the children who had been identified as in need, and did so with 69 per cent of its children's social care budget. By comparison, Shire 1 was caring for only 27 per cent of its children who were in need, but it was using 67 per cent of its budget to look after them.

Information about the costs of care in the six authorities is set out in Table 2.3. The first line gives the published data on the unit costs per week of placing a child in residential or foster care in the participating authorities for the period during which data were collected for the sample children. At face value the unit costs suggest that provision was most costly in the high need London boroughs, and least costly in the low need shire counties. The Welsh figures do not show this unit cost, so we do not know the position of Unitary 2, while Unitary 1 came somewhere between the London authorities and the shire counties. Within the matched pairs, the published costs were 21 per cent higher in London 1 than in London 2 and also 21 per cent higher in Shire 2 than in Shire 1. However, as has already been noted, some of the differences between the authorities may have been attributable to inconsistencies in the way the costs were calculated – a view that is strengthened by evidence of significant year on year changes in the published figures at this time. Moreover, in order to understand the reasons for such differences as did exist, it is necessary to look more closely at some of the factors that impacted on the costs of service delivery.

Factors contributing to cost variations

One factor that contributes to the cost of care is the proportion of time children spend in residential units. Residential care can be considerably more costly than foster care or placements with parents (see Chapter 3); indeed, the published figures showed that, for the six participating

Table 2.3: Differences in weekly costs of care and types of provision between the paired authorities

	Authority					
	London 1	*London 2*	*Shire 1*	*Shire 2*	*Unitary 1*	*Unitary 2*
Weekly cost of looking after a child in foster or residential care[a]	£605	£498	£387	£468	£480	Not available
% children in children's homes outside authority boundary[b]	74	51	26	39	56	Not available
% children in foster placements outside authority boundary[c]	53	62	11	11	20	7[d]
% placement days in residential accommodation[e]	25	16	12	6	13	7[f]

Key:

a Key Indicators Graphical System year ending 31 March 2001, minor changes made to preserve anonymity of local authorities (The Information Centre for Health and Social Care 2007).

b Children Looked After statistics for year ending 31 March 2001 (Department of Health 2002d).

c Calculated from Key Indicators Graphical System for year ending 31 March 2001 (The Information Centre for Health and Social Care 2007).

d Personal Social Services Statistics Wales, year ending 31 March 2001 (Local Government Data Unit Wales 2003).

e Calculated from the PSSEX1 return, 2000–1 (Department of Health 2001b).

f Calculated from Personal Social Services Statistics Wales for year ending 31 March 2002 – data not available (Local Government Data Unit Wales 2003).

authorities, at the time the sample was selected, the weekly cost of residential care could be up to four times the cost of foster care (The Information Centre for Health and Social Care 2007). Table 2.3 shows there were substantial differences between the participating authorities in the percentage of days their care population spent in the different types of provision: the two high need London boroughs provided the highest proportion of residential care, reaching 25 per cent of all placement time in London 1. In Shire 1 and Unitary 1 12–13 per cent of placement days were in residential care, while Unitary 2 and Shire 2 used it the least frequently (6–7% of placement days).

A further factor that may impact on unit costs is the use made of out-of-authority placements. An SSI inspection of children's social care services undertaken at the time the sample was selected, found that the majority of local authorities were faced with insufficient appropriate placements to meet the needs of their looked after children (Cooper 2002). One response has been to place increasing numbers outside the area of the authority. Some such placements may be close to the child's home, especially in inner London, where administrative boundaries are somewhat arbitrary. Other out-of-area placements, however, may be at long distances from the responsible authority, thus requiring extensive travelling time and higher levels of activity from professionals to support them properly, both of which elements add to their costs (Cooper 2002). Out-of-authority placements also tend to be unpopular with children: the young people we interviewed made comments such as the following concerning them:

> I'm happy in this home, but not in the area. It's too far away from my friends… I've no family or friends nearby and few people in my family here. (Young man, 18, foster care)

The extensive use of out-of-authority placements is a continuing issue, to be addressed by the new legislation (Department for Education and Skills 2007a, p.60). It is noteworthy that the three authorities with the highest rates of looked after children (London 1, London 2 and Unitary 1) also had the highest proportion of children placed outside their boundaries (see Table 2.3). This may have contributed to their costs, although the London authorities emphasized that their out-of-authority placements were often no further from the child's home than those within their boundaries.

Some authorities also make substantial use of the independent sector, often for specialist placements which may well be also outside the authority. As the national statistics show, at least on the surface, placements in independent foster care in particular appear to be more costly than in-house provision (The Information Centre for Health and Social Care 2007), though there is an ongoing debate as to how far the cost is matched by improved quality of care (see Sellick 2006; Sellick and Howell 2004).

The impact on case management activities of placing children outside the authority, arranging placements in the independent sector and finding placements in residential care were all factors that might contribute to variations in costs. They were explored further in subsequent discussions with social care staff (see Chapter 3), and informed the selection of variables on which data were collected for the sample of children to build the model used for our cost calculations. While the study that forms the focus of this book produced relatively basic calculations, the cost calculator model is now being developed in such a way as to facilitate more sophisticated comparisons between the costs and the consequences of care offered by different providers and the extent to which distance impacts on case management activities (see Chapters 8 and 9).

Staffing issues

At the time that the data for the original study were collected, all of the six participating authorities reported recruitment and retention difficulties, and these are likely to have had an impact on the costs of delivering services. An inspection of children's services in London 2 identified particular difficulties with the recruitment of staff to the looked after children's teams, one of which had a vacancy rate of 50 per cent. Similar problems were noted in the children and families teams in London 1, where the staff told us that the vacancy rate was 42 per cent.

Difficulties in the recruitment and retention of field social workers were identified in the Social Services Recruitment and Retention Survey (Social and Health Care Workforce Group 2000); they remain a problem although this is yet another issue that the current White Paper on looked after children aims to address (Department for Education and Skills 2007a, p.128).

The authorities had responded to staff shortages by offering incentive schemes such as funding advanced social work qualifications for existing staff (Shire 1); offering bursaries to final year social work students (London 1 and 2 and Unitary 2); and providing affordable short-term housing to new social workers (London 1).

They also competed with neighbouring authorities by offering higher salaries. Considerable variations in levels of pay were evident, with salaries in the London boroughs higher by 27 per cent for social workers and administrative staff, and by 19 per cent for frontline managers, than in Unitary 2, the authority where pay was the lowest.

Problems with staff recruitment and retention graphically demonstrate the difficulties of interpreting the associations between costs and outcomes. Lower salary scales mean lower costs, but may exacerbate difficulties in retaining staff. Fewer staff mean a reduction in the salary bill, but poor or non-existent service delivery. However local authorities do not have the option of refusing to deliver statutory services because of a shortfall in the workforce. Recruitment drives can become lengthy and expensive processes, particularly when, as in Unitary 2, social work posts have to be advertised on more than one occasion. Almost all the incentives to recruit and retain staff noted above will have had a direct and continuing impact on the total expenditure for children's social services.

Moreover, high vacancy rates mean that local authorities employ agency personnel, as had happened in the two London boroughs, Shire 1 and Unitary 2, although in the latter the percentage was considered to be negligible. In London 1, 47 per cent of both social worker and management posts in the children and families teams were filled by agency staff, while in London 2 the percentage was lower, accounting for 25 per cent of social worker posts and 10 per cent of management positions. Information provided by the authorities demonstrated that agency staff were substantially more costly to employ: figures given by one authority suggested that agency social workers cost on average 25 per cent more, and managers 53 per cent more, than those employed directly. Widespread use of agency staff is thought to be a factor that impacts on the ability of a local authority to manage its budget effectively (Cooper 2002).

Moreover, it seems likely that over-dependency on such staff is likely to increase the number of changes that vulnerable children experience, as few are employed on more than a casual basis. The reliance on agency staff is yet another continuing problem that the current White Paper aims to address (Department for Education and Skills 2007a, p.128).

Table 2.4 summarizes those factors that are likely to have influenced the costs incurred by the authorities in looking after their care populations, and demonstrates the differences between the matched pairs. As we have shown, evidence of need, use of residential care, agency placements and placements outside the area of the authority, higher salary scales and employment of agency staff, all contribute to increased costs of service delivery. However, while the table puts these factors together and produces a general picture, the information can do no more than make some suggestions as to why the costs of looking after children appear to be higher in London 1 than in London 2, in Shire 2 than in Shire 1 and in Unitary 1 than in Unitary 2.

The problem is that, by presenting these contributory factors as separate indicators, we ignore the complex relationships between the costs of service provision and the needs of the children concerned. Greater understanding can be achieved by exploring how costs accrue as individual children follow different pathways through care, or indeed any other child welfare system, and then by identifying patterns between those with similar attributes. In order to do this, we need data on both the characteristics and experiences of the children concerned, and the likely costs of the services accessed by those with different needs.

The children

Selection of sample

Within the three pairs of matched local authorities, we aimed to identify a sample of 600 looked after children, and follow their care careers for a period of about two years. While national data concerning the number of children looked after and the placements they receive have been collected

Table 2.4: Indicators of higher costs for looked after children: Comparisons between paired authorities

Factors leading to higher costs	London 1	London 2
Higher evidence of need		
Higher numbers looked after		
Higher percentage in residential care		
Higher percentage in foster care outside authority boundary		
Higher percentage in children's homes outside authority boundary		
Greater use of agency placements		
Higher salaries		
Greater use of agency staff		

	Shire 1	Shire 2
Higher evidence of need		
Higher numbers looked after		
Higher percentage in residential care		
Higher percentage in foster care outside authority boundary		
Higher percentage in children's homes outside authority boundary		
Greater use of agency placements	No information	No information
Higher salaries		

	Unitary 1	Unitary 2
Higher evidence of need		
Higher numbers looked after		
Higher percentage in residential care		
Higher percentage in foster care outside authority boundary		
Higher percentage in children's homes outside authority boundary	No information	No information

Table 2.4 *continued*

	Unitary 1	Unitary 2
Greater use of agency placements		▓▓▓
Higher salaries	▓▓▓	
Greater use of agency staff		▓▓▓

Key:

▓▓▓	Higher
░░░	Equal
	Lower

since 1952, bottom-up, child-level information about the costs of social work processes was not collected nationally until the four Children in Need Censuses were undertaken between 2000 and 2005 (Department of Health 2001a, 2002a; Department for Education and Skills 2004, 2006). During one week in the years 2000, 2001, 2003 and 2005, local authorities were required to gather information about all children in need and to calculate the amount of time and resources spent on providing services for them. All children looked after were included although, as we shall see, authorities differed in their definitions of who these should be. Because it seemed likely that the most comprehensive data relevant to exploring costs would be available for children included in the censuses, we decided that these should be used as a starting point for the study. In each authority the sample of children was drawn from the population of looked after children included in the first census, and followed until the second census date (February 2000 to October 2001).

In order to compare the relative costs and outcomes of different care careers, it was necessary to select a sample of children who were likely to have experienced a broad spread of those placements on offer. In particular it was important to include sufficient numbers of children and young people in residential care to make meaningful comparisons: these are not only the most expensive types of placement, but concerns have also been raised about the quality of care they offer (e.g. Sinclair and Gibbs 1998;

Department for Education and Skills 2007a). Younger children are, at least in theory, only rarely placed in residential units (Department of Health 1991a, although see Sempik, Ward and Darker 2008 for contradictory evidence). There are also fewer indicators of outcome that provide hard data for this age-group: examination results, school exclusions, criminal activity, entry to further education or employment are all variables which are more likely to relate to the experiences of older children and teenagers. For these two reasons – the availability of relevant outcome data and the likely spread of placements – we decided to restrict the sample to children and young people aged ten and over.

Gordon, Parker and Loughran (2000) found that 28 per cent of children looked after have significant physical, learning or emotional disabilities. More recent data from a longitudinal study of children looked after for at least a year in a representative sample of English authorities found that at entry to care, 50 per cent had identifiable emotional or behavioural difficulties, 28 per cent had a statement of special educational need or one pending and 52 per cent had a health condition of sufficient severity to require referral to a specialist (Skuse, Macdonald and Ward 2001). Children with disabilities are likely to require the most expensive placements; they are also known to be the most vulnerable of the population who are looked after away from home (Robinson, Weston and Minkes 1995; Phillips 1998; Meltzer *et al.* 2003). We therefore decided to ensure that sufficient numbers of children with disabilities were included in the sample.

Once an authority had agreed to participate, and ethical approval had been given, the liaison officer sent the research team details of all children and young people aged ten and over who had been looked after during the week of the Children in Need Census 2000. Information was given about ages, gender, current placement and disability. In order to preserve confidentiality, names were not included. In each authority the sample of 100 young people was selected from this list. As far as possible this included 40 children and young people in residential care, 40 in foster care (of which 10 were fostered with relatives) and 20 placed with own parents or in independent living. Specified minimum numbers of children and young people in out-of-authority placements or showing evidence of disability were selected to reflect the profile of the looked after population in each authority. Efforts were also made to ensure that the gender balance in each authority was adequately reflected.

This was not intended to be a representative sample: young people were selected primarily on the basis of where they were living in February 2000, the aim being to achieve an adequate balance of different placement types for statistical comparison. All authorities were aware of both national and local concerns about the spiralling costs of residential placements, the costs and quality of care of all placements provided outside their area, and the quality of care provided to children with disabilities (see Ayres 1997). In order to ensure that adequate data were available to explore these issues, the sample was deliberately weighted to include disproportionate numbers of children in each of these categories.

The last column of Table 2.5 gives details of the numbers of children included in the sample from each of the six authorities. Shire 1 and Unitary 1 were the only two to include children looked after on a series of short-term breaks in their lists of those who met the criteria for selection. When it became apparent that other authorities had excluded them, a decision was made to remove them from the sample for the main analysis, and this accounts for the smaller numbers selected. All children who met the criteria were included in the sample selection for Unitary 2, but because this is an authority with only a small care population, the total number of those eligible only reached 77.

There was also substantial sample loss. Some of the participating authorities updated their management information systems during the study, as a result of which a number of children were identified who had been wrongly classified as looked after in the Children in Need Census 2000 (Department of Health 2001a); these had to be withdrawn from the sample. In addition a number of children did not remain looked after for the whole 20-month study period, and this had to be taken into account in some of the analysis. Altogether, data were collected on 478 of the expected 600 children; 301 of them remained looked after for the full study period.

The absence of data on certain variables was also problematic. For instance, the initial management information system data from Shire 2 did not differentiate between placements with local authority foster carers and those with friends or relatives, or between in and out of area placements; this later had to be pieced together from case files after the sample had been selected. Once again, we have to accept that the sample is less than satisfactory, although it fits the research plan as far as was practical at the time of selection. The distribution of first placements is shown in Table 2.5.

Only four authorities were able to identify children who had been registered as disabled on their management information systems. Even where they could, it later became evident that criteria for registration varied from one authority to another and did not produce a true record because it was voluntary. There was also considerable confusion as to whether emotional or behavioural difficulties were included in the definition of disability. Again, many of the children with physical or learning disabilities or emotional or behavioural difficulties were only identified from case file data after the sample selection.

As we shall see, physical and learning disabilities and emotional and behavioural problems all had a major impact on the costs of care episodes; the pilot of the Cost Calculator demonstrated that, even after implementation of the Integrated Children's System, this item is not always accessible on electronic recording systems (see Chapter 8), and this remains an issue in the current phase of the research and development programme, where the Cost Calculator is being implemented in a number of local authorities. In this context, the proposal in the current White Paper on looked after Children, to consider introducing a new indicator on the emotional and behavioural difficulties of children in care within the new local authority performance management framework (Department for Education and Skills 2007a, p.93), is to be welcomed.

At the start of the study 146 (31%) sample children were in residential care, 188 (39%) were in foster care, 55 (11%) were placed with relatives and 85 (18%) were in independent living or placed with own parents. Table 2.5 shows the breakdown of these numbers between the different local authorities in the study. Eighty children and young people (17%) were in agency foster or residential homes, and 134 (28%) were placed out of area. Nearly one in five (91:19%) were known to have physical and/or learning disabilities. In line with the national statistics there were more boys (260:54%) than girls (218:46%).

Table 2.5: Placements at start of study for sample children (n = 478)

Authority	Residential care	LA foster care	Fostered with relatives	Placed with parents/ independent living	Other	Total
Planned selection in each authority	40	30	10	20	0	100
London 1	35	30	8	17	0	90
London 2	30	46	7	14	1	98
Shire 1	16	21	8	10	0	55
Shire 2	29	28	7	15	3	82
Unitary 1	25	24	12	15	0	76
Unitary 2	11	39	13	14	0	77
Total	**146**	**188**	**55**	**85**	**4**	**478**

Information collected about the sample children

The authorities were advised of the children selected for the research sample, and asked to provide additional data concerning their needs, the services they had received while looked after and their outcomes. Because the purpose of the project was to produce a model that calculated costs and that authorities would be able to use for themselves, as far as possible the variable list was restricted to those items on which data were already required as part of the Performance Assessment Framework (Department of Health 2003b) or for other government returns. The research team anticipated that most of these data could be downloaded directly from management information systems. All but one of the authorities in the original study were able to produce data in electronic format on key variables concerning placement histories, length of care episodes and primary need codes.

The proliferation of returns now required by central government, together with increased expectations of evidence-based planning, the improved potential of new technology and the implementation of the Integrated Children's System, have all meant that most authorities are now increasing their capacity to handle quantitative data (see Pinnock and Garnett 2002; Friedman, Garnett and Pinnock 2005; Cleaver et al. 2007a). Several of those in the original study were able to provide more comprehensive data in 2002 than in 2001. Authorities that are now implementing the Cost Calculator need to access a similar dataset; most of them find it relatively simple to provide data required for government returns on looked after children, although there can be difficulties in bringing together other items held on different databases. There are also continuing problems in accessing electronically held child-level data on outcomes.

Local authorities have been required to provide data on outcomes for looked after children, such as educational achievements, access to health care and offending behaviour, since 2000. However these returns have often been pieced together from data provided directly from other agencies involved in the care of the child (education departments, youth offending teams and health authorities). Because of concerns about data protection, these have often only been accessible in aggregate form. There have been real concerns that such a process has meant that agencies lost the opportunity to use these data as a basis for identifying those individual children who need additional support (Gatehouse, Statham and Ward 2004). Although the Integrated Children's System is expected to change this (Ward 2002; Department of Health 2002b), the Cost Calculator pilot authority, chosen because it was also trialling the ICS, was still collating these data from a variety of sources in 2005, and many of the items were not routinely inputted onto the management information system (Ward, Holmes and Soper 2005).

Data collected for the original Costs and Consequences study were accessed through social services departments in the participating authorities. At the time there was little evidence of data sharing between agencies, and plans to identify how costs, experiences and outcomes of social care linked with those of other welfare agencies had to be abandoned. However the original study was undertaken before the implementation of the Children Act 2004, which led to the establishment of children's services departments in 2006, integrating social services, education, and some other children's services. As a result, issues concerning data protection have since been further explored, and appropriate information sharing is now a more realistic possibility (Cleaver *et al.* 2007a). Education systems hold comprehensive data on disability, emotional and behavioural difficulties and educational outcomes, filling a gap that was evident in social services systems. Integration between these two agencies has also made it possible to examine how the methodology for calculating costs and exploring the relationship to outcomes for looked after children described in this book can be extended to all children with special educational needs (Holmes *et al.* forthcoming). Implementation of the Integrated Children's System has also been accompanied by further initiatives to explore how, and to what extent, information held on health systems can be accessed by children's services and vice versa (Cleaver *et al.* 2007a). Moreover, joint commissioning of services between NHS Trusts and local authorities has created an incentive to explore how the cost calculator methodology can be further extended to include the costs of health provision (see Chapter 9).

Case files

However, while there are encouraging signs for the future, and indeed, all data for the implementation of the Cost Calculator for Children's Services are currently imported from management information systems, much of the necessary data for the original study were not accessible electronically, and had to be extracted painstakingly from case files.

The research team gathered data from files on the 478 sample children, visiting each authority on two separate occasions, with about a year's interval between. There was considerable variation in the quality of recorded information. Key data were sometimes missing or differed from those held on the management information system. The percentage of missing data for particular variables varied greatly between the authorities; for instance available data on teenage pregnancy ranged from 10 per cent in Unitary 1 to 72 per cent in London 2.

There was some indication that the more social workers allocated to any child, the less accurate or complete was the information on the case file; on the other hand sometimes a change of social worker meant that a very detailed and useful summary was prepared. Major discrepancies in areas such as placement histories were reported back to the authorities in order to help them improve the quality of the information held both at individual and at strategic level.

The one data item consistently conspicuous by its absence from both the case files and the management information systems was clear information concerning the specialist services that children and young people had received. Visits to doctors, dentists and orthodontists; support from physiotherapists and speech therapists; special help with education; psychotherapy and counselling were rarely recorded in a consistent manner, making it impossible to tell from case notes how frequently children and young people were able to access services provided by other child welfare agencies while they were looked after by the authority (see also Beecham and Knapp 2001). Nor were these data held in other parts of the system; where there was a financial record of the authority having bought in a particular service from another agency, the detail was often insufficient to identify how many or indeed which children benefited. Accurate child-level data about services children have received is necessary if packages of care are to be satisfactorily costed. Yet their absence remains a persistent problem, noted in the pilot of the Integrated Children's System (Cleaver *et al.* 2007a) and in the preparatory study for a new children in need data collection (Gatehouse, Ward and Holmes 2008).

Interviews with children

Data collected from management information systems and case files provide little insight into children's perceptions of their experience. Children and young people can tell us not so much what services cost, but how far they are valued, and we arranged to interview a small group of those in the sample to find out what they thought were the positive and negative aspects of their experience. The aim was to interview 16 children in each authority. Because so little is known about their experiences of care, we decided to select an interview sample in which at least half the children and young people had been identified as having a physical or learning disability (or both).

Heptinstall (2000) has demonstrated how the process of gaining access to looked after children for research interviews is both lengthy and complicated. Researchers cannot approach children and young people directly because to do so would entail their receiving identifying information, such as names and addresses, before consent had been given. Thus the children and young people were selected from the anonymized dataset and a formal procedure was agreed through which the authority, acting on behalf of the research team, sought agreement from social workers, carers and/or parents and children for each interview to go ahead.

We have discussed elsewhere how complex research governance procedures, introduced with the laudable intention of protecting vulnerable people from unwarranted intrusion, can inadvertently exclude young people who may wish to participate in a research study, and will almost always result in a biased sample (Munro, Holmes and Ward 2005). These issues were very apparent in this study; we had considerable difficulties in accessing a sample, and different requirements in the local authorities meant that two of them were considerably under-represented. Eventually 37 children and young people were interviewed; 10 who were in residential care at the time of the first interview, 19 who were in foster care, four placed with own parents and four in independent living. Twenty-one of these young people had physical or learning disabilities. Twenty-five young people were interviewed twice, with an interval of between 11 and 28 months.

Interviews were semi-structured and explored the relationship between the needs of the children and young people, the services they received and their perceptions of outcome. Because there was so little recorded information about their access to specialist services, interviewees were also asked to complete a service provision checklist, detailing all services they had received during the course of the preceding three months. The interviewees each received a £10 token in return for their participation.

We anticipated that some children and young people would have communication difficulties that the research team might not be able to overcome, and therefore all interviewees were asked to choose a 'trusted adult' who could be with them during the interview. In the event, most participants chose carers or parents, which meant that they may not have spoken freely about their perceptions of their current placement; on the other hand, the 'trusted adults' provided invaluable assistance in helping to complete the service provision checklist as few children and young people could recall what additional support they had received over the preceding three months without prompting. Forty such checklists were completed. The information collected from the interviews has been utilized throughout this book, although it has been of particular value in the discussion on need, cost and services in Chapter 6, and the relationship between costs and value, in Chapter 7. Data from the service provision checklists were specifically used to complete the timelines that illustrate Chapter 5.

In addition to the data concerning needs, outcomes and perceptions, it was also necessary to gather information that would make it possible to estimate the costs of children's care careers. The following chapter describes how we identified a series of social care processes that underpin the provision of services for looked after children. Through focused discussions with local authority personnel, we collected activity and financial data that would allow us to calculate basic unit costs and a number of variations for each process in the series. These two types of information, child level data about needs, experiences and outcomes, and unit costs of the processes that underpin the delivery of care, form the core elements from which cost calculations were made.

Conclusion

This chapter has explored how the types of data required for government returns indicate variations in the demand for local authority care, and in service responses. Many of these responses are costly, especially if choices are limited and demands are excessive. Many of the data items explored at local authority level show why there are variations in the costs of care, and have indicated variables to be included in our costing model. However to understand how costs accrue and why they fluctuate, we need to look more closely at the population served. The sample of 478 children, looked after by the six authorities, was selected with the aim of providing information that would enable us to compare the different costs and outcomes of contrasting care careers. Outcomes data are important because an exploration of the cost of providing services to vulnerable children must take account of the wellbeing of service users as well as financial expenditure. However child level data on outcomes were difficult to access from electronic systems, particularly if they were more likely to be held by health, education or youth justice agencies, rather than the social services departments that held lead responsibility for the children. There are, however, encouraging signs that the integration of children's services introduced by the Children Act 2004 has led to improvements in this area.

The next few chapters of this book describe how we used the data about individual children to calculate cost pathways and explore relationships between needs, costs and outcomes; these calculations were then used as the basis for developing the first version of the Cost Calculator for Children's Services.

Summary of the key points from Chapter 2

- The purpose of the original Costs and Consequences study was to explore how variations in the costs of placing children in the care of local authorities could be better understood. Three matched pairs of local authorities agreed to participate in an empirical study. Analysis of the data provided for government returns gave some indication of the differential demands for services and cost-related service responses, suggesting a number of variables to be included in cost calculations. However child-level data were necessary to explore how costs accrue over time, and to gain further understanding of the relationship between needs, costs and outcomes.

- The authors therefore undertook a prospective longitudinal study, designed to explore both quantitative and qualitative data concerning the background, needs and experiences of a population of 478 children looked after by the three matched pairs of local authorities over a 20-month period. The sample was restricted to children aged ten years and over and was weighted to include disproportionate numbers of children with disabilities and/or in residential units in order to provide sufficient data for meaningful analysis.

- Data on children's needs and experiences were collected from management information systems, case files and from structured interviews with children and young people and their carers.

- Data on access to specialist services and outcomes were conspicuously absent from management information systems. However there are encouraging signs that at least the latter are becoming more accessible following integration of children's services.

- Data items included in the empirical study were based on research findings about the needs and experiences of looked after children. They were later linked to the unit costs of services the children received (see Chapter 3) and the database used to construct a cost calculation model that would eventually allow each authority to calculate the probable relationship between costs and outcome of different types of placement for children with different needs. This model became the prototype of the Cost Calculator for Children's Services.

Chapter 3

The Development of Unit Costs
for Social Care Processes

Introduction

The children whose care experiences were explored in the original study were all looked after during the week of the first Children in Need Census in February 2000. We have already seen (Chapter 2) that at the time there was extensive variance between authorities in the recorded costs of providing both residential and foster care, and indeed these formed one of our criteria for the selection of participants.

The latest national figures (2005/6) show even greater variance, and this becomes particularly marked when the different kinds of placement providers are taken into account. Own provision foster care ranges from £81 (Sheffield) to £564 (Kensington and Chelsea) while expenditure on agency foster care varies between £82 (Leeds) and £3286 (Gateshead). The figures for own provision residential care range from £659 (Northamptonshire) to £6620 (Wokingham), while those for agency residential care from £785 (York) to £6776 (Northamptonshire) (The Information Centre for Health and Social Care 2007).

Such significant differences in costs, both between authorities and between types of care, clearly need to be explored further and a number of questions answered. Why does it cost one local authority seven times as much as another to provide a child with foster care? Why is the average weekly expenditure per placement in agency foster care 40 times greater for one local authority than for another? Comparing overall average figures, why does residential care cost five and a half times as much as foster care? Most importantly, how far does the difference in cost to the authority represent a difference in children's perceptions of the service they use and, ultimately, a difference in outcomes?

Among the early reasons why there were such apparent disparities in the costs of delivering services to looked after children were substantial variations in the way that costs were calculated. For instance, our recent discussions with local authority finance officers suggest that the overhead costs of top-level management are allocated to individual services in varying ways in different local authorities. When it was introduced, the Children in Need Census aimed to bring greater uniformity into cost calculations by providing an explicit methodology that all local authorities were asked to use (Beecham 2000). The intention was to enable better comparisons to be made, and to allow the reasons for genuine differences to be pinpointed. Moreover, the aim of the Children in Need Census was 'to link services and the costs of services with the children in need' who are served (Department of Health 2003c, p.39). Our original study had a complementary aim, to link the costs of services more closely with the children concerned by costing social care processes and identifying those factors that related to significant variations both in costs and outcomes (see Chapters 4, 5 and 6).

Before we consider the various issues concerning the development of unit costs in the original study, the boundaries need to be revisited. As Chapter 1 explained, this study was restricted to developing unit costs that are directly attributable to social care for the period that children are looked after. The authors are well aware that many children will have received extensive services from children's social care and other agencies before they enter the care system, throughout the care episode and indeed after they leave (Statham 2000). However, this study was part of a wider research initiative in which 14 research teams all used a methodology for developing unit costs of children's social care similar to that employed in the Children in Need Census (Beecham 2000; Beecham and Sinclair 2007).

Other studies in the initiative explored the costs and outcomes of undertaking initial and core assessments (Cleaver, Walker and Meadows 2004); delivering family support services (Carpenter *et al.* 2003); deflecting adolescents from care (Biehal 2005); leaving care (Dixon *et al.* 2006) and placing children for adoption (Selwyn *et al.* 2006). By developing unit costs for care episodes, our original study sought to complete one part of this wider picture to which the whole initiative contributed. As our methodology has subsequently extended to cover costs for all children in need, we have used costs developed by other studies in the initiative as a starting point for further cost calculations (see Chapter 9).

It should also be noted that our original study focused on developing unit costs for the provision of social care. However, social work interventions are only some among a range of services provided to looked after children, many of whom, as subsequent chapters will show, also require additional support from education, health, child and adolescent mental health services (CAMHS) and other agencies. Where costs to agencies other than social care are taken into account, as in Chapter 5, our study utilized unit costs that had already been calculated by others, many of which are included in the compendium published annually by PSSRU (see Netten and Curtis 2002; Curtis 2007). More detailed analyses of these costs to other agencies will be included in future versions of the cost calculator model that are now under development. Developing methodologies for calculating the costs to the public purse of providing a range of services to a much wider population of children in need and linking these to outcomes is the focus of an ongoing research and development programme that arose from the original study (see Chapter 9).

Selection of processes to cost

The processes for which unit costs of care episodes were derived were modelled on the nine case management operations that underpin the task of looking after a child in care or accommodation, outlined in the Core Information Requirements (Process Model, Version 2) Level Two Process 1.4 (Department of Health 2001c). It proved necessary to make a number of adjustments to the published model, mainly because social care staff found it difficult to separate out some of their activity into predetermined blocks. One additional process, maintaining the placement, also had to be added in order to provide a true picture of the costs of looking after a child. The following eight processes were costed:

Process 1: Deciding child needs to be looked after and finding a first placement

Process 2: Care planning

Process 3: Maintaining the placement

Process 4: Leaving care/accommodation

Process 5: Finding a subsequent placement

Process 6: Review

Process 7: Legal interventions

Process 8: Transition to leaving care services.

All looked after children will go through the first four processes during the time they spend in care or accommodation. In every case, a decision has to be made as to whether a child needs to be looked after, and a first placement has to be agreed and found, even when this is a *de facto* placement with parents or relatives. Decisions are based primarily on the core assessment, which is likely to have been completed as part of a process outside the parameters of our initial study, and has not, therefore, been included in our cost calculations. More specialist assessments should be made of children's health, educational and developmental status, leading to personal educational plans and individual health care plans being made on the basis of the findings. These developmental plans need to be linked to the overall care plan for a looked after child, and to the placement plan, specific to each individual placement. In our study they have been included in Process 2. Once a child is in a placement, work has to be undertaken to ensure that both carers and child are adequately supported. There is also a process to be undertaken at the end of the care episode, whether the child moves on to adoption, returns home or becomes independent.

In addition, Processes 5 to 8 will need to be undertaken for some, but not all, children: those who remain looked after for a month or more will be subject to the review process; many will move to new placements, and some will require legal interventions such as emergency placement orders, care orders or residence orders to secure their position. Young people who come under the provision of the Children (Leaving Care) Act 2000 (Department of Health 2000b) will also be entitled to leaving care services. Some of these processes will be reiterated as children remain in the care system and their progress is monitored or circumstances change.

Data sources

In order to allow us to estimate their costs, the eight processes were broken down into those activities undertaken by field social workers, family placement workers, team managers, administrative staff and other personnel either within or outside children's social care. Activities were further broken down into those that involved direct or indirect client-related activity, following the methodology used in the Children in Need Census (see Beecham 2000). Focused discussions were held within team meetings to collect information about the amount of time routinely spent on each activity within each of the eight processes by each member of staff involved. Meetings were structured around the information from the local procedural documents issued to staff by each authority. Calculations were based on the extent to which staff *actually* followed local guidance rather than on the authority's expectations. For each process, the amounts of time spent by all participants were costed as proportions of salaries, overheads were added and all the values were totalled to arrive at the unit cost used in the study. The unit costs were derived from data collected from 17 meetings attended by 104 social workers, 23 family placement workers, 13 team managers, and two independent reviewing officers. A minimum of two meetings were held in each of the participating authorities, each lasting from between 30 minutes to 1¾ hours.

The focus group discussions revealed little difference in the views of staff, both within and between the six authorities, concerning the mean amount of time they spent on each process, major disparities being clearly attributable to differences in children's needs, the types of placement they received or specific local factors (see below). The information was verified and gaps filled in at a workshop at which representatives from four author-

ities met with the research team, and through responses to structured questionnaires sent out after the meetings. Of the 33 questionnaires that were
sent out, ten were returned. These proved particularly valuable for gather-
ing data from administrative staff and for obtaining information about
ceasing to be looked after and legal processes. Additional information
about staffing levels, calculations concerning the weekly costs of maintaining children in foster and residential care presented for the Children in
Need Census (Department of Health 2002a) and salary scales were gathered with the help of the liaison person in each authority. Customized unit
costs were calculated from these data for each authority participating in the
original study, and then used in the calculations shown in the following
chapters. Mean costs were calculated by averaging the unit costs for all six
participating authorities; mean out-of-London costs are the averages of the
unit costs for Shires 1 and 2 and Unitaries 1 and 2; mean London costs are
the averages of the costs from the two London boroughs.

In some instances, particularly for variations of processes that occur
only under certain conditions, the data gathered were rudimentary and
informed cost estimates had to be made by the research team. It was necessary to do this rather than ignore some elements of the processes, since the
research team were aware that activities such as deciding whether children
needed to be looked after, finding placements or making arrangements for
care leavers had actually happened. While the reliability of such estimates
may not have been high, they were the best available at the time. Subsequent studies are now collecting further activity data with the purpose of
improving on these estimates and facilitating more accurate cost calculations (Ward *et al.* 2008).

The focus group consensus approach has been shown to have internal
reliability; it has also provided a valuable starting point for developing unit
costs for social care processes and identifying factors that lead to variations. However, it is open to criticism. There are concerns that estimates of
activity could be biased by the group dynamics of the meetings, by the
views of the more vociferous participants and by the tendency for memo-
ries to focus on the more complex cases and ignore those that were more
straightforward. The research team is now in the process of triangulating
the information gathered from focus groups by also requesting

practitioners to complete event records designed to capture the time spent on specific processes in individual cases (Ward *et al.* 2008). Activity data that have been more thoroughly validated will inspire greater confidence in unit costs.

Mean costs for a looked after child

Table 3.1 demonstrates how the types of activity undertaken by the various protagonists to complete Process 1 (deciding a child needs to be looked after and finding a first placement) can be broken down into their separate parts. If a core assessment (costed outside the care processes) indicates that a child's needs might best be met in care or accommodation, the social worker needs to explore with senior managers whether placement would be both appropriate and acceptable to the authority. All the authorities required the field social worker to make a case to senior managers and obtain their agreement before any child could be placed. Obtaining such agreement was by no means easy, for accommodating children and young people can be a lengthy and costly business, and senior managers were rightly concerned to act as gatekeepers, and needed to weigh up the potential benefits to the child against the expenditure of scarce resources.

Other activities undertaken by the field social worker as part of this process included meetings with the child and his/her family, obtaining their consent to placement, exploring whether other family members or friends could accommodate the child, discussions with the family placement team, completing paperwork and arranging introductory visits. If a placement away from home was agreed, the family placement team was expected to approach potential carers and complete the necessary paperwork. A chronic shortage of appropriate placements in the participating authorities meant that finding a foster carer or a residential home with a vacancy could be a lengthy business.[1]

While the majority of the activity supporting Process 1 was undertaken by field social workers and family placement workers, other staff were also involved: administrative staff arranged resource allocation meetings and ensured that data were entered on to the management information system; team managers held additional consultations with social workers and helped prepare the case for admission; senior managers reviewed the application, assessed the probable cost and gave – or sometimes withheld – permission for the child to be placed. As the table shows, the process of admission and first placement was almost entirely undertaken by social care personnel; although professionals from other agencies were routinely consulted and involved in some of the other case management processes, it was rare for them to participate at this stage unless joint funding was being sought.

As Table 3.1 shows, on average it took 10¼ hours field social worker time; six hours family placement worker time; ¼ hour administrative time; two hours team manager time and 1¾ hours senior manager time to decide that a child needed to be accommodated, agree funding and to find a first placement with a local authority foster carer. The mean, out-of-London, unit cost of £639[2] for this process was then derived by calculating the time spent as a proportion of annual salaries and overheads for each participant, and averaging the customised costs for the four relevant authorities (see Beecham 2000).

By breaking down the processes into their component parts, it was also possible to analyse how the work was divided between the different participants. As can be seen from Table 3.1, the time-consuming, and therefore the costly, parts of Process 1 were the family placement worker's task of finding the placement and the work undertaken by the fieldworker in negotiating with the child and his/her family and obtaining their consent, as well as putting a case for admission to senior managers. Exploring the breakdown of activities in this way also immediately demonstrated areas that overlapped. For instance, in each of the processes some of the tasks undertaken by administrative staff might have been automatically generated by the development of more user-friendly IT systems for field social workers and family placement workers (see Gatehouse, Statham and Ward 2004). Some of the work of the family placement teams appeared to overlap with work undertaken by field social workers: for instance, they both claimed to support young people in placement and to chase up payments to foster carers (see also Poirier, Chamberland and Ward 2006).

While a breakdown of activities such as this can obviously be explored to identify whether duplication of tasks (and therefore higher costs) is necessary, there is a careful balance to be maintained between cost saving and children's wellbeing. Cutting some of the tasks may be ill-advised. For

Table 3.1: Activity supporting Process 1: Decide a child needs to be looked after and find first placement

Who	Type of activity	Total time taken
Field social worker	*Direct client related activity:* e.g. Meetings, visits, phone calls to child and birth family; exploring possibility of a kinship placement; introducing child to new carers *Indirect client related activity:* Completion of paperwork (e.g. LAC forms), meetings and discussion with colleagues and other professionals	10¼ hours
Administrative staff	e.g. Completion of paperwork; arranging meetings; notification of placement; data entry	¼ hour
Team manager	e.g. Discussions and meetings with social worker; representations to senior colleagues; attendance at resource allocation meeting	2 hours
Family placement social worker	Discussion with field social worker; finding placement; consultation with prospective carers	6 hours
Family placement team manager	Agree funding: consultation with family placement worker	3 hours
Other personnel within social services	Senior managers: preparation for and attendance at resource allocation meeting	1¾ hours
Other personnel outside social services: e.g. education and health	Joint funding arrangements	Variable

example, reducing the amount of time the social worker spends in direct contact with a child and his/her family may lower the costs of admission or maintaining the placement, but is also likely to have a negative impact on the wellbeing of the child. Some processes, such as the care plan or the review, were often skimped or overlooked: the comparatively low cost of Process 2 (care planning) reflects the small amount of time devoted to this activity; 54 per cent of reviews for children in the sample were not carried out within the statutory timescale. Reducing the time spent on these processes may cut the immediate financial costs to the authority, but again may decrease the child's wellbeing (see Sinclair 1984) and may have longer-term impacts if the child drifts in care without a proper permanence plan.

Each of the case management processes for a looked after child was broken down into its component parts and costs estimated in a similar manner to that described for Process 1. While some, such as Process 1, largely involved costs to children's social care, others, such as Process 2 (care planning), and Process 6 (review) involved substantial costs to other agencies, for increased integration of children's services together with the introduction of personal education plans and individual health assessments has meant that professionals from health and education have – or should have – significant involvement in the planning and review processes. The unit costs that were calculated in the initial research project include the contribution made by staff from health, education and youth offending teams to the eight social care processes. Other contributions, however, such as the support services provided by CAMHS to some placements, were not routinely costed owing to a lack of available data. As the growing potential of the cost calculator model has become apparent, further research projects have been commissioned to estimate costs to education and to health as well as to children's social care. The ultimate aim is to include also the costs of processes undertaken by youth justice teams so that when the costs to the different agencies are aggregated, the total cost to public funds will be shown (see Chapters 5 and 9).

Costs were calculated by developing a basic unit cost for each process and then identifying numerous variations (see below). The basic unit costs were all based on the simplest scenario: that the child was accommodated under the Children Act 1989, Section 20, placed with local authority foster carers within the area of the authority and there were no factors that made it hard to find an appropriate placement. Table 3.2 shows the basic unit costs for each of these processes, illustrated for a child placed in an authority outside London. These unit costs were used in the construction of the first version of the cost calculator model, used to calculate the costs incurred by the sample children in the original study, and later developed into a practical software application for use by children's services (see Chapter 8).

Table 3.2: Basic costs to children's social care of case management processes for a looked after child in foster care (outside London)

	Process	Cost (updated to 2006–7 prices)
Process 1	Deciding child needs to be looked after and finding a first placement	£639
Process 2	Care planning	£120
Process 3	Maintaining the placement (per month)	£1,689
Process 4	Exit from care/accommodation	£263
Process 5	Finding a subsequent placement	£205
Process 6	Review	£408
Process 7	Legal processes	£2,765
Process 8	Transition to leaving care services	£1,164

It is a relatively simple task to identify the frequency with which each of these processes is undertaken for a particular child; by attaching unit costs to them it is possible to calculate the total cost of a care episode. The costs of Processes 3 and 7 are calculated slightly differently from the others. Maintaining the placement (Process 3) represents an ongoing cost incurred throughout the care episode rather than on a number of discrete occasions, and is therefore calculated by multiplying the unit cost by the number of days, weeks or months the child is looked after. The cost of this process comprises both social care activity in supporting the placement and the fee or allowance paid for the placement. Where the child is subject to a care order[3] or other legal order, the cost of Process 7 is added to the full cost of the care episode. Since the model calculates the cost of each placement individually, the one-off investment cost of obtaining the care order is spread over the expected duration of the care episode (from the date of the order until age 18) with part of the cost being allocated to each placement.

Variations

While the methodology described above could be used to calculate the basic costs incurred by any agency in the process of fulfilling its responsibilities for looked after children, there were a number of specific factors that resulted in substantial variations in the time spent on some of the component tasks and thus the process costs. Such variations were engendered by particular factors within the local authority, within the types of placement used or within the population of looked after children. The remainder of this chapter explores these factors and considers how far they are likely to explain the substantial variations between local authorities in the costs of placing children away from home that are evident in the national returns.

Local authority factors leading to variations in costs

Factors within the local authorities that were thought to contribute to variations in the costs of service delivery could be attributed to geography, local policies and procedures, staffing and the availability of resources.

The focus group discussions showed that staff in all the participating local authorities recognised the extent to which geography affected the cost of service delivery: in the large shire counties children could be placed within the area, but nevertheless several miles from both their birth family home and the social workers' office, thus adding to the costs of statutory visits, contact arrangements and any meetings where it was important to bring all interested parties together. In the smaller Unitary 2, poor road networks and the number of placements in remote rural locations also meant that travelling time was excessive. The variation between local authorities could be substantial: for instance social workers in Shire 1 claimed that some statutory visits to children placed within the authority area could take up to a full working day because of the distances involved, while those in Unitary 1 argued that no 'in county' placements took more than 20 minutes to reach.

Local policies and procedures also had a major impact on costs. The local authorities had all introduced procedures designed to reduce the numbers of looked after children or the use of the more expensive placements. However, these gatekeeping procedures could be extremely costly in themselves. For instance, Shire 1 attributed its success in keeping down the numbers of children it looked after to the strict thresholds operating through its 'children's allocation meeting'. Social workers in this authority who wished to place a child had to make a written case and present it to a meeting of senior managers. The cost of social workers' preparation for the meeting and managers' involvement added £536 (at 2006–7 prices) to the unit cost of Process 1 in this authority. However, the cost saving of such a rigorous gatekeeping procedure may have been considerable, for this sum represented only nine days of a foster placement. Moreover, such meetings were only held once a week and the deadlines for notification of a potential case to be heard were apparently rigorously implemented – both factors that are likely to have served to reduce the numbers of children considered and therefore placed. The numbers of children looked after had substantially reduced in Shire 1, though the evidence from the study could not show whether, or how far, this could be attributed to the introduction of this procedure. Nor could our data demonstrate whether the reduction in numbers of looked after children meant that there were more children in the community with unmet needs. The published national data discussed in Chapter 2 do, however, show that the proportionate spend on children in need was above average in this authority, suggesting that by reducing their looked after population managers had succeeded in channelling more resources into family support services for children living at home.

In Shire 1 the involvement of several senior managers in the process of deciding whether a child needed to be looked after appeared to reduce the numbers, and therefore overall costs, of children in care. However, involving senior staff unnecessarily in decisions can obviously be a costly business. The level at which decisions had to be made accounted for a number of variations in the costs of service delivery. London 1, for instance, had recently decided to lower the level at which a decision to fund an agency placement could be made – another area where gatekeeping procedures were usually in place – from group manager to the more accessible service manager, thus reducing the costs of this decision-making process. In Unitary 1, resource allocation meetings had been abandoned, presumably on the grounds of unnecessary expense. In this authority the decision to place a child was less costly than in Shire 1, though it seems probable that the threshold for admission was not so rigorously enforced: 22 per cent of children in need were looked after in Shire 1 in comparison with 28 per cent in Unitary 1 (Department of Health 2003b).

Differences in salaries paid and the mix of staff employed also accounted for variations in the costs of service delivery. Shire 1, for instance, paid its team managers substantially more than did Shire 2, while the median pay for its field social workers was slightly less. As Chapter 2 pointed out, all the authorities had unfilled vacancies: differences in recruitment packages, such as assistance with housing or bursaries for social work trainees, accounted for some of the variations in the costs of employing staff. The costs of appointing agency staff were not incorporated into the unit cost calculations in the original study, as precise details of the percentage employed in each authority were not available; had it been possible to include them they would undoubtedly have added to the costs of service delivery in some authorities.

Authorities can, of course, reduce costs by employing fewer staff. However, a reduced workforce is likely to result in higher caseloads and more children remaining unallocated. The largest caseloads were to be found in Unitary 1 and the greatest number of unallocated cases in London 1, suggesting that there might have been additional negative impacts on the children's wellbeing in these authorities.

Placement factors leading to variations in costs

A number of placement factors also contributed substantially to variations in the costs of looking after a child. The unit costs to children's social care for maintaining the placement (Process 3) developed in the study encompassed the subsistence, salary and capital costs of the placement as calculated by the authorities, together with the costs of supporting it through visits to child and birth family, contact arrangements, travelling and paperwork (social worker time); typing letters, filing and other paperwork, telephone calls, arranging payments to carers (administrative staff time); and supporting foster carers (family placement worker time).

Table 3.3 shows the unit cost for Process 3, maintaining one month's stay in each of the five main types of placement: residential care; foster care; placed with relatives; placed with own parents; and independent living, as calculated through the study.

Table 3.3: Unit costs to local authorities of Process 3: Maintaining the placement (within the authority, outside London) by placement type per month[a]

	Average placement cost	Average process / activity cost	Total cost
Foster care	£595	£1,094	£1,689
Kinship care	£287	£1,157	£1,444
Own parents	£0	£698	£698
Residential unit	£12,716	£698	£13,416
Independence	£1,907	£698	£2,605

a Reported unit costs published in government returns and given in earlier chapters (Tables 2.2 and 2.3) are for weekly placement costs. Monthly costs were used in the study because they are more easily linked with other data items in calculating costs of care episodes and their variations.

As Table 3.3 demonstrates, there were substantial variations in the cost of this process, according to the type of placement used. The greatest variations are due to differences in placement costs (fees).

The costs of providing and staffing accommodation mean that placements in residential units are likely to be more expensive than those within family homes, particularly as the local authority's responsibility to foster carers does not usually encompass the costs of buying, renting or maintaining property. Truly comparable costs for different types of placement would take costs to foster carers – including opportunity costs – into account, something outside the remit of our research programme.

However, between the authorities there were also substantial differences in the costs of different placement types. The weekly placement cost in a local authority residential unit as calculated by the authorities and updated to 2006–7 prices varied from £2934 in Shire 2 to £2379 in London 2. While factors such as staffing levels and the provision of specialist health or education facilities in some placements make comparisons difficult, there were also substantial, and probably genuine, differences between the authorities in the payments made to foster carers. The exceptionally high foster care allowance paid by the London authorities no doubt reflects prices within the capital, but there were also disparities in the amounts paid by the authorities outside London. Between the two shire authorities there was a £38 difference in the weekly payment to carers looking after a 15-year-old, and between the three local authorities outside London for which information was available, a £50 a week difference in the payments made to carers looking after a 16-year-old. The picture was further complicated by provision in at least two of the local authorities to make additional payments to more skilled or specialist foster carers: in Shire 1 the basic foster care allowance could be supplemented by four increments according to skills levels – the rates for the most skilled foster carers in this authority were commensurate with the placement fees for some residential units.

Placing children in the care of relatives or friends was a substantially less costly option than placing them in local authority residential or foster care. Of the four local authorities for which we have information, one had *ad hoc* arrangements to pay an allowance only to those kinship carers who 'require financial assistance in order to be able to look after the child', although they would then pay them the same as they paid their own foster carers (skill level one). The other authorities all paid kinship carers between a quarter and a third of the amount they paid their own foster carers. The Children Act 1989 requires practitioners to investigate first whether a child can be accommodated by members of his or her extended family before seeking a placement with strangers (S.23.6). Kinship care is thought to be most beneficial to the child (see, for instance, Broad 2001), though recent research from both the USA and the UK suggests that outcomes are not always satisfactory (Sinclair, Wilson and Gibbs 2001; Taussig 2003; Ward, Munro and Dearden 2006). Certainly it is the least costly option for the authority, though it seems probable that the low payments also reflect the continuing debate concerning the extent to which the state should support families in fulfilling private responsibilities towards children (Ward forthcoming a). Since the data were collected for the original study, an important legal judgement (R v. Manchester City Council 2001) – has required local authorities to pay the same rates of allowance to their approved foster carers, regardless of whether they are related to the child placed with them.

Placements in independent living have sometimes been regarded as an inexpensive option. However in our study the social workers claimed that young people placed independently received as much support as those in foster care, and the placement costs, which include rent, were substantially higher. The activity costs may be directly related to the implementation of the Children (Leaving Care) Act 2000 and the dedicated support provided by leaving care teams.

There were other important variations in the costs of supporting placements. For instance, some, though not all, social workers visited children and young people in residential care less frequently than those in other placements, on the grounds that the residential key worker would be fulfilling much of their role. This is yet another issue which the current White Paper on looked after children aims to address (Department for Education and Skills 2007a, p.63). Contact arrangements, which took up a substantial amount of the field social workers' time, were also less complex in residential units, where they could be supervised by staff members on site. On the other hand the process of finding a residential placement – which was usually undertaken by social workers – took about ten hours longer than the process of finding a foster home.

Family placement workers tended to visit kinship carers more frequently than local authority foster carers, thus adding to the costs of supporting the former. The least costly placements were of course those with children's own parents, for there was no subsistence allowance to pay, and fewer contact arrangements to supervise. Practitioners claimed that these children received some extra support, as their reviews were held twice as frequently as those for children in other placements, presumably in order to monitor closely the extent to which their needs were being met; however the data from case files and management information systems did not support this assertion.

All the authorities placed children in residential units run by private or voluntary bodies. In the 1980s, Knapp (1984) wrote a paper arguing that the fees then charged by private children's homes were lower than the costs of local authority provision, even after standardization. Some of the agency residential placements used by the local authorities in our study still appeared to be less costly than the equivalent in-house provision, especially those used by London 1. However, there was a huge difference in the weekly charge for these placements, which included a very wide range of different types of facilities. It was almost impossible to make direct comparisons based on the data that we had available. Moreover the costs of maintaining children and young people in agency residential units, where the authority only pays for the beds it fills, should be offset against the costs of keeping open in-house units which could be under-occupied, but again the data were not sufficiently detailed or comprehensive to make these calculations. All we can say is that the fees charged by agencies for providing placements often appeared to be high – but these frequently included the provision of specialist health and/or educational care, other support, and management costs, a finding that concurs with the work of Sellick and Connolly (2002). Further work therefore needs to be undertaken to determine the true cost of such placements in comparison with those provided in-house, and particularly the relationship between costs and children's wellbeing. Whatever the actual cost, the majority of such placements were perceived by local authority personnel to be an expensive, specialist resource, something that Knapp's paper predicted would eventually happen as the needs of the looked after population became more challenging.

Our study was, however, able to explore the additional costs of the supporting processes of finding and maintaining agency placements, all of which accounted for substantial variations in the mean unit costs. In response to the apparent expense of such placements, many authorities operated gatekeeping procedures to try to reduce their usage. Agency foster placements were particularly costly both to find and to maintain, although they were used by all the authorities, and extensively so by the two London boroughs. In one authority the process of placing children with agency foster carers took up to 18 hours more of a family placement worker's time (£589) than for those provided in-house, as all local resources had to be explored before a decision for funding could be made.

In all authorities agreement for funding also had to be obtained from a senior level of management – and in one authority the initial approval from a service manager had to be further ratified by a business development unit. Agencies in some authorities also required the family placement team to liaise with any other responsible authorities to ascertain the appropriateness of placements where other foster children were already present. On the other hand, agencies usually supported their own foster carers, so the task of the local authority family placement team was reduced.

Table 3.4: Comparison between the costs (out of London) of maintaining in-house and agency placements (costs updated to reflect 2006–7 prices)

Placement type	Provider	Cost
Foster care	In house	£1,689 (per month)
Foster care	Agency (in local authority)	£5,433 (per month)
Residential unit	In house	£13,416 (per month)
Residential unit	Agency (in local authority)	£10,248 (per month)

Table 3.4 shows the difference in average costs between maintaining agency foster and residential placements and those provided in house. As is evident, the process of maintaining agency foster homes was costly and may have materially contributed to differences between authorities in the total costs of their care populations. Nevertheless it is also noteworthy that in this study the *average* unit costs of placements in agency residential units were lower than those provided in house: however such a finding should be treated with caution as it could be an artefact, attributable to the wide range of placement costs.

Many agency residential and foster placements attracted additional costs because they were also outside the area of the local authorities. They were particularly expensive to support, because of the travelling time involved. Some of their placement reviews were also held on a three-monthly basis, partly to compensate for social workers' inability to complete all the statutory visits required; again repeated reviews added to their cost.

It is evident from the above discussion that the variation in costs between the different types and providers of placements led to significant disparities in the unit cost of Process 3 – maintaining the placement. This is the most costly of the eight social care processes. Disparities in the proportionate use of the main placement types may have contributed substantially to the variations in the total costs of service delivery between the participating authorities, a point explored further in Chapters 4 and 6.

Child factors

As well as the organizational and the placement factors, there were also a number of child-related factors that contributed to the variations between authorities. Children's needs, the type of placement that they are most likely to require, their probable pathways through the care system, and the provision of additional support services from agencies outside children's social care: all of these factors affect the overall cost of service delivery and are likely to account for some of the variations between authorities. The focus group discussions identified how cost-related factors such as disabilities or offending behaviour impacted on the eight social care processes; case files were searched for evidence of such items in order to build up cost profiles of each child in the sample.

Child factors affecting placement type and support services

There is increasing evidence that the population of children and young people who come into the care of local authorities has a high incidence of health, educational and social need that will require considerable compensatory services if they are to achieve satisfactory wellbeing in adulthood (Meltzer *et al.* 2003; Skuse and Ward 2003; Darker, Ward and Caulfield 2008; Sempik, Ward and Darker 2008). Such services will add to the costs to the public purse of providing placements. In addition, a relatively high proportion of looked after children have extensive needs due to physical or learning disability or emotional or behavioural problems: the prevalence of such children in the care population of a local authority will substantially influence the costs of providing services.

Children with disabilities

In addition to the 8700 children with a need code of 'disability of child' who were looked after in the year ending 31 March 2007 under at least one agreed series of short-term placements (Department for Education and Skills 2007b), about 10 per cent of long-term looked after children and young people are thought to have learning or physical disabilities of sufficient severity to require specialist nursing care (Ward and Wynn forthcoming). The children with disabilities in the study had entered the care system at a slightly (though not significantly) younger age than the rest of the sample; a significantly higher percentage (52%:22%) were placed in residential care at the time of the first round of data collection, though the latter finding is likely to have been influenced by the way the sample was selected. The weekly placement costs of most (though not all) specialist foster homes and residential units for children with disabilities were higher than those for children requiring non-specialist care: one agency home, for instance, charged an additional 30 per cent for providing extra night-time supervision. Placement costs did not always include additional support services such as special educational provision, physiotherapy and speech therapy, some of which had to be bought in by social care providers. There were significant differences between some of the authorities in the proportion of their sample children who had disabilities – the range was between 12 per cent (Unitary 2) and 34 per cent (Shire 1).[4] This is one more factor that accounts for the variance in the cost of their service delivery; it is explored further in Chapters 5 and 6.

Emotional or behavioural difficulties

Somewhere between 40 per cent and 60 per cent of children looked after away from home in the UK are thought to have emotional or behavioural problems of a severity that would warrant referral for clinical support (Meltzer *et al.* 2003). As Quinton and Murray (2002) point out, these difficulties are mostly focused around conduct problems, although emotional disturbances involving high levels of anxiety and unhappiness are also common. The prevalence of children with such disorders adds to the costs of care provision in a number of ways. First, children with emotional or behavioural difficulties should be receiving mental health support – one of the additional services that add to the costs of placements, even if not charged to children's social care. Second, these children cannot always be accommodated by foster carers with only basic skills. They are likely to require more specialist – and therefore more expensive – placements. However, many children and young people with such difficulties are not immediately placed in specialist care – they frequently appear to run the gamut of foster and residential placements, only achieving specialist support after a number of other options have proved unsatisfactory.

Over half (54%) of the children and young people in the sample were identified as having emotional or behavioural difficulties.[5] Scott and colleagues (2001) have demonstrated the long-term public costs of such problems. Our study confirmed some of these findings by demonstrating that children and young people in the care system who have emotional or behavioural difficulties are substantially more costly to children's social care than their peers: those in the sample were at least twice as likely to be offered the more expensive agency placements and/or to be placed in residential care; they were half as likely as their peers to be accommodated by relatives or friends. In addition, a high proportion of these young people spent time in temporary relief placements, provided by the local authorities to support their permanent carers. Differences in the prevalence of children with these attributes within their looked after population therefore account for a substantial amount of the variation in the costs of service delivery between local authorities (see Chapters 5 and 6).

Young offenders

It was evident that offending behaviour affected the costs of looking after young people rather differently from other forms of emotional or behavioural disturbance. Young people who commit offences incur additional costs to youth offending teams, to the police and to the courts, as well as extra costs to children's social care. The latter are required by the courts to find placements for young people remanded to their care, and have little control over such decisions. This means that the case management processes are less onerous, and therefore less costly, but that the placement costs are likely to be greater, as many of these children will be in residential units, some of them with secure provision. Moreover, as one might expect, these young people tend to move frequently from one placement to another, and the costs of finding a new placement tends to increase with each move (see Chapter 4).

Unaccompanied asylum-seeking children

One further group whose prevalence is likely to account for some of the variation in costs of looking after children are unaccompanied asylum seekers. A number of factors reduce the cost of providing them with care or accommodation: unaccompanied asylum-seeking children are, *de facto*, children in need, and therefore there is no complex decision-making procedure before they can be placed. There are also no contact arrangements to be made with relatives. On the other hand, costs are likely to be increased, at least at the start of a care episode, by the probability that an interpreter will be needed for all case management processes. While these factors almost balance each other out, over time the costs of providing care to unaccompanied asylum-seeking children are likely to be higher than those for some other groups because of the length of the care episode. Almost all will need to remain looked after until they reach adulthood, although they tend to enter care at a later age than many other children and young people (see Chapters 5 and 6). Unaccompanied asylum-seeking children are also likely to incur costs to other agencies: for instance there will be extra costs for providing language support in schools and for processing asylum-seeking applications.

Children with exceptionally high support needs

Almost all local authorities have a number of children and young people with physical or learning disabilities and emotional or behavioural problems in their care population. For the reasons discussed above, the proportion displaying such attributes will substantially affect the cost of providing care or accommodation to the total care population, particularly if they become looked after at an early age and are unlikely to leave before they reach adulthood. Moreover, some children in each authority will display a combination of disability, emotional or behavioural problems and offending behaviour. These children and young people are likely to be very few in number: about ten per cent of the sample in four of the participating authorities, although more in others. Nevertheless, the combination of the factors discussed above may add substantially to the costs of supporting these young people, so they may account for a disproportionate amount of the budget.

Child factors affecting social care processes

The prevalence of some of these child-related factors not only affects the cost of placements, but also the costs of social care processes. Where children have profound physical or learning disabilities, care planning is slightly less costly, because some of the work involved in developing the personal education plan has already been undertaken as part of the process of obtaining statements of special educational need. Process 3, maintaining the placement, is also less costly because relatives tend to arrange their own, unsupervised, contact and there is less need for social worker involvement. On the other hand, the process of deciding if a child needs to be looked after and then finding placements is more costly, as there is more negotiation between the various agencies involved, particularly if joint funding is being considered.

Data collected in the course of the study showed that the child-related factors discussed above had a significant impact on the length of placements. The average length of a placement was reduced by 198 days if a child or young person displayed emotional or behavioural difficulties, and by a further 135 days if convicted of an offence. On the other hand, it was increased by 162 days if the child or young person had a physical or learning disability. Length of placements was related to mobility within the care system rather than to the length of the overall care episode – children with emotional or behavioural difficulties tend to change placement significantly more frequently than those with physical or learning disabilities. Changes of placement are not always indicative of negative outcomes – for instance, children may experience positive moves from unsatisfactory placements to others that more closely meet their needs. As Chapter 7 demonstrates, some children who were unhappy in placements found that they could only move from them if they behaved badly. Conversely, stable placements are not necessarily always positive: a number of social workers we spoke to raised concerns about the institutionalization of children with disabilities in long-term residential placements.

Nevertheless, all changes are costly to the local authority, and frequent changes are likely to have a negative impact on the child's wellbeing. The mean unit cost for Process 5, finding a second or subsequent placement with local authority foster carers, was £205[6]; it rose to £463 if a residential placement was sought, and to £718 if the child was placed with agency foster carers outside the authority area. Moreover, it is evident that some children, particularly those with emotional or behavioural difficulties, enter a vicious circle in which frequent movement from one placement to another exacerbates their problems, with the result that the pattern of instability continues. Such children become 'difficult to place',[7] and the costs of finding them further placements increase substantially. The data from the study suggest that the cost of finding a subsequent placement is increased by a further £430 (210%) in foster care, and £574 (124%) in residential care once the child has acquired this reputation.

Table 3.5 illustrates how the costs of providing care over a six-month period to a child (Child 1) who shows no evidence of disability or emotional or behavioural difficulties and who stays in the same foster placement throughout that period, compare with the those of providing care to a child (Child 2) with a behavioural problem who experiences the breakdown of placements in one local authority and one agency foster home over the same six months and is eventually placed in a residential unit. For the sake of simplicity it is assumed that both young people are accommodated under the Children Act 1989, Section 20.

The table demonstrates how the costs of each process can be calculated and then added together to show the costs incurred both to children's social care and to other agencies over specific periods of time. It also shows how children can incur very different costs over a similar time period as their needs become more evident. It is noteworthy that, as Child 2's difficulties become more apparent, not only do placements become more

Table 3.5: Comparison between care costs of two children with different pathways over six months (outside London)

Child 1

Activity	Cost to children's social care	Cost to other agency
Review	£408	£48[a]
New care plan (Process 2)		£148[b]
Maintain placement with local authority foster carers for 6 months including process and placement costs (Process 3)	£10,134	

Child 2

Activity	Cost to children's social care	Cost to other agency
Review	£408	£48*
New care plan (Process 2). Decision to provide mental health support	£120	£148*
Maintain placement with local authority foster carers for 2 months including process and placement costs (Process 3)	£3,378	£580* (weekly sessions with clinical psychologist)
Change of placement to agency carers in local authority (Process 5)	£962	
Maintain placement with agency carers within local authority for 2½ months (Process 3)	£13,583	£725* (weekly sessions with clinical psychologist)
Change of placement to residential care in local authority (child now difficult to place) (Process 5)	£1,037	

Child 1

Review (Process 6)	£408	£48
Total	**£11,070**	**£244**

Child 2

Maintain placement in residential home for 1½ months (Process 3)	£20,124	£435* (weekly sessions with clinical psychologist)
Review (Process 6)	£815	£211[c]
Total	**£40,427**	**£2,147**

a Attendance by an education representative.

b Completion of care plan and personal education plan by other agency professionals.

c Attended by education and clinical representatives because child now receiving mental health support.

* Calculated from Curtis (2007), p.115.

costly, but the costs of routine processes such as holding a review or finding a new placement also increase.

Translating the methodology into a practical application

Once the unit costs and their numerous variations had been calculated in the manner described above, it was possible to develop a cost calculator model that could link the costs to data collected from case files about children's needs, the frequency of social care processes, types of placements and other services received over specific time periods. The costs incurred over the study timeframe by each of the 478 children in the sample were calculated; these are discussed in the next three chapters. Relationships between costs and the relatively limited outcomes information available could also be explored (see Chapter 6). However the calculations are based on a selected sample of children and young people chosen to illustrate how and why costs vary, and to explore the extent to which costs relate to experience and outcome. Since the study was undertaken, the original research instrument has been translated into a practical tool that local authorities and other agencies are using to inform decision-making at both child and authority level, to facilitate strategic planning and to introduce greater transparency into the commissioning process. Cost calculations that were originally somewhat theoretical and illustrative are now being used to support practical decisions about children currently in care or accommodation. As part of the programme to develop the model for a more practical purpose, adjustments have been made in order both to facilitate calculations and to increase their accuracy.

Increasing the accuracy of calculations

Many of the unit costs used in the research model are based on average costs incurred by six local authorities. A further authority piloted the model to assess its practical uses (Ward, Holmes and Soper 2005) and there are now 11 more authorities working on the research and development programme. Data collected through this programme will continue to inform the development of unit costs – and of course average costs from 18 authorities are likely to reflect reality more closely than those based on data from only six.

However, average costs can only produce a relatively broad picture; it is evident that those authorities which decide to make substantial use of the Cost Calculator for Children's Services to support routine decisions will wish to move away from averages to calculate their own customized unit costs and import them into the model. A unit costs database has now been developed and incorporated into the cost calculator programme to facilitate this. For each process authorities can import their own activity data together with information about salaries to develop their own unit costs. Overheads are automatically calculated following an accepted formula (see Curtis 2007) and included. Because the collection of activity data and the identification of variations can be time-consuming, the database allows for limited as well as complete customization: authorities can explore the mean activity and finance data collected from others and only make changes where their own situation appears to be substantially different.

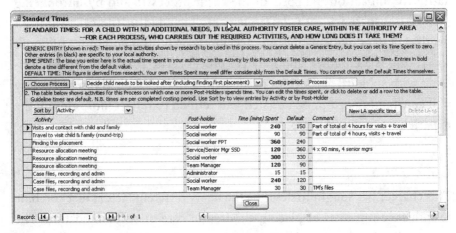

Figure 3.1: Screenshot from the Unit Cost Database
Note: Default times reflect the average activity times for each process collected from authorities that have so far contributed to the research and development programme.

In the initial study, over 90 per cent of the costs of care episodes were accounted for by Process 3 (maintaining the placement); the cost of running the residential unit, the allowance to the foster carer or the fee paid to the agency providing the placement was the most costly element in this process. The use of average costs for the different placement types is particularly problematic both because they encompass such a high proportion of the overall costs of care episodes and because there are extensive variations around the mean (see Table 3.3). In developing the facility to customize the model, one of the first considerations has been to allow authorities to calculate individual Process 3 costs for each placement. This can be done by importing the actual fees and allowances paid for individual placements, or by defining a customized cost sheet and substituting in it the average fees actually paid for particular types of placements instead of the default figures already provided. The development of the Cost Calculator for Children's Services is discussed further in Chapter 8.

Chapter 9 describes the continuing programme of research and development that has followed the original study. This currently includes studies that aim to further refine the unit costs described in this chapter by identifying more specifically how placements at a distance from the authority impact on the costs of the eight processes and by introducing greater transparency into those elements included in the calculation of overheads. It is evident that the development of unit costs for children's social care is a complex and iterative process. The basic unit costs developed with six local authorities participating in the original research study will constantly need to be updated and refined to reflect more closely the experiences of a wider group.

Conclusion

This chapter has sought to describe the many different factors that combine to influence the costs of placing children in care or accommodation. The costs of the eight key social care processes that support the case management of a looked after child have been calculated, using data gathered through focus groups and responses to questionnaires from staff in the six local authorities that participated in the original study. Placement costs incorporating fee payments and foster care allowances have also been added. Variations to the costs of social care may be attributed to factors within the organization of the authority, the proportionate use of different placement types and to differences in the characteristics of the population looked after: these issues are explored in greater depth in Chapters 4, 5 and 6.

Some costs to agencies outside children's social care have also been considered: although these are not necessarily charged to children's services departments they nevertheless represent a cost to the public purse. To understand more fully the costs incurred when children are placed in care or accommodation, the routine costs of health, education, socio-legal and youth justice processes would need to be linked to the costs of social care; these issues are now being explored in the ongoing research and development programme (see Chapter 9).

The unit costs shown in this chapter are based on data concerning activities, placement fees and salaries provided by the six authorities that participated in the original study. Increasing numbers of authorities participating in the research programme will produce more realistic average costs. Other authorities using the cost calculator model as a practical tool to support decision-making may produce different figures; however if the same methodology is used their calculations will be comparable, making it possible to identify where differences lie. Developing accurate unit costs in this area is a complex process that constantly needs to be updated and refined.

Summary of the key points from Chapter 3

- Eight processes which support the case management of looked after children have been identified and costed: deciding a child needs to be looked after and finding the first placement; care planning; maintaining the placement; exit from care/accommodation; finding a subsequent placement; review; legal processes; transition to leaving care services.

- Activity data were collected from focused discussions held with practitioners and managers who were asked to break down each process into its component parts and calculate the amount of time it took each staff group to complete the separate tasks. Unit costs were calculated using these data, together with information about salaries and placement fees.

- Variations in unit costs can be attributed to authority factors, placement factors and/or child-related factors.

- Authority factors include, for example: geography; policies and procedures; staffing and resources.

- Placement factors are related to placement type, placement fee or cost, provider (e.g. agency or local authority) and location. The extensive range of costs of residential placements provided both by authorities and agencies may produce misleading calculations when averages are used.

- Child-related factors include: disability, emotional or behavioural difficulty, and offending behaviour. The circumstances of asylum-seeking children also produce different cost pathways.

- Translating the research methodology into a practical application for use by local authorities and other agencies requires a continuing programme to compare, customize and refine unit costs.

Notes

1   These calculations do not yet include the cost of recruitment, training and assessment of carers. This work is currently being undertaken as part of our ongoing programme, so that future cost calculations will include these elements.

2   In order to facilitate comparisons, throughout this book all 2000–1 unit costs calculated as part of the original study have been inflated using PSSRU pay and prices inflators to 2005–6 (the latest year for which they are available) and the Treasury GDP deflator estimate to 2006–7. The inflation over the period was estimated at 25.8 per cent.

3   Care orders were the main legal processes that affected the children and young people in the original study. While unit costs have been derived for this process, further work still needs to be undertaken to develop unit costs for emergency protection orders, interim care orders, special guardianship orders, and so on.

4   ($\chi^2 = 8.16$, $df = 1$, $p = 0.004$, continuity corrected); there were also significant differences between Shire 1 and Unitary 2 ($\chi^2 = 4.80$, $df = 1$, $p = 0.028$, continuity corrected).

5   Children and young people were identified as having emotional or behavioural difficulties if they met one or more of the following criteria within the study timeframe: they were permanently excluded from school; they had a statement of special educational need in response to emotional or behavioural difficulties; they attended a school for children with emotional or behavioural difficulties; they

experienced more than one placement breakdown as a result of their behaviour; they had either received or been offered and refused mental health support services during the timeframe; they had exhibited self-harming behaviour patterns; they were engaged in prostitution; they had an eating disorder.

6   Updated to 2006–7 prices.

7   In this study the definition of a 'difficult to place' child was one who had emotional or behavioural difficulty and disability, or emotional or behavioural difficulty and was a frequent mover (in accordance with Performance Assessment Framework indicators).

Chapter 4

Placement Patterns, Processes and Costs

Introduction

The previous chapter explored the factors that impact on the costs of placing children in local authority care. We demonstrated how the costs of social care are made up of two elements: the costs of case management processes and the day-to-day costs of placement provision. We showed how the amount of time spent on various activities by staff at different levels of an organization can be calculated and then translated into the costs of case management, and how the daily costs of placements differ according to type, locality and provider. We also noted that a number of factors related to local authority policy and practice, the needs and characteristics of the population served and the types of placement available lie behind substantial variations in the overall costs of service delivery. Once the unit costs have been calculated and the numerous variations taken into account, it is possible to multiply these by the number of times a case management process has been undertaken and the number of days or hours a child has spent in placement over a specific time period and thereby calculate the social care costs of a care episode. Of course, social care is only one of a range of services available to children looked after away from home; there will also be costs to education, health and possibly Connexions, youth services, mental health, youth justice and socio-legal services. As part of our current research and development programme we are mapping out and developing unit costs for several of these other children and young people's services so that they can be included in subsequent versions of the model (see Chapter 9). However it is easiest to understand the rationale for these calculations if we focus initially on one specific area, in this instance social care.

In this chapter we take the unit costs calculated in the manner demonstrated in Chapter 3 and link these with the data from the sample of children whose care experiences were followed for the 20 months of our original study to explore further how different patterns of placements and processes are likely to have affected the costs and complexity of their care pathways. Calculations of probable costs to the authorities involved demonstrate how such patterns are likely to account for substantial differences in the costs of service delivery. Chapters 5 and 6 then seek to shed further light on such differences by exploring how far they are related to the characteristics of the children concerned, while Chapters 6 and 7 explore relationships between costs and outcome.

The sample

Chapter 2 gave details of the sample children and described how they were selected. As we shall see (Chapters 5 and 6) costs are closely related to children's needs. It will be remembered that all children aged ten and over and looked after by the local authorities during the first Children in Need Census week (February 2000) were eligible for selection. However, the sample was stratified to include sufficient numbers for meaningful analysis of children with disabilities and young people placed in residential care. This means that the group studied is likely to include rather more children and young people with emotional or behavioural difficulties, or with physical and learning disabilities than might be found in a normative population of looked after children, and is a point that should be taken into account when considering these findings. It was not possible to weight the sample in this way in Unitary 2 because of their small total number of looked after children; this may be one reason for differences between costs and experiences in this authority as compared with the five others.

Estimating costs

Chapter 2 (Table 2.5) also showed that, for various reasons, there were considerable differences in the sample numbers of children from each of the six authorities. Because of these disparities, percentages are used throughout this chapter in order to make comparisons more meaningful. There were also differences in the length of care episodes, as 177 children (37%) ceased to be looked after during the study period. Moreover within the timeframe of the study there were also substantial differences in the proportion of children who left the care of the authorities, ranging from 14 (25%) in Shire 1 to 39 (48%) in Shire 2. In order to facilitate comparisons, many of the calculations shown in this chapter do not display the raw data, but instead have used them as a basis for estimating the annual costs incurred by a care population of 100 children looked after by each authority. Estimated costs have been calculated by dividing each cost by the number of placement days to which they relate (giving costs per day for the process) and then multiplying by the number of days for which 100 children would be looked after for a year (36,500).

Costs within the study timeframe

Table 4.1 gives details of the comparative social care costs of looking after a sample group of a hundred children in each of the six local authorities for a year. As Chapter 3 showed, the costs are made up of the range of social care processes that are undertaken during a care episode, together with the costs of providing a home and the activities required to support the child within it. The table itemizes the costs of these processes in separate columns. As in other chapters, for ease of comparison costs have been inflated to 2006–7 prices. The costs data set out in Table 4.1 are described in the following sections and presented as charts to illustrate cost comparisons between the authorities.

As was evident from Chapter 3, the vast majority of costs for looked after children are incurred by Process 3 (maintaining the placement). This process accounted for between 95 per cent and 97 per cent of the total costs in each authority within the study timeframe. It is therefore unsurprising that differences in placement costs account for most of the variation between authorities.

Figure 4.1 plots the estimated annual costs incurred by a hundred children in each authority, using data from two columns of Table 4.1, namely

Table 4.1: Estimated yearly costs incurred by 100 children looked after in each authority (costs inflated to 2006-7 prices to facilitate comparisons)

	No of children	Process 1 Admission	Process 2 Care plan^a	Process 3 Maintain placement	Process 4 Exit	Process 5 Next placement	Process 6 Review^a	Process 7 Legal	Process 8 Transition to leaving care services	Total estimated annual costs
London 1	100	N/A	£30,119	£6,739,657	N/A	£83,216	£197,932	£21,840	£18,862	£7,091,626
London 2	100	N/A	£30,356	£6,823,627	N/A	£65,608	£150,019	£25,781	£19,597	£7,114,988
Shire 1	100	N/A	£18,784	£7,211,361	N/A	£31,088	£144,132	£19,565	£10,513	£7,435,443
Shire 2	100	N/A	£22,037	£6,698,770	N/A	£60,062	£144,725	£18,211	£18,109	£6,961,914
Unitary 1	100	N/A	£21,056	£5,992,809	N/A	£63,574	£131,594	£21,629	£11,596	£6,242,258
Unitary 2	100	N/A	£20,662	£3,726,437	N/A	£30,809	£100,204	£23,431	£13,720	£3,915,263
Total			**£143,014**	**£37,192,661**		**£334,357**	**£868,606**	**£130,457**	**£92,397**	**£38,761,492**

a Based on estimated frequency.

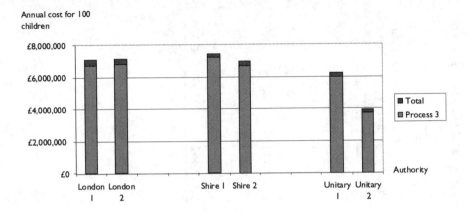

Figure 4.1: Maintaining the placement as a proportion of estimated annual costs for a care population of 100 children in each authority (Costs inflated to 2006–7 prices)

Process 3, maintaining the placement', and 'Total estimated annual costs'. The areas of the two blocks shown for each authority therefore illustrate the proportionate costs of maintaining the placement. These estimated annual costs show substantial differences between some, but by no means all, the authorities. Costs to London 1 and 2 and Shire 2 were all fairly similar, with differences of only one or two per cent between them; however costs in the two unitary authorities were at least 11 per cent less than those in the other authorities, and those in Unitary 2 only 62 per cent of those in Unitary 1. Estimated costs in Shire 1 are particularly intriguing, for, as we have seen, this authority had taken extensive measures to reduce the overall costs of providing care or accommodation and had succeeded in reducing the numbers looked after, yet its placement costs were higher than those of all the other authorities. This chapter will seek to find an explanation for this anomaly.

Placement types

Figure 4.2 demonstrates the percentage of months the children spent in each of the different placement types within the timeframe of the study. As can be seen, there were substantial differences between the authorities.

These are likely to account for much of the variation in placement costs noted above. The average unit cost for maintaining a child for a week in a residential placement was 4.5 times that of an independent living arrangement, eight times that of the cost for foster care, 9.5 times that of a placement with family and friends and more than 12.5 times that of a placement with own parents (see Chapter 3, Table 3.3). High percentages of placement months in foster care and slightly lower percentages in residential care are likely to provide some explanation as to why placement costs are lower in Shire 2 and Unitary 2 than in their paired authorities. In both Shire 1 and Unitary 1, the high proportion of time spent in placements with parents or relatives (30% and 35%) balances out some of the costs incurred by extensive use of residential care. This may also be one reason why, in spite of its higher use of residential care, placement costs are lower in London 1 than in London 2.

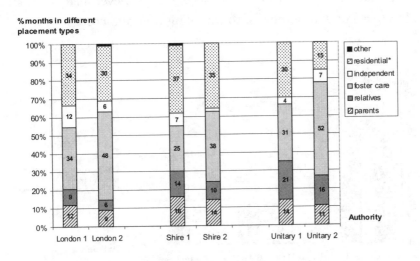

Figure 4.2: Percentage of placement months spent in different placement types by authority (n=1004 placements; 7633 months)

* Includes children's homes, mother and baby units and secure units.

The picture is also complicated by the use of out-of-authority and agency placements. Placements outside the area of the authority cost about £125 (at 2006–7 prices) more per month to maintain than those within it, because of the increased hours spent by fieldworkers in providing support, largely due to the longer travelling times for statutory visits. Figure 4.3 depicts the percentage of placement months that sample children were known to have spent in out-of-area and agency placements. The numbers used for this chart are likely to be underestimates, as only those placements that were clearly identified as being out-of-authority or provided by an agency were included in this category. Where this was not explicitly stated, placements were assumed to have been provided by the authority and within its area. Figure 4.3 shows that children in Unitary 1 spent over a quarter (27%) of their time placed out-of-area in comparison with only eight per cent of time spent in such placements in Unitary 2. This may provide a further reason why costs in the latter authority were low, and perhaps indicates one explanation for the relatively high costs in the former. In both the two London authorities, children spent about half their time (51% and 50%) in out-of-area placements; however many of these were in other London boroughs, so travelling time and costs were low.

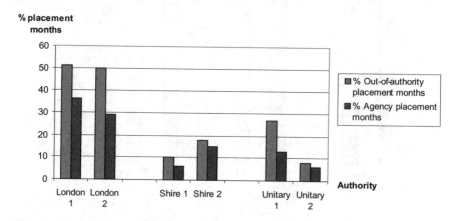

Figure 4.3: Percentage of months in out-of-authority and agency provided placements by local authority (n=1004 placements; 7633 months)[a]

a These figures are likely to be an underestimate, as only those placements that were clearly identified as being out-of-authority or provided by an agency were included in this category. Where this was not explicitly stated, placements were assumed to have been provided by the authority and within its area.

Although there is considerable range in the costs of maintaining agency residential placements, and some are less costly than those provided in-house, as a rule they are one of the most expensive types of care. This is at least partly because many include provision for health or education as well as for social care. Agency foster placements are particularly expensive, costing on average three times as much to maintain as those provided by the authorities. Extensive use of such placements by the London authorities – particularly agency foster care in London 2 – is a further reason for their high costs. On the other hand, children in Shire 1 and Unitary 2 spent only six per cent of their time in agency placements, another explanation for low costs in the latter (but not the former) authority.

Movement

All the sample children were already looked after at the start of the study, and so Process 1 (the decision to look after a child and finding the first placement) occurred outside the timeframe for all but 21 children who left care or accommodation and were then readmitted, four of them twice. Figure 4.4 shows the comparative estimated costs for undertaking this process for 100 children in each authority (with no readmissions).

The high costs for Process 1 in Shire 1 reflect the strict gatekeeping procedures designed to reduce the numbers of children looked after and discussed in Chapter 3. These may be regarded as investment costs, for not only is there evidence that this authority was placing fewer children in care or accommodation (see Chapter 2), but also this and subsequent chapters will show that those children who *were* looked after by this authority tended to receive placements more appropriate to their needs and to change them less frequently than in some of the others, perhaps reflecting more efficient strategic planning. Variations in costs in all the authorities also reflect the types of placement chosen: high Process 1 costs in the two London authorities may reflect their extensive use of out-of-authority or agency placements, which required additional activity; low costs in Unitary 2 reflect the small number of out-of-authority, agency or residential placements used.

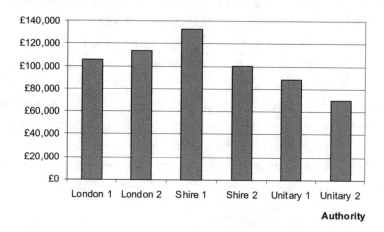

Figure 4.4: Costs of Process 1: Decision to look after and finding first placement, by local authority (annual estimated costs for a care population of 100 children with no readmissions, updated to 2006–7 prices[a])

a Costs of Process 1 (decide to look after and find first placement) do not include costs of initial and core assessments, each estimated at £873 to social services and £161 to other agencies (2006–7 prices) (see Cleaver, Walker and Meadows 2004).

Costs of moving from one placement to another are reflected in Process 5 (finding second and subsequent placement). There were 533 placement moves during the 20-month timeframe. These were experienced by 199 children, and include six who moved more than ten times. Figure 4.5 uses these data to estimate the number of moves experienced annually by a care population of 100 children in each authority. The number of placement changes was markedly higher in Shire 2, where they were just over twice as frequent as in Unitary 2. A single child experiencing a high number of placement changes could skew the figures, as may have happened in London 2 and Shire 2, where one child experienced 21, and one 20 placements within the 20 months of the study. However, in Shire 2 there were also more children who experienced four or more placements (18:22%) during the study than in the other authorities; moreover, even if all those children who moved more than ten times are excluded from the analysis, there was still more than twice as much movement in this authority as in

Unitary 2[1]. Differences in the number of changes in placement between authorities almost reaches statistical significance.[2] This is more apparent if the six children who moved placement more than ten times are excluded.[3]

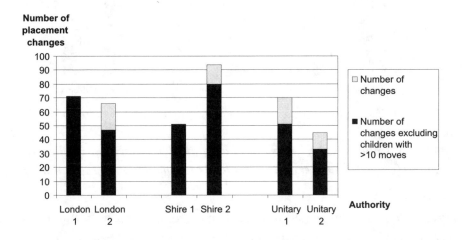

Figure 4.5: Placement changes by local authority (estimated number of changes over a year for a care population of 100 children)

We have already indicated in Chapter 3 that the more frequently children move, the more difficult they become to place, and as a result the placement costs tend to increase. Placement changes entail both a financial cost to the authority and a wellbeing cost to the children concerned. In our wider research and development programme on costing children's services, the definition of a frequent mover is based on the PAF indicator, 'CF/A1: The percentage of looked after children at 31 March with three or more placements during the last financial year' (now replaced by the indicators N1 62 and 63) (Department of Communities and Local Government 2007). Three or more placements in 12 months would be equivalent to five or more in the 20 months of the study time period. The numbers of children experiencing this level of movement are shown in Figure 4.6. As can be seen, the highest number of frequent movers is to be found in London 1 and Shire 2, and the lowest in Shire 1 and Unitary 2.

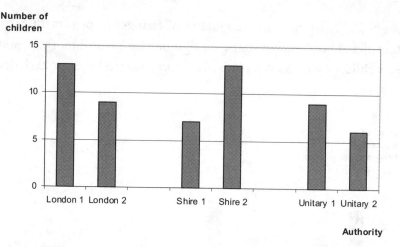

Figure 4.6: Children experiencing three or more placements annually by local authority (estimated numbers over a year for a care population of 100 children)

Figure 4.7 shows the variation in costs incurred by Process 5 (finding a second or subsequent placement) in the six authorities. The data demonstrate how changes of placement are a costly process, and particularly so if the child is a frequent mover, or if he or she moves between residential or agency placements which require additional assessment procedures or approval at a higher level of management.

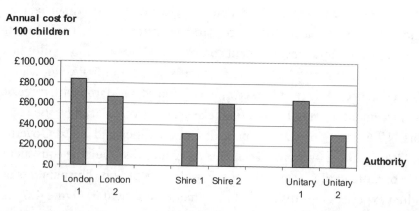

Figure 4.7: Costs of Process 5: Finding second or subsequent placements by local authority (annual estimated costs for a care population of 100 children, updated to 2006–7 prices)

The exceptionally high costs for this process in London 1, for instance, reflect the frequent placement moves as well as the high number of out-of-authority and agency placements used by this authority, although children did not spend significantly more months in them than in London 2. However the frequent changes of placement found in Shire 2 are not reflected in similarly high costs. The standard unit cost for this process in this authority was £229 (at 2006–7 prices), only slightly higher than that in Unitary 2, and lower than that in all the other authorities, being only 69 per cent of the unit cost (£332) in Shire 1. For Shire 2, the frequent occurrences of Process 5 are to some extent balanced out by their relatively low cost. For Shire 1, the high cost of the process is balanced out by the much smaller amount of movement. The figures also show how infrequent changes of placement in Unitary 2 are reflected in costs that are less than half those incurred by some of the other authorities.

Finally, large numbers of children moved out of the care of the authorities within the study timeframe – in Shire 2 and the two unitaries this amounted to over 40 per cent of the original sample. We have used these data to estimate the different costs to the authorities of undertaking this process over a 12-month period, as shown in Figure 4.8. The impact of the length of care episodes on costs is discussed in greater detail below.

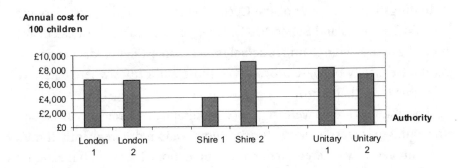

Figure 4.8: Costs of Process 4: Ceasing to be looked after (annual estimated costs for a care population of 100 children, updated to 2006–7 prices)

Planning processes

There are three planning processes that may occur during a care episode: Process 2 (care plan), Process 6 (review) and Process 8 (transition to leaving care). Process 2 encompasses a number of different elements: the personal education plan; the individual health plan; for some children and young people, the permanency plan; as well as the care plan itself. The management information systems in the six authorities in the original study held very little precise data on this process. It was not always possible to calculate how many children had a care plan, or how frequently these were updated. For the purposes of developing the original version of the cost calculator model, we calculated the costs and frequency of planning processes from information obtained in the meetings with social care staff, where the consensus was that all children would have a care plan and that at least some of these elements would be updated following a six-monthly review. Practitioners also stated that care plans for children with disabilities were updated less frequently because their circumstances were less likely to change, and they were less likely to move placements. The calculations therefore include an assumption that care plans for children with disabilities were updated annually rather than on a six-monthly basis.

The introduction of the Integrated Children's System between 2003 and 2007 has meant that electronic data on the frequency of all social care processes are now more likely to be accessible, an expectation supported by findings from the pilot of the Cost Calculator for Children's Services (see Ward, Holmes and Soper 2005). Later versions of the cost calculator model have been able to utilize actual rather than estimated data concerning the frequency of these processes in those authorities where dates are accessible (see Chapter 8).

Local authorities have a statutory requirement to review all looked after children at least once every six months – and more frequently if they have only recently entered care or accommodation. This would mean that over the 20-month period of the initial study all children in the sample should have had at least three reviews, and many of them considerably more.

Figure 4.9 shows the estimated costs of plans and reviews in the participating authorities, as calculated using the unit costs developed for the
study. Differences in the costs of reviews reflect differences in frequency
when children are disabled or placed out-of-authority. In all but one of the
authorities, social care staff indicated that reviews for children in
out-of-authority placements or placed with own parents were undertaken
twice as frequently as those for children looked after within the authority
or in other placements; the prevalence of children in these placements is
one reason for the high costs of reviews in London 1. Low staff salaries, as
well as the small number of children in these placements, are among the
reasons for the substantially lower costs of reviews in Unitary 2. In Shire 1,
where there were also very few children in out-of-authority or agency
placements, the savings are balanced by higher staff salaries and by a high
proportion of children with physical or learning disabilities whose reviews
were less frequent, but entailed higher costs due to the attendance of
additional health care personnel.

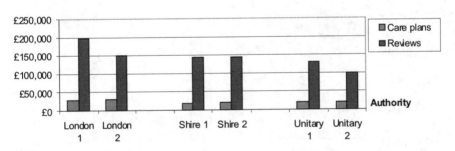

Figure 4.9: Costs of Processes 2 and 6: Care plans and reviews by local authority
(annual estimated costs for a care population of 100 children, updated to
2006–7 prices)

The greatest amount of social care activity supporting Process 8 (transition
to leaving care) is taken up with constructing the pathway plan. The social
care staff who contributed to the development of the unit costs calculated
that on average this activity took 39 hours to complete because it was

necessary to develop a relationship with the young person as part of the process in order for the pathway plan to be fully appropriate. The larger set of activity data that is being compiled through the current programme of research, development and implementation of the cost calculator model (see Chapter 9), will provide opportunities to test out and verify these calculations. Eighty-one young people in the sample reached the age of 16 and made the transition to leaving care services during the course of the study. Figure 4.10 shows two different, but related, variables. The annual estimated costs to each authority of the transition to leaving care are illustrated by the shaded columns and the values shown on the left hand axis; the estimated numbers per 100 children in each authority who make the transition to adulthood each year are shown by the line, the values of which are reflected on the right hand axis. As Figure 4.10 shows, the proportionate numbers ranged from 13 in Unitary 1 to 21 in Shire 2, increasing the costs of case management during the study timeframe for the latter authority.

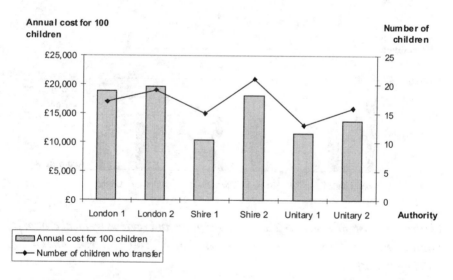

Figure 4.10: Costs of Process 8: Transition to leaving care by local authority (annual estimated costs for a care population of 100 children, updated to 2006–7 prices[a])

a In the original study this process was not costed for children with disabilities or for unaccompanied asylum seekers who moved to different systems. Subsequent changes in practice are now reflected in our current programme of work which costs this process for all care leavers..

Legal processes

Finally, 266 (56%) of the children in the sample were made the subject of care orders. Legal processes are costly to both social services and other agencies; they add substantially to the costs of care episodes. Moreover, the costs illustrated in Figure 4.11 below only include the costs of social care; legal and court costs would add substantially to the costs to the public purse of each care order (see Selwyn *et al.* 2006). We also know that the costs of care orders are subject to substantial variations, reflecting factors such as the type of court involved, the number of interim hearings, the extent to which the order is contested and so on; this clearly warrants further study, although it has so far been outside the remit of our cost calculation programme. We can, however, demonstrate that there are considerable differences between authorities in the frequency with which care proceedings are undertaken; in the initial study the proportion of children subject to care orders ranged from 47 per cent in Shire 1 to 66 per cent in Unitary 2 (see Figure 4.11). The costs of a care order are spread evenly across the care episode, from the date of the order to the young person's 18th birthday, when the majority come to an end (see also Chapter 3).

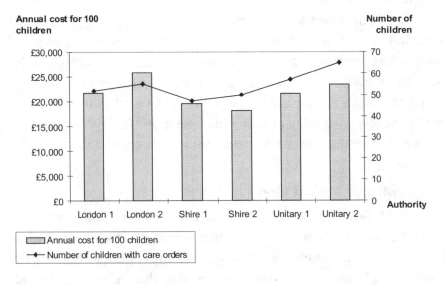

Figure 4.11: Costs of Process 7: Children with care orders by local authority (estimated annual costs for a care population of 100 children, updated to 2006–7 prices)

TOURO COLLEGE LIBRARY

Thus the older the young person is at the time the order is made, the greater the annual cost. High salary costs in Shire 1 and a different age structure of the sample mean that the costs of this process were in fact lowest in Shire 2.

Total costs

Table 4.1 (at the beginning of this chapter) shows in detail the data discussed and puts them together to show the costs of care pathways for an estimated sample of 100 children looked after for 12 months, with costs updated to reflect 2006–7 prices. As is evident, the cost of maintaining placements dominates all other costs, so that those authorities which use the most expensive placements incur the greatest overall costs. Placements are often closely related to need, and authorities may have little choice over their selection when children have extensive needs (see Chapter 6). The cost of other processes also has some influence: the costs of maintaining placements in London 1, for instance, are about £84,000 lower than those in London 2, probably because their high use of placements with parents and relatives offsets their extensive use of residential care; however frequent movement in this authority not only contributes to the overall costs, but also has a knock-on effect on the cost of maintaining placements, as children tend to move from cheaper to more costly provision; frequent use of agency and out-of-authority placements also leads to an increase in the costs of reviews in this authority. The whole results in this authority having total costs that are only about £23,000 lower than its pair. Conversely, the low costs of maintaining placements in Unitary Two are also compounded by the low rate of movement and its knock-on effects.

Length of time looked after

While Table 4.1 demonstrates the estimated annual social care costs incurred by a care population of 100 children in each of the six authorities, it does not show how variations in the costs of care episodes are materially affected by a further factor – the length of time that children are looked after. This, together with the types of placement that children receive, accounts for the major costs of the service. Annual returns, which show

TURO COLLEGE LIBRARY

that the average lengths of care episodes are gradually increasing, support concerns about spiralling costs (Statham *et al.* 2002; Department for Education and Skills 2007b).

A large number of the sample children had entered care or accommodation many months, if not years, before the study began. By this date, 239 (50%) had been continuously looked after for more than three years, 153 (32%) for more than five years and 42 (9%) for more than ten years. Only 108 (23%) had been in care or accommodation for less than a year (see Figure 4.12). Of the 42 children who had been looked after for more than ten years, 13 (30%) had entered care or accommodation before their first birthday and 26 (62%) before they were five.

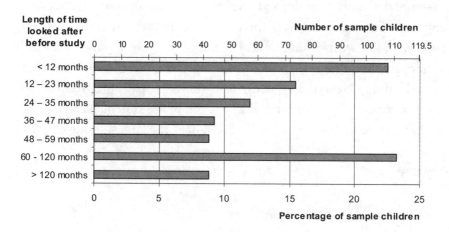

Figure 4.12: Length of time looked after before the study began (n = 478)

Such lengthy periods in care or accommodation are difficult to evaluate. On the one hand, they are likely to have been extremely costly to the authorities involved, and the negative outcomes of being looked after are well known (see Jackson and Thomas 1999; Jackson 2001; Kufeldt and Stein 2005). On the other hand, there is emerging evidence to suggest that many children benefit from being looked after (Skuse and Ward 2003), that those who stay long in care tend to do better academically (Social Exclusion Unit 2003), and that, while swift rehabilitation may bring financial benefits to the authority, the costs to the children's wellbeing can be considerable, particularly if insufficient work has been undertaken to address the difficulties within the birth family that precipitated the initial intervention (see Sinclair *et al.* 2003; Ward, Munro and Dearden 2006). There is some evidence that those children who stayed long in care or accommodation had a relatively high chance of finding stable placements: 30 (68%) of this group had been in their current placement for two years or more, as compared with 144 (30%) of the sample as a whole (see also Ward forthcoming b).

Figure 4.13 shows the differences between the authorities in the length of time that the sample children had been looked after before the study began. As the graph demonstrates, there were nearly 15 per cent of children in the sample from London 1, as compared with none from Shire 1 who had already been looked after for ten years or more; in fact mean lengths of care episodes were three years six months in Shire 1 as compared with four years four months in London 1. Shire 1 was also the only authority with no sample children who had first entered care before their fourth birthday. Nevertheless if, as one would anticipate, the group of long stayers remains fairly static until they age out of the system, it seems possible that, two years further on, Shire 1 will have the largest group of young

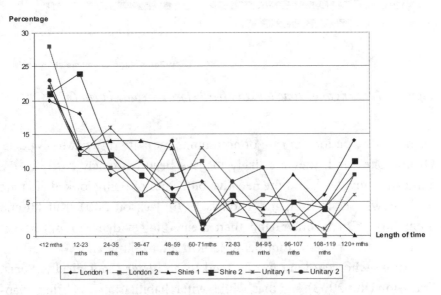

Figure 4.13: Length of time looked after by authority (n = 478)

people looked after for ten years or more; clusters of children moving through the system, as shown in this graph, can materially influence the overall costs of services from one year to the next.

Table 4.1 (from the beginning of this chapter) is repeated below and juxtaposed with Table 4.2 so as to facilitate comparisons of the estimated annual costs of providing care to 100 children in the six authorities with the estimated costs of their full care episodes. The latter amount to several times the annual costs, demonstrating how costs escalate when children stay long in care. This is not simply because costs of maintaining placements grow with each month in care or accommodation. The data from the study demonstrate that those children who remained in care were significantly more likely to be those with the greatest needs, for example, children with profound physical disabilities; conversely, those children who left before the end of the timeframe tended be those who were least costly to maintain.

Moreover, while some children will experience relatively uneventful care episodes, the longer that others remain looked after, the greater the risk that costs will escalate as they experience a sequence of placements, each one more costly than the one before, and each move entailing increased social care activity. Costs may further accelerate as young people enter their teens, for the older children are, the harder they are to place, particularly if they have a history of behavioural problems. The timelines shown in Chapter 5 illustrate how costs can escalate when children and young people follow complex pathways through care.

Skewed costs

Tables 4.1 and 4.2 also indicate that there are specific issues relating to costs in some authorities. When the estimated costs of whole care episodes are taken into account, expenditure in Unitary 1 is greater than in Shire 2, although the annual costs are less. This is probably because the unitary authority had twice as many young people who had been looked after for eight years or more. However anomalies are particularly evident in the costs incurred by Shire 1. We have already seen that this authority had successfully introduced measures to reduce the numbers of children placed in

Table 4.1: Estimated yearly costs incurred by 100 children looked after in each authority (costs inflated to 2006–7 prices to facilitate comparisons)

	No of children	Process 1 Admission	Process 2 Care plan*	Process 3 Maintain placement	Process 4 Exit	Process 5 Next placement	Process 6 Review[a]	Process 7 Legal	Process 8 Transition to leaving care services	Total estimated annual costs
London 1	100	N/A	£30,119	£6,739,657	N/A	£83,216	£197,932	£21,840	£18,862	£7,091,626
London 2	100	N/A	£30,356	£6,823,627	N/A	£65,608	£150,019	£25,781	£19,597	£7,114,988
Shire 1	100	N/A	£18,784	£7,211,361	N/A	£31,088	£144,132	£19,565	£10,513	£7,435,443
Shire 2	100	N/A	£22,037	£6,698,770	N/A	£60,062	£144,725	£18,211	£18,109	£6,961,914
Unitary 1	100	N/A	£21,056	£5,992,809	N/A	£63,574	£131,594	£21,629	£11,596	£6,242,258
Unitary 2	100	N/A	£20,662	£3,726,437	N/A	£30,809	£100,204	£23,431	£13,720	£3,915,263
Total			£143,014	£37,192,661		£334,357	£868,606	£130,457	£92,397	£38,761,492

a Based on estimated frequency.

Table 4.2: Estimated costs of care episodes for 100 children looked after in each authority (entry to care / accommodation to end of study period or exit if earlier) (costs inflated to 2006–7 prices to facilitate comparisons)

	No of children	Process 1 Admission	Process 2 Care plan[a]	Process 3 Maintain Placement	Process 4 Exit	Process 5 Next placement	Process 6 Review[a]	Process 7 Legal	Process 8 Transition to leaving care services	Total
London 1	100	£105,855	£154,042	£29,063,607	£11,184	£287,189	£997,719	£138,285	£65,423	£30,823,304
London 2	100	£113,607	£145,355	£31,909,410	£11,004	£278,866	£744,887	£138,960	£48,715	£33,390,804
Shire 1	100	£132,355	£84,208	£30,768,736	£6,725	£167,202	£618,073	£98,334	£40,242	£31,915,875
Shire 2	100	£100,487	£103,130	£24,820,006	£15,223	£285,684	£635,644	£85,666	£43,333	£26,089,173
Unitary 1	100	£89,037	£96,986	£28,437,119	£13,508	£221,575	£639,740	£113,310	£30,622	£29,641,897
Unitary 2	100	£70,284	£112,191	£16,388,562	£11,969	£156,101	£521,644	£114,660	£37,211	£17,412,622

a Based on estimated frequency.

care or accommodation. While its costs for Process 1 (decision to admit) were high, it had successfully reduced costs in a number of other areas: it had the smallest proportion of children on care orders; on average its children were looked after for the shortest periods; it made little use of out-of-authority or agency placements; it had one of the highest percentages (30%) of children placed with own parents or relatives; it had fewer changes of placement than all but one other authority. On all the above criteria it most closely resembled Unitary 2, the least costly authority; and yet, as Tables 4.1 and 4.2 demonstrate, Shire 1 incurred the highest estimated annual expenditure of all authorities and the second highest estimated expenditure overall throughout the care episodes of the sample children. Some salaries in this authority were higher than those in other authorities outside London, but these are not sufficient to account for the disparities.

In each authority there are a small number of children with very extensive needs who require highly specialized and extremely expensive care. The explanation for the high total costs in Shire 1, notwithstanding all the indicators that these would be low, lies in the preponderance of such children. In the sample groups from each of the London authorities, and from Shire 2 and Unitary 1, there were between five and seven children whose care cost over £12,500 per month (over £18,500 per month for two children in London 2). These children represented between 5 and 8 per cent of the sample from these authorities. There were no children incurring commensurate costs in Unitary 2. However, there were 12 such children in Shire 1, representing 22 per cent of the sample from this authority. The costs of caring for these 12 children came to 58 per cent of the costs of looking after the sample children in this authority during the study period, thereby distorting the pattern of expenditure. All but two of these were children with physical or learning disabilities. Staff in this authority claimed that some families moved to the locality in order to access its exceptionally high quality services for children with disabilities; it is the presence of these children that accounts for a major part of the expenditure in this authority.

Conclusion: Calculating the costs of care episodes

This last point suggests that variations in the costs of providing care and accommodation can be compared and explained by exploring the relative costs and frequency of social care processes in supposedly similar authorities, but they cannot be properly understood without looking more specifically at the characteristics of the care population – the subject of the following two chapters.

As Chapter 5 will also demonstrate, it is possible to use the methodology illustrated in this chapter as the basis for compiling timelines that illustrate how costs accrue, and in some cases escalate, over the care pathways of individual children. The Integrated Children's System (ICS) (Department of Health 2002b) has been developed with the aim of ensuring that the necessary information concerning children's characteristics, social care processes and placement patterns is collected at case management level as an integral part of social care practice and inputted directly into management information systems. Much of these data are also required for national returns; the data collated for this purpose are more likely to be complete than those available from individual case records, though they are not always easy to relate to individual children (Ward 2002). Where child-level data items are available it is possible to link them to unit costs, compiled as indicated in Chapter 3, so as to produce both aggregate costs for groups of children as well as individual costs for each child. Information on activities by children's social care and other agencies for all children in need is also increasingly available, so that eventually it should be possible to cost complete social care interventions over time.

The ultimate objective would be to link such costs to outcome data – also collected through the ICS and national returns, though as yet not always available in electronic format (see Ward, Holmes and Soper 2005). As we shall see in Chapter 8, all these data can be collated from a range of sources and inputted into the cost calculator model to produce calculations similar to those shown in this chapter. The model is at present being developed so that it can establish the current costs of care episodes for a population of looked after children and link these to outcomes; subsequent plans include a project to explore how such data can be used to predict the likely costs and consequences of services accessed by future populations of children in need.

Summary of the key points from Chapter 4

- Process 3 (maintaining the placement) accounts for between 95 per cent and 97 per cent of all costs. Variance in costs between authorities reflects differences in the percentage of months spent in each placement type, and in agency foster care and out-of-area placements.

- Frequent changes of placement are not only costly in themselves, but also have a knock-on effect on the costs of other processes. Children who become difficult to place are more likely to require out-of-authority placements that incur additional support costs and more expensive reviews.

- One authority in the original study had invested highly in the costs of Process 1 (deciding to admit and finding first placement). This authority showed evidence of cost reductions in other areas; its children were looked after for the shortest periods, it had the lowest number of care orders, it made little use of agency or out-of-authority placements, it had one of the highest percentages of children placed with own parents and fewer changes of placement than all but one other authority. This may indicate a number of dividends arising from careful planning at entry to care/accommodation, and effective strategic planning overall, though the causal link would require further exploration.

- Costs are substantially influenced by the length of time that children are looked after. Long-stay children tend to remain fairly static until they age out of the system. It should be possible to identify clusters of children moving through the system who will materially influence the overall costs of providing services from one year to the next.

- Up to a point (but see Chapter 6) placement types reflect children's needs. A small number of children with very extensive needs will require exceptionally costly placements and can skew the costs of the whole care population in an authority. Comparisons between authorities must not only consider process costs but also the characteristics of the care population.

- Implementation of the Integrated Children's System should ensure that the necessary information concerning social care processes and placement patterns is collected at case management level and inputted directly into management information systems. The majority of the necessary data items are already collated for national returns. The cost calculator model can link this information to unit costs, so as to produce both aggregate costs for groups of children and individual costs for each child over a specific timeframe.

Notes

1 The average number of moves over the course of the 20-month study was 1.35 in Shire 2 compared with 0.55 in Unitary 2.

2 Kruskal–Wallis Test: $\chi^2 = 10.92$, $df = 5$, $p = 0.053$.

3 Kruskal–Wallis Test: $\chi^2 = 11.93$, $df = 5$, $p = 0.036$.

Chapter 5

Children and Costs

Introduction

The previous chapter demonstrated that, during the period of the study, there were substantial differences between the participating authorities in the costs of providing care and accommodation. The major variations are attributable to the differences in the costs of placement types and the frequency with which they are used. Smaller variations occur because of differences in the costs and frequency of case management processes such as arranging new placements, undertaking reviews and applying for care orders.

Calculations such as those undertaken in Chapter 4 can demonstrate that substantial differences in the costs of care provision occur, and can indicate their sources, but they do little to improve understanding of the underlying factors or explore why additional expenditure may be necessary. Without such understanding there is a temptation to introduce measures to reduce costs that fail to take account of the consequences for children's wellbeing. This chapter takes a closer look at the child-related factors identified in the focused discussions with social care personnel as likely to have a bearing on the costs of service delivery, and explores how far they can explain the variations between authorities. The following chapter (Chapter 6) considers the relationship between such factors, the need for – and delivery of – services, and outcomes.

Children's characteristics

As Chapter 3 demonstrated, children's characteristics have cost implications for the authorities that place them. Children's ages, and to some extent their primary need at admission, influence the length of time they will require care or accommodation; other characteristics such as ethnicity and first language may have implications for the recruitment of carers and the provision of services, while the extent of their needs will influence the type and cost of placements, the frequency and complexity of case management processes and the range of additional support services that they require.

Age at start of current care episode

Age at entry has obvious implications for the costs of periods spent in care or accommodation. The longer children are looked after, the less likely they are to return to their families (Millham *et al.* 1986; Bullock, Gooch and Little 1998). While very young children who cannot be placed with relatives or return to their birth families may be placed for adoption, the older they are, the less likely they are to find adoptive families (see, for instance, Selwyn *et al.* 2006). A very high percentage of those children who enter care or accommodation at an early age, and are not swiftly reunited or adopted, may need to be looked after for several years, until they are old enough to cope independently, with obvious implications for the long-term costs of service delivery.

The left hand vertical axis on Figure 5.1 indicates the number of children in each age group and has a maximum value of 475, the total number of children for whom data were available. That value therefore corresponds to 100 per cent of the children, and so it aligns with the maximum value on the right hand axis. Both the histogram blocks and the line on the chart showing cumulative values can be read against either vertical axis, the left hand one showing the actual numbers of children and the right hand one the corresponding percentage. The chart shows the age of the sample children at the start of their current care episode. As we saw in Chapter 4 (Figure 4.12), although one of the criteria for sample entry was that children were aged ten and over, many of them had already been looked after

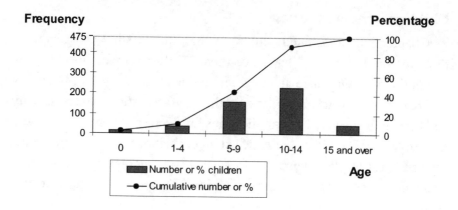

Figure 5.1: Age at start of current care episode (n = 475)

for several years by the time they were selected. As Figure 5.1 shows, 49 (10%) had been looked after continuously from before their fifth birthday – and 13 of these (3%) from before their first. A further 156 children had entered care or accommodation between their fifth and their tenth birthdays, making a total of 43 per cent looked after continuously since before they were ten. Only 9 per cent (43 children) had entered care or accommodation after their 15th birthday, with only a few years left before they reached adulthood. It is also noteworthy that there were substantial, although not statistically significant, differences in the sample age structure between authorities: for instance, Shire 1 had no sample children continuously looked after since before their third birthday, and only one (2%) before his fifth; the comparison authority, Shire 2, had four (5%) children admitted before their third birthday, and ten (12%) before their fifth.

Primary needs

Figure 5.2 shows the primary need of the sample children, as given in the Children in Need Census. There is a relationship between children's needs and the length of time that they are likely to be looked after. Children with disabilities or those looked after following abuse or neglect are the most likely to remain in care or accommodation for longer, and accounted for nearly three quarters (74%) of the group who became looked after before the age of five. Unaccompanied asylum-seeking children (UASC), who mostly become looked after because of 'absent parenting', are likely to remain in care or accommodation for a much shorter time period: all the UASC in this sample were aged 15 and over when they first approached the authorities, and were therefore unlikely to remain their responsibility for more than a few years.

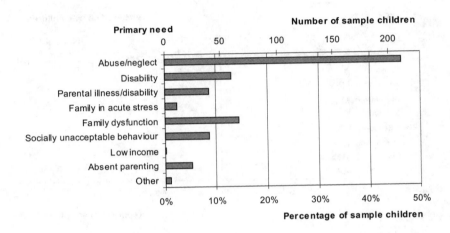

Figure 5.2: Primary needs of sample as given in the CIN census (n = 457)

Ethnic origin

The ethnic origin of the sample children is given in Figure 5.3. As can be seen, 73 per cent of them were white British and 27 per cent from other ethnic groups. The care population was relatively homogeneous in the four authorities outside London, where only 8 per cent of the sample children were from groups other than white British. In contrast, the population in both the London authorities was much more diverse: only just over half of the sample children from London 1 were white British: 44 (51%) in London 1, and just over a third (36%) in London 2. However, as one might expect, in both these authorities the population from minority groups came from many different ethnic and cultural backgrounds. The sample from London 2, for instance, included 21 children of mixed heritage, 11

Afro-Caribbean children; 15 black Africans, one Asian child, seven white European children and five white Irish children. This authority had recently held a recruitment drive for black carers, which had resulted in greatly improved choice of placements. Nevertheless, providing a service that attempts to meet the linguistic, religious and cultural needs of such a diverse population has major implications for its costs.

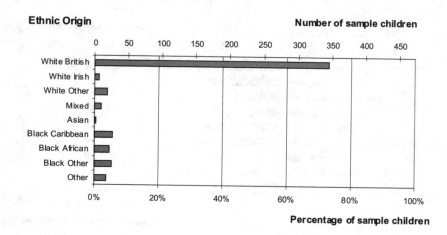

Figure 5.3: Ethnic origin of sample children (n = 472)

Ward, Munro and Dearden (2006) found that very young children from minority ethnic groups were frequently placed with temporary carers, pending a more suitably matched placement becoming available; as we have already seen, movement is a costly process, both in terms of resources and children's wellbeing. Evidence from the sample presented in this book suggests that these issues do not always arise: the white British children in this study had significantly more placement moves than other children.[1] This may be because there was a greater choice of black carers in one authority with a very diverse population, or because the children were older; however it is also likely to reflect the complex relationship between a range of children's needs and the services they received in different authorities, as discussed below.

Gender balance

The study showed no clear evidence of a relationship between ethnicity and underlying factors that influence the cost and type of placements, such as emotional or behavioural difficulty, or physical or learning disability.[2] However there was evidence that gender could be a proxy indicator for the presence of such factors. In line with the national statistics there was a higher proportion (54%) of boys than girls (46%) in the sample as a whole. Boys were often more costly to look after than girls, not for any intrinsic reason, but because they were more likely to display characteristics such as emotional or behavioural difficulty (56%:52%) and offending behaviour (36%:17%), and, particularly, combinations of these factors,[3] that added to the costs of service provision. It may be for this reason that a significantly higher proportion of boys had been placed in residential units at the start of this study (32%:23%),[4] and a notably lower proportion in foster care (36%:44%). Although the girls had, on average, spent about 7.5 months longer in the care system than the boys, these additional costs were unlikely to cancel out the extra costs incurred by boys.

Exceptional child-related factors

As Chapter 3 indicated, children's specific needs are likely to impact both on the types of placement they are offered, and on the demand for additional support services by other agencies such as education, health and CAMHS. Information from practitioners and managers, gathered as part of the process of developing unit costs, indicated that the prevalence of children within the care population who display the following attributes – or combinations of them – is likely to have a direct impact on the cost of placements: physical and learning disabilities; emotional or behavioural difficulties; and offending behaviour. Unaccompanied asylum-seeking children comprise a further group whose circumstances, rather than their attributes, engender a different pattern of costs. In any population of looked after children, some will display none of these additional support needs: we expect that those authorities with a higher proportion of these children in care or accommodation will incur lower costs per looked after child, though their overall expenditure on children's services may be greater, for such authorities may place a higher proportion of their whole population of children in need away from home than do those with better developed family support services.

Such an issue requires further exploration. Our initial study was restricted to exploring those factors that affect the costs and consequences of different placement options. However a subsequent study is now extending the cost calculator methodology to explore further the relationship between costs, services and outcomes for all children in need, and to consider additional factors within children's birth families and within the communities in which they live as well as those within the children themselves, that might relate to the costs and consequences of service provision (see Ward *et al.* 2008).

Prevalence of factors that potentially affect costs

The focus group discussions with practitioners and managers identified four types of additional support need that impact on the costs of service provision. The various different combinations of these needs produces 11 groups of children: five simple groups, who display none or one of the additional, cost-related needs, and six complex groups, of children who display two or more. As Chapter 3 indicated, it seems likely that the higher the proportion of children in the complex groups, the greater the costs of providing care or accommodation.

The five simple groups are:

1. None: Children and young people with no evidence of additional support needs (129, 27%).

2. EBD: Children and young people with emotional or behavioural difficulties (129, 27%).

3. Offend: Young offenders (46, 10%).

4. UASC: Unaccompanied asylum-seeking children and young people (10, 2%).

5. CWD: Children and young people with a physical or learning disability (30, 6%).

The six complex groups are:

1. CWD + EBD: Children and young people with both a disability and emotional or behavioural difficulties (46, 10%).

2. EBD + Offend: Children and young people with emotional or behavioural difficulties who are also young offenders (72, 15%).

3. UASC + EBD: Unaccompanied asylum-seeking children and young people, with emotional or behavioural difficulties (4, 1%).

4. CWD + Offend: Children and young people with disabilities who are also young offenders (2, –%).

5. CWD + EBD + Offend: Children and young people with both a disability and emotional or behavioural difficulties who are also young offenders (9, 2%).

6. UASC + CWD + EBD: Unaccompanied asylum-seeking children and young people with both a disability and emotional or behavioural difficulties (1, –%).

Our definition of a young offender was someone who received a reprimand, final warning or conviction within the timeframe of the study.

The children with no additional needs, the four other simple groups and six complex groups are shown in Figure 5.4. As can be seen, 129 (27%) children showed no evidence of additional support needs – an important point to note both because the prevalence of such children in the care system is often ignored and because this is the group who are most likely to have relatively simple pathways through care or accommodation, incurring few additional costs either to children's social care or to other agencies. A total of 215 (45%) of the children displayed one high support need; 124 (26%) children displayed combinations of two; and a very small group of children (10:2%) displayed combinations of three or more.

While there may not always be a close relationship between the cost of placements and needs, it does seem likely that the children with the more complex needs will require the more expensive placements. The profile of the care population in each of the participating authorities shows considerable differences in the proportions of children in each of these groups (see below and Chapter 6). This may offer some explanation for the differ-

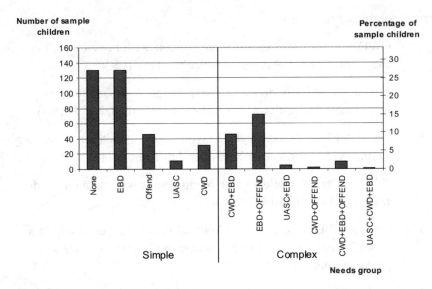

Figure 5.4: Children in each of the groups as a frequency and a percentage (n = 478)

ences in placement patterns, processes and costs between the authorities, shown in the previous chapter. The study also showed emerging relationships between need, cost and outcome, an issue that will be explored further in Chapter 6.

The following case studies illustrate the differences between costs and experiences for children in each of the first seven of these groups, and also one group with three needs: disabilities, emotional or behavioural difficulties and offending behaviour. Within each group, the case for illustration has been randomly selected from those in the sample for whom there was detailed service provision information available either on the case file or from an interview.

Children with no evidence of additional support needs

Children with no evidence of additional support needs experienced fewer changes of placements and were also more likely to be placed within the area of the authority, either in a kinship placement or with local authority foster carers (see example below). The costs of both placements and social care processes are therefore likely to be relatively low for these children.

The highest percentage of these children was found in the care population of Unitary 1 (37%) and the lowest in Shires 1 and 2 (22% and 21%) (see Chapter 6: Figure 6.8). As noted in Chapter 2, at the time of sample selection the proportion of children in need who became looked after was much higher in Unitary 1 (98 per 10,000) than in the two shire counties (41 per 10,000 in Shire 1 and 55 per 10,000 in Shire 2); we also know that strategies had been successfully introduced in Shire 1 to reduce the number of looked after children. This may offer some explanation for this differential, although the two London authorities also had a very high proportion of children in care or accommodation (122 and 140 per 10,000) but a relatively low proportion with no additional support needs.

Child A – no evidence of additional support needs

Child A was a girl of white British origin, aged 11 at the start of the study. She first became looked after at the age of ten, as the result of neglect. Initially she was placed with her birth mother and stepfather under a care order and she remained with them for a year. She then moved to live with her birth father in a placement that lasted for three months. After this she was placed with long-term, local authority foster carers in Month 2 of the study, and she remained in the placement until the end of the study timeframe (Month 20). Child A attended mainstream school and made the transition to secondary schooling in Month 7. During the time that she was placed with foster carers she maintained contact with her birth family, seeing her birth mother and stepfather monthly and her birth father and brother fortnightly.

Figure 5.5 provides a timeline illustration of the experiences of this adolescent girl during the timeframe of the study, and Table 5.1 demonstrates how these might be costed. It is noteworthy that Child A had relatively inexpensive placements with her family and with local authority foster carers. She incurred some educational costs, in that she attended school, and some health care costs, but there was no exceptional expenditure. She was likely to have 'developed a secure attachment to carers' while retaining a relationship with her birth parents, and to have 'gained maximum life chance benefits

Table 5.1: Costs for Child A – no evidence of additional support needs

At the start of the time period shown Child A was placed with her birth father; she then moved to a placement with local authority foster carers, in the area of the local authority. Four reviews were held during the timeframe of the study and her care plan was updated following each review. She attended mainstream school, making an age-related transition to secondary school in Month 7. She attended six-monthly dental checks and an annual looked after child health assessment.

Costs of processes (at 2006–7 prices)

Process	Cost to LA	Total	Cost to other agencies	Total
2 – Care planning	£120 x 4	£479	£148 x 4	£591
3 – Maintaining the placement	£39,306 plus £393 minus £2,044[a]	£37,654		
5 – Find subsequent placement	£204	£204	£204	
6 – Review	£408 x 4	£1,630	£47 x 4	£189

Costs of services (at 2006–7 prices)

Service	Cost	Total
Mainstream schooling	£22[c] per day	£6,822
Dentist	£7[c] x 3	£22
LAC Health assessment	£34[d]	£34
		£6,878

| 7 – Legal | £7[b] x 87 | £595 | £13 x 87 | £1,157 | £1,937 |
| | | **£40,562** | | | |

Total cost incurred by children's social care to look after Child A during study period		**£40,562**
Total cost incurred by other agencies for Child A during study period		**£8,815**
Total cost incurred during study period at 20 months (87 weeks) (at 2006–7 prices)		**£49,377**

The displayed values of the costs estimates and totals have been rounded to the nearest integer. It therefore may not be possible to exactly reproduce the totals from the rounded cost estimates that are displayed.

a This cost includes the payment made for the placements and all activity to support the placements. There is an increase in cost in the first three months of a placement due to increased social worker activity. There is a reduction in cost as a result of reduced activity once the placement has lasted for more than one year.

b The cost of obtaining a care order has been divided over the total number of weeks between the date of the order and the child's eighteenth birthday.

c Unit cost taken from Berridge et al. 2002 (costs inflated to 2006–7 prices).

d Based on the unit cost of a surgery consultation with a general practitioner (Curtis 2007, p.127).

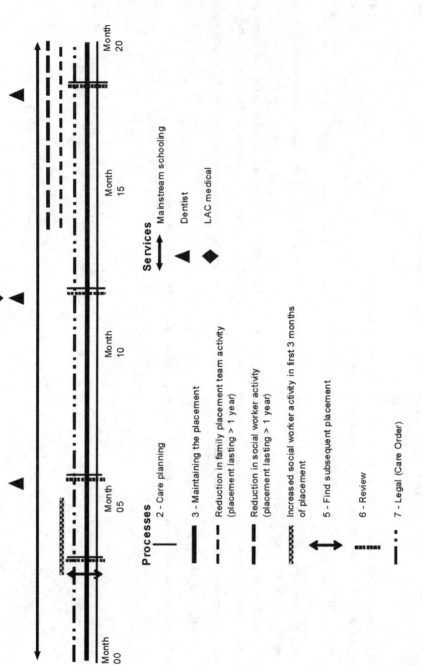

Processes

2 - Care planning

3 - Maintaining the placement

Reduction in family placement team activity
(placement lasting > 1 year)

Reduction in social worker activity
(placement lasting > 1 year)

Increased social worker activity in first 3 months
of placement

5 - Find subsequent placement

6 - Review

7 - Legal (Care Order)

Services

Mainstream schooling

Dentist

LAC medical

Month 00   Month 05   Month 10   Month 15   Month 20

Figure 5.5: Timeline for Child A – no evidence of additional support needs

from educational opportunities, health care and social care'. She was being equipped to make a successful transition to adulthood.

Children with emotional or behavioural difficulties

Emotional or behavioural difficulties were identified in Chapter 3 as a factor that impacts on care costs. Children in this group were more likely to be placed in out-of-authority, agency (and therefore higher cost) placements. Furthermore, they were also more likely to have experienced shorter placements that changed frequently, both factors that have been identified as increasing costs. The overall proportion of children with emotional or behavioural difficulties alone, and not displaying any of the other factors was 27 per cent. This ranged from 41 per cent in Shire 2 to 18 per cent in Shire 1 (see Figure 6.8). Child B is illustrative of a child in this group.

Child B – emotional or behavioural difficulties

Child B was a young woman of black Caribbean origin, aged 17 at the start of the study. She first became looked after at the age of 14, the reason being described as 'preventative'. The primary need code was recorded as 'socially unacceptable behaviour'. Before the start of the study this young person had experienced four different placements; her fifth placement, which lasted up until the time that she ceased to be looked after, was of nine months duration. Her first placement was with local authority foster carers, but all subsequent placements were in residential units, all of them out of the area of the placing authority. Child B suffered from depression and an eating disorder (anorexia nervosa); she also had a history of self-harm. She had a history of drug and alcohol use and also smoked regularly. During the months of the study period, while she was looked after, this young woman had regular sessions with a clinical psychologist. Although all residential placements provided education facilities as well as specialist health care to address her eating disorder, this young woman did not complete her statutory education. Throughout the time that Child B was accommodated she had no contact with her birth family. She ceased to be looked after in Month 4 of the study, when her case was transferred to the community mental health team, although she remained in the same placement throughout the transition.

The timeline in Figure 5.6 illustrates the experiences for Child B during the timeframe of the study; the associated costs are estimated in Table 5.2. Costs to children's social care were high, because she was placed in specialist residential care. They would have been about £176,000 higher, had she not ceased to be accommodated on reaching the age of eighteen, sixteen weeks into the study. Most of the additional health and education costs are incorporated into the placement costs, as these services were provided in-house. The only substantial additional cost was for sessions with a clinical psychologist, which continued when this young woman transferred to adult services. Her mother refused to let her have contact with any member of her birth family and she had little chance of developing substitute attachments, as no placement lasted for longer than nine months. She left care with no qualifications and with continuing mental health problems; her transition to independent adult life would be difficult. This young woman had extensive needs; she received a substantial package of services while looked after; there is insufficient evidence to show how far they impacted on long-term outcomes.

Young offenders

More than a quarter (27%) of the children in the sample were convicted of a criminal offence during the timeframe of the study, thereby incurring additional costs to youth offending teams, the police and the criminal courts. Some young people also committed criminal offences both before and during the study. It should be noted, however, that the sample of young people selected for this study was deliberately skewed towards those with additional support needs in order to ensure sufficient numbers in residential care, and does not reflect a normative care population. Detailed information concerning offending behaviour amongst young people in care or accommodation can be found in Darker, Ward and Caulfield (2008).

One of the reasons why offending behaviour can lead to higher costs is because young people can be remanded to the care of the local authority. Some of these young people need higher cost, possibly secure placements; local authorities have little control over these costs, for although they have

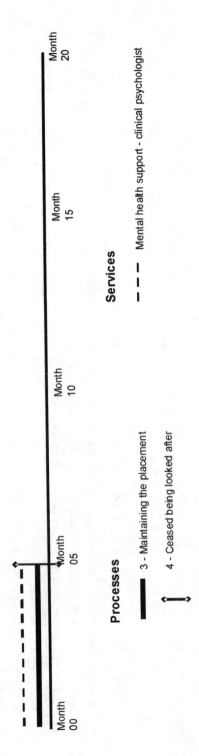

Figure 5.6: Timeline for Child B – emotional or behavioural difficulties

Table 5.2: Costs for Child B – emotional or behavioural difficulties

Child B was placed in a specialist, agency residential unit which provided both education and health facilities until Month 4 when she ceased being looked after. Reviews were held at six-monthly intervals and this young person's care plan was also updated six monthly. This young person also attended weekly, hour long sessions with a clinical psychologist.

Costs of processes (at 2006–7 prices)

Process	Cost to LA	Total	Cost to other agencies	Total
3 – Maintaining the placement	£2484 x 16 weeks[a]	£39,737		
4 – Ceased being looked after	£263	£263		
		£40,000		

Costs of services (at 2006–7 prices)

Service	Cost	Total
Clinical psychology	£67[b] x 16 weeks	£1,072
		£1,072

Total cost incurred by children's social care to look after child B during 16 weeks of study period **£40,000**

Total cost incurred by other agencies for Child B during 16 weeks of study period **£1,072**

Total cost incurred during 16 weeks of study period (at 2006–7 prices) **£41,072**

The displayed values of the costs estimates and totals have been rounded to the nearest integer. It therefore may not be possible to exactly reproduce the totals from the rounded cost estimates that are displayed.

a This cost includes the payment made for the placement and all activity to support the placement. Child B ceased being looked after in Month 4; therefore the time period being costed is 16 weeks.

b Unit cost taken from Curtis 2007, p.115.

to find the placement, it is the courts that make the decision that the young offender will need to be placed away from home. Seven per cent of the young people who had committed a criminal offence were remanded to the care of the participating authorities. The proportion was highest in Shire 1, where 13 per cent of the sample children had been remanded to care; on the other hand there were no remands to care in Unitary 2.

While most young offenders also showed evidence of other cost-related attributes, 46 (35%) did not. The proportion of young offenders who did not meet the criteria for inclusion in any of the other groups was highest in Unitary 2 (18%) and lowest in Shire 2 (4%). Child C is illustrative of a child in this group.

Child C – young offender

> Child C was a boy of black African origin who was aged 16 at the start of the study. He first became looked after at the age of four as a result of his parents' health. During this time he experienced seven different placements, five of which were in residential units. The year before the study began he was placed with his parents and remained with them until its end. This young man completed his statutory schooling in Month 5, although he did not take any exams and had been permanently excluded on four occasions. He then enrolled at college but did not attend. From Month 6 until the end of the study he was unemployed, although he was trying to establish himself as a DJ. In Month 12 he became a father; throughout the study he maintained a relationship with the mother of his child and had regular contact with his daughter. Three years before the study began, whilst living in residential care, this young person had started committing criminal offences. This activity continued until the end of the study, by which time he had five separate convictions for criminal damage, burglary and vehicle theft.

The timeline in Figure 5.7 illustrates the experiences for Child C within the study period, with the costs being set out in Table 5.3. Although Child C had obviously incurred high costs to children's social care earlier in his care career, during the study period these were relatively low because he

Table 5.3: Costs for Child C – young offender

During the timeframe shown, Child C was placed with his parents. Reviews were held at six-monthly intervals and his care plan was also updated six-monthly. In Month 5 his case was transferred to the leaving care team. This young person attended mainstream school until he completed his statutory schooling, also in Month 5. For the remainder of the time period shown he was unemployed. Regular dental checks and a looked after child health assessment were both refused by this young person. During the timeframe shown this young person committed three criminal offences, two counts of vehicle theft and one of burglary. He was convicted for all of the offences.

Costs of processes (at 2006–7 prices)

Process	Cost to LA	Total	Cost to other agencies	Total
2 – Care planning	£163 x 3	£490	£181 x 3	£542
3 – Maintaining the placement	£332[a] x 87 weeks	£28,913	£64 x 87 weeks	£5,582
6 – Review	£1021 x 3 + £125[b]	£3,188	£172 x 3	£515
7 – Legal	£5[c] x 87 weeks	£441	£8 x 87 weeks	£660

Costs of services (at 2006–7 prices)

Service	Cost	Total
Mainstream Schooling	£22[d] per day	£2,044
YOT involvement/ criminal costs	£200[e] x 87 weeks	£17,400
		£17,444

| 8 – Transition to leaving care | £1,164 | £1,164 | £7,299 | £34,195 |

Total cost incurred by children's social care to look after Child C during study period **£34,195**

Total cost incurred by other agencies for Child C during study period **£26,743**

Total cost incurred during study period of 20 months (87 weeks) (at 2006–7 prices) **£60,938**

The displayed values of the costs estimates and totals have been rounded to the nearest integer. It therefore may not be possible to exactly reproduce the totals from the rounded cost estimates that are displayed.

a This cost includes the activity to support the placement.

b An additional cost is incurred for the first 16+ review.

c The cost to obtain a care order has been divided over the total number of weeks between the date of the order and the child's 18th birthday.

d Unit cost taken from Berridge *et al.* 2002 (costs inflated to 2006–7 prices).

e Unit cost taken from Liddle 1998, p.105.

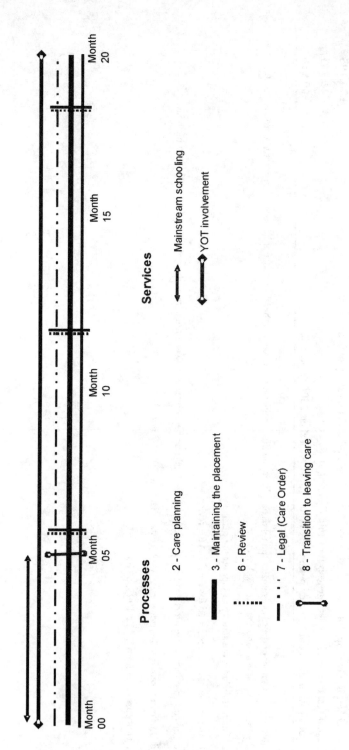

Figure 5.7: Timeline for Child C – young offender

was placed with his own parents. There were also no health care costs because he refused to visit the dentist 131or to attend his looked after medical. Costs to education would have ceased six months into the study, when he completed his statutory education. However, Child C provides a clear illustration of one of the themes that recur throughout the whole programme of research that supports the development of the cost calculator model – that the corollary of low financial costs to children's social care may be high wellbeing costs to the young people concerned, and also what one might term high 'negative' costs to other agencies such as the police. This young man left school with no qualifications and was unemployed for at least the next 15 months. Unless his employment prospects improved he would probably need to claim income support both for himself and his daughter. He committed three offences within the timeframe of the study – at a cost of £17,400 in police, court and youth offending team (YOT) time. The only supportive services he received were involvement from children's social care and the YOT team.

Unaccompanied asylum-seeking children (UASC)

The fourth group of children and young people whose circumstances have been identified as having an impact on costs are unaccompanied asylum seekers. Although some of the variations in the activity required to support these children reduce and some increase costs (see Chapter 3), overall our calculations suggest that they incur an additional cost of about £204 per month. Only a small proportion of the sample were unaccompanied asylum-seeking children (3%) and an even smaller percentage did not meet the criteria for inclusion in any of the other groups (2%). UASC are only present in the sample from three of the participating authorities (London 1, London 2 and Unitary 1). Child D (below) is illustrative of a child in this group.

Child D – unaccompanied asylum-seeking child

> Child D was a girl of black African origin who was aged 16 at the start of the study. She first became looked after at the age of 15, when she arrived in England from Ethiopia to seek asylum. This young woman was initially placed in a residential unit before being found a home with local authority foster carers, with whom she remained for the timeframe of the study. She attended a specialist education provision for young people for whom English is not their first language, and completed her statutory schooling. She subsequently started an NVQ in social care in Month 7, and was still attending college at the end of the study.

The timeline in Figure 5.8 illustrates the experiences for Child D within the study period and the costs are set out in Table 5.4. Additional costs have been included in all the social care processes to take account of the possible need for translations or an interpreter. In the first year of the study educational costs were relatively high because this young woman received specialist tuition; however, she later moved into mainstream education to do her NVQ. Outcomes appear to have been relatively positive in that she had a stable placement throughout the study period, and moved on to further education.

Children with disabilities

The proportion of children in the sample with disabilities alone was 6 per cent. This figure was highest in London 1 and Shire 1 (9%) and lowest in Unitary 2 (1%) (see Chapter 6: Figure 6.8). As indicated in Chapter 3, disability is a factor that potentially impacts on costs both because a specialist placement has to be provided and because additional support services are also likely to be required. Children in this group are illustrated by Child E.

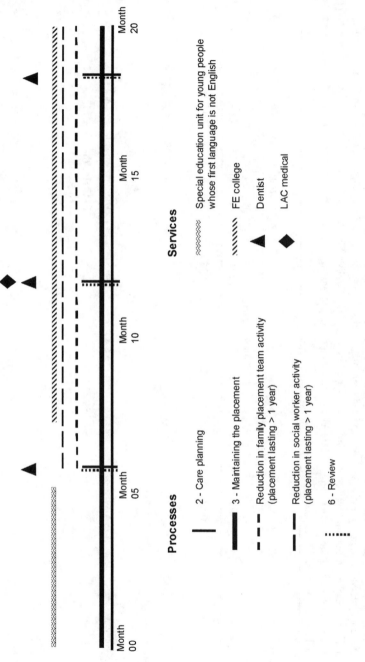

Figure 5.8: Timeline for Child D – unaccompanied asylum-seeking child

Processes

| 2 - Care planning |
| 3 - Maintaining the placement |
| Reduction in family placement team activity (placement lasting > 1 year) |
| Reduction in social worker activity (placement lasting > 1 year) |
| 6 - Review |

Services

| Special education unit for young people whose first language is not English |
| FE college |
| Dentist |
| LAC medical |

Table 5.4: Costs for Child D – unaccompanied asylum-seeking child

Child D was placed with local authority foster carers within the area of the authority during the timeframe shown. Reviews were held at six-monthly intervals and her care plan was also updated every six months. For the first school year shown until Month 5, this young person attended a special education unit for young people whose first language is not English. She then progressed on to a further education college in Month 7 and continued her studies there until the end of the time period. This young person attended six-monthly dental appointments and her annual looked after child health assessment.

Costs of processes (at 2006–7 prices)

Process	Cost to LA[a]	Total	Cost to other agencies	Total
2 – Care planning	£310 x 3	£931	£148 x 3	£443
3 – Maintaining the placement	£695 x 87 weeks minus £6227[b]	£54,213		
6 – Review	£748 x 3	£2,243	£47 x 3	£142
		£57,387		**£585**

Costs of services (at 2006–7 prices)

Service	Cost	Total
Special education unit	£67[c] per day	£6,334
FE College	£22[d] per day	£4,777
Dentist	£7[c] x 3	£22
LAC Health Assessment	£34[e]	£34

Total cost incurred by children's social care to look after Child D during study period	£11,167
Total cost incurred by other agencies for Child D during study period	£57,387
Total cost incurred during study period of 20 months (87 weeks) (at 2006–7 prices)	£11,752
	£69,139

The displayed values of the costs estimates and totals have been rounded to the nearest integer. It therefore may not be possible to exactly reproduce the totals from the rounded cost estimates that are displayed.

a The cost of translations and/or an interpreter are included in all the processes.

b This cost includes the payment made for the placement and all activity to support the placement. There is a reduction in cost as a result of reduced activity once the placement has lasted for more than one year.

c Unit cost taken from Berridge et al. 2002 (costs inflated to 2006–7 prices).

d Provisional cost based on the cost of mainstream schooling taken from Berridge et al. 2002.

e Based on the unit cost of a surgery consultation with a general practitioner (from Curtis 2007, p.127).

Child E – physical and learning disabilities

Child E was a girl of white British origin, aged 13 at the start of the study. She first became looked after at the age of 11 as a result of abuse/neglect. She had physical and learning disabilities, cerebral palsy, spastic quadriplegia, and a global developmental delay. This young person was placed in a residential unit when she first became looked after and then moved to a foster placement with agency carers out of the area of the authority. This placement was supported with ongoing respite relief for the carers. Child E had health support input from both speech therapists and occupational therapy; she also spent some time as a hospital inpatient during the timeframe of the study. This young person had a statement of special educational needs and attended a special day school. In addition she also had a personal teaching assistant. She did not have any contact with her birth family.

The timeline in Figure 5.9 illustrates the experiences of this child during the timeframe of the study, and Table 5.5 shows how these might be costed. It is noteworthy that the costs to children's social care were relatively high, because of the out-of-authority placement with agency carers, which included ongoing respite support. This was also a stable placement, where Child E had an opportunity for developing secure attachments and where she had access to a range of additional health and educational services. While the costs to other agencies were also high, these were for services designed to meet her needs.

Complex groups

The cost of looking after children may be substantially increased if they display a combination of additional support needs, both because they may require more expensive placements and also because additional support services may be necessary. The costs of some of the social care processes may also be greater as more intensive activity may be required. A total of 134 children, 28 per cent of the sample, displayed a combination of additional support needs, and therefore belonged to a complex group.

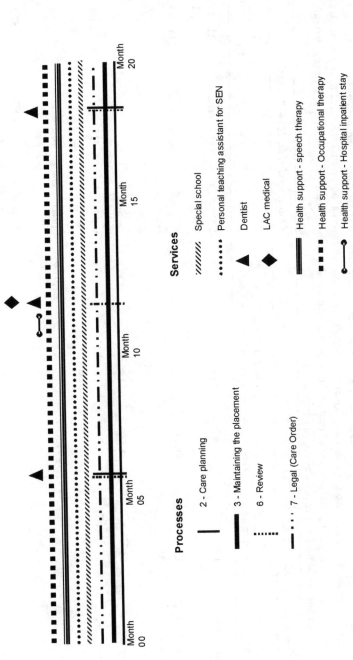

Processes

	2 - Care planning
	3 - Maintaining the placement
	6 - Review
	7 - Legal (Care Order)

Services

///////	Special school
•••••••	Personal teaching assistant for SEN
▲	Dentist
◆	LAC medical
	Health support - speech therapy
	Health support - Occupational therapy
	Health support - Hospital inpatient stay

Figure 5.9: Timeline for Child E – disabilities

Table 5.5: Costs for Child E – disabilities

During the time period shown above Child E was placed with agency foster carers out of the area of the placing authority. Reviews were held at six-monthly intervals and as a child with disabilities her care plan was updated annually. A care order was obtained for this young person when she first became looked after at the age of 11. She attended a special day school for the duration of the study period and was supported by a personal teaching assistant on a daily basis. Six-monthly dental appointments were attended as was a looked after child health assessment. Health support was provided to this young person by the occupational therapy team and she also attended weekly, hour-long speech therapy sessions. She also stayed in hospital for two weeks following an operation.

Costs of processes (at 2006–7 prices)

Process	Cost to LA	Total	Cost to other agencies	Total
2 – Care planning	£81 x 2	£163	£148 x 2	£296
3 – Maintaining the placement	£1019 x 87 weeks[a]	£88,637		
6 – Review	£1021 x 2	£2,042	£186 x 2	£371
7 – Legal	£11[b] x 87 weeks	£939	£16 x 87 weeks	£1,408
		£91,781		£2,074

Costs of services (at 2006–7 prices)

Service	Cost	Total
Special day school	£67[c] per day	£21,136
Personal teaching assistant	£36[c] per hour	£11,494
Dentist	£7 x 3[c]	£22
LAC Health assessment	£34[d]	£34
Speech therapy	£42[e] x 87 weeks	£3,654
Occupational therapy	£56[f] x 87 weeks	£4,872

Hospital inpatient stay	£235[g] x 14 days	£3,290
		£44,502
Total cost incurred by children's social care to look after Child E during study period		**£91,781**
Total cost incurred by other agencies for Child E during study period		**£46,576**
Total cost incurred during study period of 20 months (87 weeks) (at 2006–7 prices)		**£138,357**

The displayed values of the costs estimates and totals have been rounded to the nearest integer. It therefore may not be possible to exactly reproduce the totals from the rounded cost estimates that are displayed.

a This cost includes the payment made for the placement and all activity to support the placement. There are additional costs as a result of the placement being out of the area of the local authority.

b The cost to obtain a care order has been divided over the total number of weeks between the date of the order and the child's eighteenth birthday.

c Unit cost taken from Berridge et al. 2002 (costs inflated to 2006–7 prices).

d Based on the unit cost of a surgery consultation with a general practitioner (Curtis 2007, p.127).

e Unit cost taken from Curtis 2007, p.113.

f Unit cost taken from Curtis 2007, p.137.

g Unit cost taken from Curtis 2007, p.99.

Percent

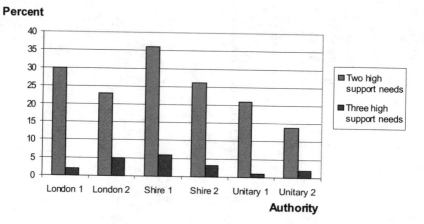

Figure 5.10: Children who display combinations of high support needs by authority

Figure 5.10 shows the percentage of children in each of the participating authorities who displayed combinations of either two or three additional support needs. There were fewer in the two unitaries than in the other authorities. The highest percentage of children in the sample who displayed a combination of three additional support needs were in Shire 1. Similarly, Shire 1 had the highest percentage (36%) of children in the sample who displayed a combination of two additional support needs. This finding supports the earlier hypothesis that the costs per child looked after in Shire 1 were likely to be relatively high, although the overall costs of delivering a service to children in need may have been reduced, as the authority appears to have concentrated its resources on looking after children with exceptional needs, and to have left children with less extensive needs, who might have been placed in care or accommodation had they lived in different authorities, with their families in the community. There is, as we have seen, some evidence that additional resources had been given to family support services in this authority, though we do not know how extensive or effective they were.

The combinations of additional support needs that occurred most frequently among the children in the sample were disability together with emotional or behavioural difficulties (10% of the sample) and emotional or behavioural difficulties plus offending behaviour (15% of the sample).

Disability and emotional or behavioural difficulties

Shire 1 had the highest percentage (20%) of children with both a disability and emotional or behavioural difficulties. Information on activity to support looked after children gathered from social care staff as part of the focus group discussions indicated that this group of children were the most difficult to place and often required specialist agency placements. However, some children in this group were placed with local authority carers; see Child F below.

Child F – disability and emotional or behavioural difficulties

> Child F was a boy of white British origin who was aged 11 at the start of the study. He first became looked after at the age of ten, following the death of his mother, and a care order was obtained. He had physical disabilities and related mobility problems. He was also formally assessed during the timeframe of the study and identified as having emotional or behavioural difficulties. This young man was initially placed with his grandmother; however, because of her non-compliance with children's social services and concerns about his excessive weight gain, in Month 4 he was placed with local authority foster carers. While he was placed with these carers this young man had ongoing sessions with a dietician and the occupational therapy team were involved to oversee the necessary modifications to the foster carers' home. During the study period this young man attended mainstream school with the support of a personal teaching assistant. He had fortnightly, unsupervised contact with his grandmother.

The timeline in Figure 5.11 illustrates the experiences and Table 5.6 shows the costs for Child F. Costs to children's social care are relatively low, largely because he was placed either with kinship carers or with local authority foster carers within the area of the authority throughout the study period. There were relatively high costs to other agencies, designed to meet both his health and his educational needs.

Table 5.6: Costs for Child F – disabilities and emotional or behavioural difficulties

At the start of the study time period until Child F was placed with kinship carers where he stayed until Month 4. He then changed to a placement with local authority foster carers within the area of the authority. A care order was obtained for this young person when he first became looked after, ten months before the start of the study. During the timeframe two review meetings were held and his care plan was also updated twice. Child F attended two different mainstream schools during the time period shown; there was an unscheduled change of school because of transport difficulties. At both schools this young person was supported by a personal teaching assistant on a daily basis. This young person attended six-monthly dental appointments and also his annual looked after child health assessment. From the time that he was placed with local authority foster carers he attended weekly sessions with a dietician. During this time, there was also ongoing involvement from the occupational therapy team to address the changes that needed to be made to the foster carers' house as a result of the young person's mobility difficulties.

Costs of processes (at 2006–7 prices)

Process	Cost to LA	Total	Cost to other agencies	Total
2 – Care planning	60 x 2	£120	£118 x 2	£296
3 – Maintaining the placement	£40,360 plus £287 minus £1195[a]	£39,452		
5 – Find subsequent placement	£365	£365		
6 – Review	£408 x 2	£815	£148 x 2	£371

Costs of services (at 2006–7 prices)

Service	Cost	Total
Mainstream schooling	£22[c] per day	£6,822
Personal teaching assistant	£36[c] per hour	£11,494
Dentist	£7[c] x 3	£22
LAC Health assessment	£34[d]	£34

7 – Legal	$£7^b$ x 87 weeks	£590	£10 x 87 weeks	£1,145		**£1,812**			
Occupational therapy	$£56^e$ x 70 weeks	£3,920							
Dietician	$£30^f$ x 70 weeks	£2,100							
							£24,392		

Total cost incurred by children's social care to look after Child F during study time period	**£41,342**
Total cost incurred by other agencies for Child F during study time period	**£26,204**
Total cost incurred during study time period of 20 months (87 weeks) (at 2006–7 prices)	**£67,546**

The displayed values of the costs estimates and totals have been rounded to the nearest integer. It therefore may not be possible to exactly reproduce the totals from the rounded cost estimates that are displayed.

a This cost includes the payment made for the placements and all activity to support them. There is an increase in cost in the first three months of a placement due to increased social worker activity. There is a reduction in cost as a result of reduced activity once the placement has lasted for more than one year.

b The cost to obtain a care order has been divided over the total number of weeks between the date of the order and the child's 18th birthday.

c Unit cost taken from Berridge et al. 2002 (costs inflated to 2006–7 prices).

d Based on the unit cost of a surgery consultation with a general practitioner (from Curtis 2007, p.127)

e Unit cost taken from Curtis 2007, p.137.

f Unit cost taken from Curtis 2007, p.158.

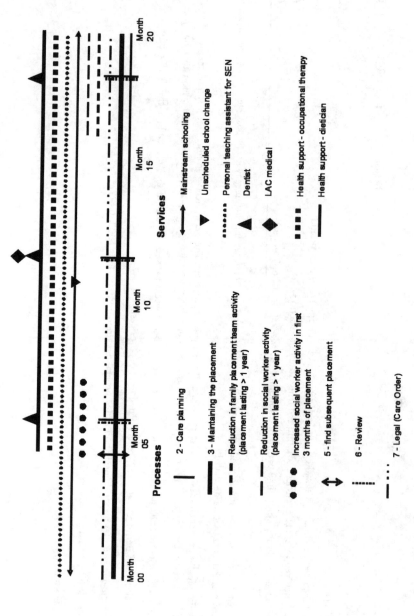

Processes

2 - Care planning

3 - Maintaining the placement

Reduction in family placement team activity
(placement lasting > 1 year)

Reduction in social worker activity
(placement lasting > 1 year)

Increased social worker activity in first
3 months of placement

5 - find subsequent placement

6 - Review

7 - Legal (Care Order)

Services

Mainstream schooling

Unscheduled school change

Personal teaching assistant for SEN

Dentist

LAC medical

Health support - occupational therapy

Health support - dietician

Figure 5.11: Timeline for Child F – disabilities and emotional or behavioural difficulties

Emotional or behavioural difficulties plus offending behaviour

The highest proportion of children with emotional or behavioural difficulties who were also young offenders occurred in London 1 (21%) and the lowest in Unitary 2 (6%). The case study of Child G provides an example of a child who displayed the combination of factors found in this group.

Child G – behavioural difficulties and offending

Child G was a girl of black Caribbean origin, aged 15 at the start of the study. She first became looked after at the age of eight, as a result of abuse. In the seven years between entry to care and the start of the study she had experienced 21 different placements. Child G then had a further six placements within the 20 months of the study: she was placed in three different agency residential units, two of which were out of the area of the placing authority. She then moved on to a series of three semi-independent placements within the local authority. All of the placement changes were recorded as placement breakdowns as a result of her behaviour; she also had a history of absconding.

Child G completed her statutory schooling at a special SEN day school in Month 5. Prior to this she attended seven other secondary education provisions including mainstream school and residential special schools; she was also educated for a short time in a secure unit.

During the study time period Child G was involved in drug taking (cannabis) and drug dealing; she was also known to be involved in prostitution. Child G was involved in other criminal activities, including physical violence and injury and criminal damage both prior to and during the timeframe of the study, although there was no evidence of her continuing to offend after Month 10.

Child G refused to attend her annual looked after child health assessment, or any dental appointments. She also refused all mental health support.

The timeline in Figure 5.12 demonstrates the experiences and Table 5.7 shows the costs for Child G within the timeframe of the study. Costs to children's social care for looking after this young woman were very high, both because she moved through a number of expensive placements, and

Table 5.7: Costs for Child G – emotional or behavioural difficulties plus offending behaviour

During the time period shown, Child G experienced six different placements. The first three were in residential units, two of them out of the area of the authority. In Month 11 she then moved to her first semi-independent placement within the area of the authority. After two weeks that placement broke down and she was then placed in another semi-independent placement for just over four months. In Month 16 she moved to a third semi-independent placement. During the time period shown two review meetings were held and her care plan was also updated twice. This young person attended a special day school until Month 5 when she completed her statutory schooling. Child G committed and was convicted of six criminal offences within the 12 months prior to Month 6, and received ongoing input from the youth offending team until Month 10. This young person refused to attend both dental appointments and her looked after child health assessment.

Costs of processes (at 2006–7 prices)

Process	Cost to LA	Total	Cost to other agencies	Total
2 – Care planning	£120 x 2	£240	£144 x 2	£287
3 – Maintaining the placement	£145,271 plus £1781[a]	£147,052	£47 x 87	£4,079
5 – Find subsequent placement	£5,132	£5,132		
6 – Review	£1223 + £125[b]	£1,348	£1736 x 2	£345
7 – Legal	£5[c] x 87	£463	£10 x 87	£897

Costs of services (at 2006–7 prices)

Service	Cost	Total
Special day school	£67[d] per day	£6,365
YOT involvement/ criminal costs	£315[e] x 43	£13,545
		£19,910

8 – Transition to leaving care	£1,164	£1,164	£155,399	£5,609	£24,392

Total cost incurred by children's social care to look after Child G during study period	£155,399
Total cost incurred by other agencies for Child G during study period	£25,519
Total cost incurred during study period at 20 months (87 weeks) (at 2006–7 prices)	£180,918

The displayed values of the costs estimates and totals have been rounded to the nearest integer. It therefore may not be possible to exactly reproduce the totals from the rounded cost estimates that are displayed.

a This cost includes the payment made for the placements and all activity to support the placements. There is an increase in cost in the first three months of some placements due to increased social worker activity.

b An additional cost is incurred for the first 16+ review.

c The cost of obtaining a care order has been divided over the total number of weeks between the date of the order and the child's 18th birthday.

d Unit cost taken from Berridge et al. 2002 (costs inflated to 2006–7 prices).

e Costs taken from Liddle 1998.

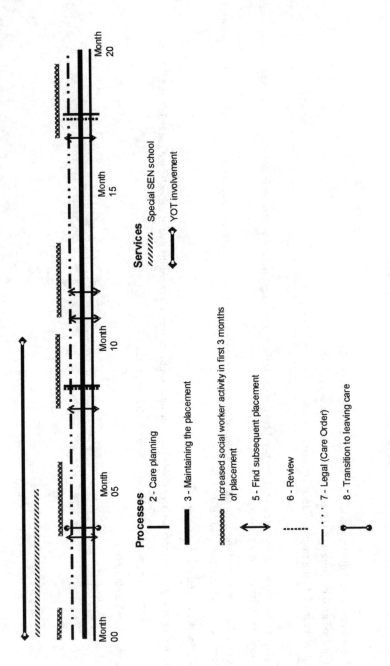

Figure 5.12: Timeline for Child G – emotional or behavioural difficulties plus offending behaviour

because finding new placements involved a substantial amount of activity. This young woman had very high additional needs and appeared to be alienated from all efforts to provide effective support throughout the study.

Other children with complex needs

The other complex needs groups were very small, none of them covering more than 2 per cent of the total sample. Because of the low numbers, these children will not be included in further analysis of the sample as a whole. However, it needs to be acknowledged that providing placements and associated support services for a child with very complex needs can skew a local authority's budget. This is particularly likely to happen where children display a combination of three additional support needs. Child H, whose case study is shown below, had both a disability and EBD; he also committed a criminal offence within the timeframe of the study.

Child H – a combination of support needs

> Child H was a boy of mixed ethnic origin, aged 15 at the start of the study. He first became looked after at the age of 13 as a result of abuse. Child H had both emotional and behavioural difficulties and displayed challenging behaviour. He also had Asperger's syndrome, learning difficulties and obsessive compulsive disorder. Child H experienced seven different placements prior to the start of the study, six in agency residential units and one in a secure unit. At the start of the study he had been in his eighth placement, a local authority residential unit, for three months. He moved to an agency residential unit in Month 1. He was then placed in a specialist residential unit in Month 5, where he received 2:1 supervision at all time. On moving to this placement Child H received a specialist package of education support, including home tuition; prior to this he was excluded from several education units at his placements.
>
> Two years before the start of the study, Child H was charged with his first criminal offence after attacking his escort when travelling to a secure placement. He was subsequently charged with four other incidents of physical violence, one of criminal damage and one threat to kill. As a result he was made the subject of a criminal supervision order in Month 19.
>
> During the study time period Child H attended regular sessions with both a clinical psychologist and a psychiatrist. He also attended hospital outpatient appointments for neurological assessments.

Table 5.8: Costs for Child H – disabilities, emotional or behavioural difficulties plus offending behaviour

During the time period shown, Child H experienced three different placements. At the start of the study he was placed in a local authority residential unit. In Month 1 he was placed in an agency residential unit, out of the area of the authority. In Month 5 he was then placed in a specialist agency residential unit where he had 2:1 supervision at all times. Four review meetings were held for this young person and his care plan was also updated four times. This young person attended the education provision in the agency residential unit until Month 2, when he was permanently excluded. A package of specialist education support was then put in place when he moved to his new placement in Month 5. During the time period shown Child H attended six-monthly dental appointments, his looked after child health assessment, weekly sessions with a clinical psychologist and fortnightly visits with a psychiatrist. He also attended two neurological assessment appointments at the hospital in Months 2 and 3. During the time period Child H committed and was convicted of six criminal offences and received ongoing support from the youth offending team.

Costs of processes (at 2006–7 prices)

Process	Cost to LA	Total	Cost to other agencies	Total
2 – Care planning	£81 x 4	£326	£148 x 4	£591
3 – Maintaining the placement	£323,843 + £785 minus £270[a]	£324,358		
5 – Find subsequent placement	£2,454	£2,454	£211	£211
6 – Review	£815 x 4 + £125[b]	£2,692	£349 x 4	£1,396
7 – Legal	£11[c] x 87 weeks	£925	£21 x 87 weeks	£1,797

Costs of services (at 2006–7 prices)

Service	Cost	Total
Special package of education	£585[d] per week	£25,739
Permanent exclusion	£123[e]	£123
Dentist	£7[f] x 3	£22
LAC Health assessment	£34[g]	£34
Hospital outpatient visits	£157[h] x 2	£314

8 – Transition to leaving care	£1,164	£1,164		£5,829
			Clinical psychologist	£67[i] per hour
		£3,995	Psychiatrist	£69[j] per hour £2,967
			YOT involvement/ criminal costs	£924[k] x 87 £80,420
				£115,448
	£331,919			

Total cost incurred by children's social care to look after Child H during study period **£331,919**

Total cost incurred by other agencies for Child H during study period **£119,443**

Total cost incurred during study period (at 2006–7 prices) **£451,362**

The displayed values of the costs estimates and totals have been rounded to the nearest integer. It therefore may not be possible to exactly reproduce the totals from the rounded cost estimates that are displayed.

a This cost includes the payment made for the placements and all activity to support the placements. There is an increase in cost in the first three months of a placement due to increased social worker activity. There is a reduction in activity after Month 17 when the placement has lasted for more than one year.

b An additional cost is incurred for the first 16+ review.

c The cost to obtain a care order has been divided over the total number of weeks between the date of the order and the child's 18th birthday.

d Based on unit costs of teacher per hour, from Berridge *et al.* 2002

e Unit cost taken from Parsons and Castle 1998.

f Unit cost taken from Berridge *et al.* 2002 (costs inflated to 2006–7 prices).

g Based on the unit cost of a surgery consultation with a general practitioner (from Curtis 2007, p.127)

h Unit cost taken from Curtis 2007, p.99.

i Unit cost taken from Curtis 2007, p.115.

j Unit cost taken from Curtis 2007, p. 151.

k Costs taken from Liddle 1998.

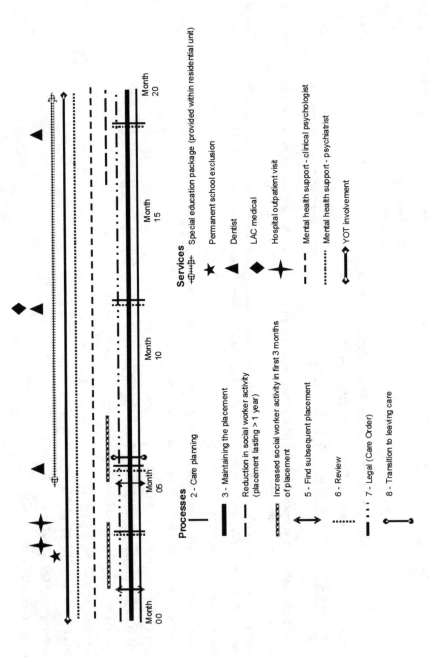

Figure 5.13: *Timeline for Child H – disabilities, emotional or behavioural difficulties plus offending behaviour*

The costs of looking after Child H, shown in Table 5.8, relate to the timeline shown in Figure 5.13. They are markedly higher than for the majority of other children in the sample. The greatest amount of expenditure was due to the high fees of the specialist residential placement that he moved to in Month 5; these were increased to account for the 2:1 supervision provided to the young person at all times. The placement was also out-of-authority and therefore required high levels of social work time to support the young person. Following a series of agency residential placements prior to the study timeframe, Child H had become 'difficult to place' and increasing amounts of social work time had to be spent on finding the rare placements that were prepared to accept him. Although charges for some residential units included education, provided on the premises, Child H was excluded from this provision at all his residential placements prior to the start of the study. In his final, specialist residential placement, a package of education support had been created specifically for his needs and this was maintained until the end of the study timeframe. Child H's very high additional support needs made it difficult to assess the impact of interventions on his education or his emotional or behavioural difficulties; however it should be noted that contact with his birth family was erratic and he had not formed substitute relationships with carers.

Both the last two case studies (Child G and Child H) illustrate instances where young people have very high support needs and it is difficult to assess how successful extremely costly services are in influencing long-term outcomes. There are several possible explanations why outcomes for these young people may appear to be unsatisfactory (see also Selwyn *et al.* 2006; Sinclair and Gibbs 1998): it may be that service responses are too reactive – offering too little, too late, instead of responding proactively to need; it may be that some placements are extremely expensive not because they provide a high quality service but because they are the only provision that will take some children with very extensive needs; on the other hand it may be that some children's needs are so great that almost any interventions will be ineffective. In view of the large sums of money involved, this is an area that would merit further research.

Table 5.9 summarizes the different costs over the 20-month time period illustrated by these case examples. In considering them, a number

Table 5.9: Summarizing the different costs over the study time period for each case study

Child	Group	Cost to children's social care	Cost to other agencies	Total costs incurred
A	No evidence of cost-specific attributes	£40,562	£8,815	£49,377
B	Emotional or behavioural difficulties	£40,000	£1,072	£41,072[a]
C	Young offender	£34,195	£26,743	£60,938
D	Unaccompanied asylum-seeking child	£57,387	£11,752	£69,139
E	Physical or learning disability	£91,781	£46,576	£138,357
F	Disability and emotional or behavioural difficulties	£41,342	£26,204	£67,546
G	Emotional or behavioural difficulties and offending	£155,399	£25,519	£180,918
H	Disability, emotional or behavioural difficulties and offending	£331,919	£119,443	£451,362

a This young person ceased to be looked after during the course of the study. Had she remained in the residential unit in which she had been placed for the full 87 weeks the costs to children's social care would have been increased by £176,000.

of points should be taken into account. First, as with all calculations in this study, these are illustrative costs based on the best information that we have available for the participating authorities – more comprehensive data would undoubtedly produce different figures. Nevertheless, they are all calculated using the methodology described in Chapter 3, and therefore the extent of variation between children and young people with different needs is likely to be fairly robust. Second, however, these calculations are based on real data concerning the child welfare activities recorded about a selection of sample children, and as such, they reflect the genuine complexity of such cases.

Much of the difference in costs is attributable to the different types of placement that children received. It is noteworthy that the children placed in residential units, Child G and Child H, incurred substantially higher costs than those in other groups. Child B would have incurred similar costs, but was only looked after for 16 weeks of the study period, after which she was transferred to adult services and a different budget. Child G and Child H also had numerous changes of placement during the study period, thereby incurring high, and therefore costly, levels of social work activity. The young offender (Child C) had begun to commit offences while in residential care, but during the study period was placed with own parents: there were therefore no placement costs, although he was sup-ported by a high level of activity from both children's social care and from the YOT. Child F, who had both physical disabilities and emotional or behavioural difficulties, incurred relatively low costs to children's social care, because he was placed first in kinship care and then with local author-ity foster carers within the area during the study period, but with ongoing health support. There was no guarantee that the very expensive place-ments adequately met children's needs any more than did the cheaper placements with own parents or relatives.

Being able to cost children's placements accurately makes it possible to compare the relative value, both in terms of costs and quality, of different packages of care, particularly if costs can be related to outcomes. Accurate cost data can make it easier to compare the value of alternative options, such as replacing the very expensive residential placements with a package of specialist foster care, accompanied by extensive support from psycho-therapeutic and special education services. Our continuing research and development programme includes a study designed to compare the cost pathways of a sample of children and young people who have spent at least six months in a pilot programme of multi-dimensional treatment foster care with data on children with similar profiles who received a different type of placement (Holmes, Westlake and Ward forthcoming a). One of the key questions will be to explore whether placement stability is signifi-cantly improved by introducing the programme.

The following chapter looks at these issues more closely, and explores whether there was a difference in the services and placements that were provided to the different groups of children in the participating authorities. In particular it focuses on the complex relationship between children and young people's needs, the cost of services and the relationship to outcomes.

Summary of the key points from Chapter 5

- While children's characteristics (ethnic origin; gender; age at start of current period in care or accommodation; primary needs) have some cost implications for local authorities, high support needs arising from factors such as disabilities, emotional or behavioural difficulties and offending are most likely to influence the type and cost of service provision.

- The children in this study fell into eleven groups categorized by single or multiple combinations of additional support needs. There were five simple groups, displaying none or one, and six complex groups, displaying two or more additional support needs.

- Twenty-seven per cent of the sample (129 children) showed no evidence of additional support needs; 215 (45%) showed evidence of one additional need; 124 (26%) displayed combinations of two; and only ten children (2%) showed evidence of three or more.

- Timelines can illustrate how costs accrue to both children's social care and to other agencies for selected children and young people in each group who show increasingly complex combinations of need.

- Variations in the prevalence of each needs-related group within the care population in each local authority are likely to explain some of the differences in placement patterns, processes, costs and outcomes.

- Children with exceptionally high support needs received extremely costly packages of care. Being able to cost children's placements accurately would facilitate comparisons between the relative value, both in terms of costs and quality, of different types of care and make it easier to weigh up the potential advantages and disadvantages of introducing a range of alternative packages of support.

Notes

1. Mann–Whitney $U = 19494.50$, $N^1 = 345$, $N^2 = 127$, $p = 0.039$.
2. $\chi^2 = 0.48$, $df = 1$, $p = 0.83$ (continuity corrected).
3. Boys were significantly more likely than girls to have additional (disability, emotional or behavioural difficulties, offending) support needs ($\chi^2 = 6.10$, $df = 1$, $p = 0.014$ (continuity corrected)).
4. $\chi^2 = 3.97$, $df = 1$, $p = 0.046$ (continuity corrected).

Chapter 6

Need, Cost, Service and Outcome

Introduction

So far we have seen that the variations between authorities in the costs of providing care or accommodation are closely related to the types of placement that children receive, and to the needs of the children and young people themselves. This chapter seeks to explore the relationship between need, cost, service and, to a limited extent, outcome. It considers questions such as whether those children who cost more gain better access to services and whether some authorities are able to provide more cost-effective services to children with similar needs. Given the complexity of the issues involved, it should be no surprise to find that there are no easy answers. Identifying relationships between costs and welfare outcomes is a particularly thorny issue, because such links are at best tenuous and can rarely be related to a single factor such as a specific intervention. Because of the difficulty in establishing true causal connections, in this chapter the exploration of outcomes focuses more closely on the extent to which specific groups of children and young people had better (or worse) *opportunities* for improved life chances than on the extent to which these were converted into improvement (or deterioration) in developmental progress. A more extended, longitudinal study would be necessary to explore the latter issue.

Relationship between need and cost

Figure 6.1 shows the substantial differences in the estimated mean annual costs of looking after a child in each of seven groups from which individual case histories were explored in Chapter 5. As with other chapters, mean annual costs were estimated by dividing each cost by the number of placement days to which they relate (giving costs per day); these mean daily costs were then multiplied by 365 to give mean annual costs. The groups are shown in ascending order of mean annual cost per child with the number of children in each needs group in the sample also indicated. As we anticipated, the mean costs of providing care or accommodation were lowest for children who displayed no evidence of additional support needs, and highest for the group of children and young people with emotional or behavioural difficulties who also committed offences. Overall, the mean cost of looking after children in the simple needs groups was less than for those in the complex groups. Groups with less than ten children in them have been excluded from this analysis. These groups all included children and young people with the most complex needs (see Chapter 5, Figure 5.4); although they contain insufficient numbers for meaningful analysis, it should be noted that these tended to be the most costly children, whose presence in the care system could skew the total budget for children's social care in a local authority (see Chapter 4).

The incremental costs of providing care and accommodation to children with more complex needs are particularly evident in the differences in mean cost between children in the simple groups with only emotional or behavioural difficulties *or* offending behaviour and those in the complex group who displayed both these attributes. Looking after a child who showed signs of emotional or behavioural difficulty *or* who offended cost the authorities on average between £51,000 and £58,000 per year (at 2006–7 prices). However when these two features were combined, the average costs were approximately doubled to £109,000. On average, children with disabilities cost more than other children, and there was a considerable increase (£21,000 per year) if they also showed evidence of emotional or behavioural problems. Costs for these children were further increased if they were convicted of offences.

The data plotted in Figure 6.1 are set out in Table 6.1, together with the coefficient of variation for each of the needs groups. As well as there being substantial differences between the mean costs for the various

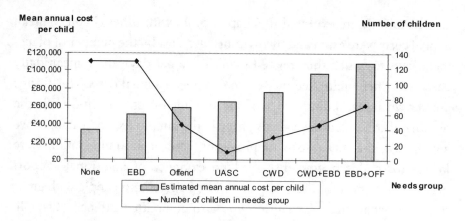

Figure 6.1: Comparative costs of looking after children with different needs (mean annual costs estimated on the basis of raw data from the study and updated to 2006–7 prices) (n = 462)

groups of children, there are also considerable variations in the costs incurred in looking after children within each of the needs groups. Since the means of the different needs groups vary so much, we thought it appropriate to use the relative measure of variability (coefficient of variation = standard deviation/mean), to compare the dispersions within them.

Table 6.1: Comparative costs of looking after children with different needs: Mean and coefficients of variation (2006–7 prices) (n = 462)

	Number in sample	Estimated mean annual cost per child (£)	Coefficient of variation
None	129	33,634	0.948
EBD	129	51,431	0.815
Offend	46	58,176	0.795
UASC	10	65,102	0.599
CWD	30	76,305	0.757
CWD + EBD	46	97,633	0.606
EBD + OFF	72	109,178	0.530
Total	**462**		

With the exception of unaccompanied asylum-seeking children, the simple needs groups displayed relatively more variability than the two complex ones. Children who showed no evidence of additional support needs had by far the lowest mean cost, but the spread of values around that mean was relatively large so that group had the biggest coefficient of variation. These cost variations are likely to reflect the considerable differences in types of care offered to children and young people with similar needs in the participating authorities. For example, young people who offended (who have the third highest coefficient of variation) spent a high proportion of time in the least expensive placements – with own parents; but some also spent time in high cost secure units. The relatively lower cost variations in the complex needs groups probably reflect how far the authorities were restricted in the types of placement they were able to offer children and young people who showed combinations of extensive support needs. Differences between the authorities will be explored further later in this chapter.

Need, cost and opportunities for developing attachments

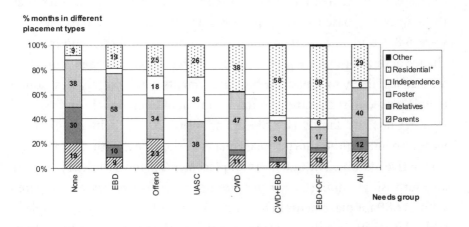

Figure 6.2: Percentage of placement months spent in different placement types, by group (n = 462 children; 936 placements; 7319 placement months)

* Includes children's homes, mother and baby units, secure units

As Chapter 4 has shown, up to 97 per cent of the costs of looking after a child in care or accommodation can be attributed to differences in the types of placement used. Figure 6.2 shows the percentage of time children in the seven most common groups spent in the five main placement types. The five placement types in the chart are set out in order of descending cost – placements with parents being generally the least costly and those in residential care the most. Children in the five simple needs groups spent a higher proportion of placement months in foster care (34–58%) and a lower proportion in more expensive residential care (9–38%). The situation is reversed for children in the two complex needs groups, who spent 58–59 per cent of their time in residential care.

Family placements, with parents, relatives or in foster homes, generally offer children better opportunities of preserving or developing secure attachments with adults, one of the key objectives for children's services (Department of Health 1999) reiterated in the current White Paper on looked after children (Department for Education and Skills 2007a). On this particular criterion there is, therefore, an inverse relationship between cost and outcome, for residential units tend to be more costly, although high staff turnover, shift working and frequent movement of children all mean that they offer fewer opportunities of developing such attachments. Placements in residential units also tend to be on average shorter than those in family based settings (in this study the respective mean lengths were 6.8 months as compared with 8.6 months), offering children less chance of developing a sense of stability. Placements in independent living are also less likely to support secure attachments with adult figures: young people placed in such settings often complain of being lonely and isolated from friends and family (see Skuse and Ward 2003; Stein 2004). They were also among the shortest placements in the study, with a mean duration of five months. The unit costs for placements in independent living are also surprisingly high (£3001 per month, at 2006–7 prices, as compared with £1689 for placements in foster care). This is because young people in such placements require substantial social work support, and the subsistence cost usually includes rent (see Chapter 3).

Children with no evidence of additional support needs and opportunities for developing attachments

Children displaying no evidence of additional support needs spent a significantly[1] higher proportion of their time (30%) in placements with relatives or friends than did others; they also spent a high proportion of time in placements with own parents (19%) or foster carers (38%) and a significantly lower proportion of time in residential units (9%) than those in the other groups.[2] They were also the group who experienced the greatest degree of stability: at the start of the study 95 (74%) of them had been in their current placement for more than two years, and 38 (29%) for more than three; 107 (83%) of the young people in this group remained in the same placement for the full 20 months of the study.

At the start of the study 31 (24%) children in this group were in out-of-authority placements. However, nine of these were placements with relatives or friends, intended to preserve family attachments although they may have been at a distance from birth parents. Only the two London authorities and Unitary Two placed children in this group in out-of-authority foster or residential care, although we have already seen that in the London boroughs such placements may have been very near at hand. As Chapter 7 shows, placements at a distance from the authority are unpopular with children, who dislike living far from familiar surroundings and the potential loss of contact with family and friends that this entails.

> I do get homesick quite a bit because I still have some friends from my old school and I don't get to see them much. When I come back here after the holidays I get very tearful and it takes a week or so to settle down. (Young woman, 18, out-of-authority residential school)

> I just want to be in a nice house with nice people. I don't mind if it's with other young people or adults, but I don't want to stay in this area. I'd like to be where I have friends. (Young woman, 18, independent living unit)

Of the 22 children and young people in this group who were placed at a distance from the authority at the start of the study, nine had spent over two years in their current placement and six more than four years. All but one of these long-stay placements were with foster carers; it seems likely that the stability they provided would have counterbalanced the disadvantages of being placed outside the authority. Nevertheless, it is noteworthy that even in this group at the start of the study, eight (6%) children and young people were in out-of-authority placements with foster carers that had lasted less than six months.

Children with disabilities and opportunities for developing attachments

Children with disabilities, including those who also had emotional or behavioural difficulties, spent less than 5 per cent of their time in placements with relatives or friends, and only a little more in placements with parents. Those with disabilities alone spent the majority of their time (47%) in foster care, although they also spent a high proportion of placement months in residential units (38%). Although they had more opportunities for developing and sustaining secure attachments with adults than many other children in the sample, they had fewer than the group of children who showed no evidence of additional support needs or those who had emotional or behavioural difficulties but no other significant problems. Similarly, children with disabilities experienced greater stability than many other children, although less than those with no additional needs. At the start of the study 21 (70%) of them had been in their current placement for more than two years, and 17 (57%) for more than three, including two children whose placements had lasted for over 11 years; 20 (67%) of these young people remained in the same placement throughout the study. Although this group had the longest mean length of placements in foster care, this was only for 14 months. About half of this group (14:47%) were in out-of-authority placements at the start of the study. These placements probably provided fewer compensatory opportunities for developing secure attachments than those for children with no evidence of additional support needs: although over half (8/14) had lasted for over two years, a high proportion were in residential care (6/14).

Children with both physical or learning disabilities and emotional or behavioural difficulties spent a significantly[3] higher proportion of their time in residential placements (58%:38%) and a significantly[4] lower proportion of time with foster carers, parents or relatives than those with disabilities alone (38%:62%). Although they spent substantially less time out of the authority than children with disabilities alone (37%:50%), they nevertheless had fewer opportunities to develop or sustain close attachments. Moreover their placements were less stable: at the start of the study only 16 (35%) had been in their current placement for two years or more, and 11 (24%) for at least three years; however almost the same proportion (29:63%) of them remained in the same placement throughout the study.

Children with complex needs and opportunities for developing attachments

The inverse relationship between cost and opportunities for developing secure attachment, already emerging in the different experiences of children with no evidence of additional support needs and those with disabilities, is thrown sharply into relief when children displaying both emotional or behavioural difficulties and offending behaviour are considered. Apart from the very small numbers of children with severe and complex needs, this was the most costly group in the sample; it was also the third largest, including 72 children, 15 per cent of the sample as a whole. Young people in this group spent the lowest proportion of their time in family placements with parents, relatives and foster carers (33%) and the highest proportion in residential units (59%). Their experiences contrast with those of the group of children and young people who displayed emotional or behavioural difficulties alone, who spent well over twice as much time in family based placements (77%) and only about a third as much (19%) in residential care. The opportunities for developing secure attachments for the group with more complex needs were further diminished by the frequency with which they moved.

Figure 6.3 shows the number of placements experienced by the sample children during the 20 months of the study. While children with no additional support needs were the most likely (83%:107) to experience just one placement during the 20-month period, less than a quarter (21%:15) of those with emotional or behavioural difficulties who also offended did so. Thirty-one children in this latter group (43%) experienced five or more

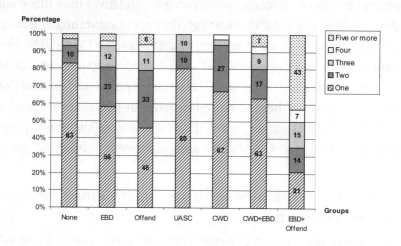

Figure 6.3: Number of placements by group (n = 462)

placements during the study period, including one young person who had 20 placements and one who had 21. The mean length of time children and young people in this group remained in each placement during the study period was three months in foster care and four in residential units. In contrast, 58 per cent (75) of those children who displayed emotional or behavioural difficulties alone remained in the same placement throughout the study, and only five (4%) had five or more placements, their average placement length being ten months in foster care and eleven months in residential care. As we shall see, not only do the frequent movements of the group with more complex needs represent an escalating spiral into more and more costly placements, they also prevent young people from forming secure attachments to other adults or to peers and make it less likely that they will access services from other agencies such as education, health and child and adolescent mental health services.

It is, of course, difficult to separate out cause from effect. The more costly placements *are* those which are the least likely to provide the conditions under which adequate attachments might be formed, and movement exacerbates this cost; moreover, the increased alienation of some of these young people is a cause, as well as an effect, of the transient circumstances of their lives. Nevertheless, these are the young people for whom the costs of providing care and accommodation are the highest – and who are at greatest risk of experiencing isolation and social exclusion in adulthood.

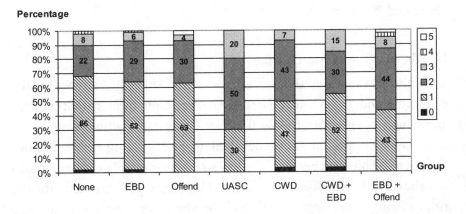

Figure 6.4: Number of social workers by group over 20-month study period (n = 462)

There is also little evidence of these young people developing secure and enduring relationships with social workers that might, perhaps, compensate for the lack of stability in other areas of their lives. Figure 6.4 shows the numbers of social workers to whom young people were allocated during the 20 months of the study. Apart from the ten asylum seekers, young people with emotional or behavioural difficulties who also offended were the least likely to have remained on the caseload of one social worker (31:43%) throughout the study and the most likely to have been allocated to four or more (3:4%), although the numbers who experienced such very frequent changes are so small as to be possibly attributable to chance. There may be valid reasons why these young people experience changes of social worker: they may be moved deliberately to practitioners whose skills are more appropriate to their needs, or with whom they are expected to be able to establish better relationships; nevertheless the young people themselves often regard such changes in a negative light:

> Social workers are constantly changing and that's difficult for me. The staff [in the residential unit] are always changing. (Young woman, 18, residential unit)

The potentially adverse effects of such changes need to be understood within the context of constant changes in domicile, home, school and social contacts that is so characteristic of these young people's lives (see Skuse and Ward 2003).

Needs, costs and life chances

So far the data appear to show an inverse relationship between cost and the conditions under which adequate attachments might form, so that children and young people who follow the least costly care pathways appear to have the best opportunities for developing and sustaining secure relationships with adults and peers, and vice versa. Young people with emotional or behavioural difficulties who are also offenders appear to be at particular risk of being drawn into a vicious circle where opportunities to develop secure attachments become increasingly limited as they become hard to place in family homes and are moved into residential units. Such placements can be impersonal, are costly and are also often of very short duration. Does the evidence also suggest a similar, inverse relationship between cost and access to those universal and specialist services that are intended to improve young people's life chances, such as health, education and child and adolescent mental health services?

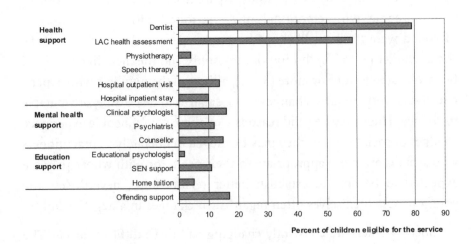

Figure 6.5: Types of service used (n = 462)

Figure 6.5 shows that, within the timeframe of the study, the sample as a whole received specialist support from a wide range of other agencies. A relatively high proportion of all children and young people went to the dentist (79%), small numbers also had speech therapy (6%) or physiotherapy (4%). Rather fewer had their annual health assessments (59%) than the national figures for the total population would suggest,[5] probably because these young people were in the age-group most likely to refuse to attend. A total of 205 children and young people (43%) received mental health support – an encouragingly high proportion, given the extent of known need amongst this population (see Meltzer *et al.* 2003). A high percentage of the sample (43%) either had statements of special educational need or had entered the statementing process, and were therefore likely to be eligible for additional educational support, although it was not always clear what help they had received. A few young people (21:5% of those eligible) received home tuition in addition to full time education, mainly in order to help them prepare for GCSEs. A similar number (22:17% of those eligible) received support such as anger management or substance abuse programmes to help them deal with offending behaviour. However while the sample as a whole appeared to gain reasonable access to a wide range of services, there were considerable disparities in the experiences of children and young people in each of the different groups.

Children with no evidence of additional support needs and life chances

Children and young people with no evidence of additional support needs had reasonable access to health care. Over 80 per cent visited the dentist and 50 per cent attended at least one annual health assessment in the course of the study. Although 29 (22%) of them refused health assessments, these were usually young people who were either placed with relatives or long-term foster carers and felt that this was a reminder that they were still looked after, or who felt that the assessment identified them as different from their friends. Others had previously been abused and refused to attend on the grounds that they did not feel comfortable with the examination. Only two of these 129 young people attended outpatients' appointments during the course of the study, and six spent time in hospital as inpatients.

It will be remembered that this group of young people had relatively stable lives while looked after, 83 per cent remaining in the same placement throughout the time period of the study. This is also reflected in the stability of their school careers: 89 per cent (109) of this group had no unscheduled changes of school during the study period, and only one young person changed more than once. Of the 13 young people who did have an unforeseen change of school, only two moved because their placements changed.

A number of young people in this group needed help with their education: 27 (21%) of them had statements of special educational need. Nevertheless the majority of those with statements (22) were in mainstream school or colleges of further education; only five were in special schools, of which three were residential. Fifteen of the young people in this group received additional educational support. Some of this was in the form of classroom assistance for those with special educational needs. However eight (47%) of the teenagers in this group received extra tuition to help prepare them for GCSEs. Authorities that introduced such schemes tended to offer extra tuition only to those who were in stable placements, with the result that young people in this, the least costly group, were most likely to benefit.

There is an interrelationship between the relative stability experienced by these young people and their educational outcomes, which, perhaps unsurprisingly, were the most positive for all groups in the study. Only seven of the young people with no additional needs were known to have missed 25 days or more schooling during either of the academic years of the study. Of those who reached school leaving age during the course of the study, 33 (51%) passed one or more GCSEs, 12 (19%) gaining five passes at grade C or above. This latter figure includes two young people who passed ten GCSEs at grades C and above, one of whom went on to gain four A levels.

However although some young people in this group had successful school careers, this was not true for all: 17 (26%) of the older teenagers had ceased to attend school by the time they reached 16, while 15 (38%) of those who had no statement of special educational needs, and 17 (63%) of those who did have statements left school without any qualifications. Only ten (50%) of the young people in this group who had left school were known to be employed at the end of the study. This was also the group with the highest percentage of teenage pregnancies: by the end of the study ten (7%) had either been pregnant or had made a girlfriend pregnant.

Unaccompanied asylum-seeking children and life chances

The small group of ten unaccompanied asylum-seeking children who showed no other additional needs were very similar in life chances profile to the group described above. They made little use of additional health care services, although only one of them refused the annual health assessment. Seven of them had up-to-date dental treatment and none refused to go to appointments. They tended to remain in stable placements throughout the study and had no unscheduled changes of school. Many of the asylum seekers had attended a specialist education provision for young people whose first language was not English, although none of them had statements of special educational need. Most of them started to be looked after at 14 years or more, and the need to adapt to a new culture and learn a new language in a short space of time, in addition to the experiences that had precipitated them into care, may explain their relatively low academic achievements: one passed one GCSE and an NVQ, and one gained an NVQ only. Four of them had ceased to attend school by the time they reached their 16th birthday. However by the end of the study at least four had gone on to colleges of further education, and only one was known to be unemployed.

Children with disabilities and life chances

We have already seen that the average annual cost of looking after children and young people with disabilities was more than twice that of providing care or accommodation for those with no evidence of additional support needs, and almost three times as much if they had emotional or behavioural difficulties as well as physical or learning disabilities. This was largely due to the high proportion of time spent in agency (26%), out-of-authority (42%) and/or residential placements (50%).

Of all the groups in the sample, children and young people with disabilities were most likely to receive routine health care in the form of dental appointments (93%) and statutory health assessments (85%). This may mean that, on at least these criteria, this group received a higher standard of health care. However, we have seen that a considerable number of young people in other groups refused statutory health assessments: only one young person with disabilities did so, suggesting that these young people may simply have been less able to object to interventions they did not wish to receive.

As one would expect, young people in these groups were most likely to receive specialist physical health care: within the timeframe of the study 43 (57%) received some form of additional health support service. Of those for whom information is available, six (8%) received physiotherapy, 15 (20%) speech therapy, 17 (22%) attended hospital as outpatients and five as inpatients. However without precise information about their health needs it is impossible to tell how far these interventions were appropriate or effective. Many of these children were similar in profile to Child E (see Chapter 5), who was moved from a residential placement to foster carers who were provided with support from community based health professionals.

All but three of the children with disabilities were known to have statements of special educational need. Many of them had learning disabilities. As a group they spent just over a quarter (27%) of their time in placements that were known to have educational facilities on the premises. No children who had disabilities alone passed one GCSE, although three of those who had disabilities plus emotional or behavioural difficulties did so.

Children with emotional or behavioural difficulties and life chances

We have already seen that the children with emotional or behavioural difficulties in this study fell into three groups: those who displayed no other additional needs, those who also had disabilities and those who were also young offenders. When children with emotional or behavioural difficulties also displayed other needs, the costs of caring for them were approximately doubled. The earlier discussion found an inverse relationship between cost and outcome for two of these groups, in that those with emotional or behavioural difficulties who were also young offenders were substantially less likely to have opportunities to develop or sustain attachments to peers and adults or to remain in a stable placement than those who displayed emotional or behavioural difficulties without showing evidence of other needs. A similar relationship between these two groups as regards their opportunities to improve their life chances is described below. By contrast, the third group of children, who had both emotional or behavioural difficulties and disabilities had costs similar to the other group with complex needs but better outcomes.

Young people with emotional or behavioural difficulties who were also young offenders were the least likely of all the sample to access routine medical care; only 29 (40%) of them had a health assessment and less than half of them (34:47%) saw a dentist within the study period. The only health service that these young people did frequently access was admission to hospital: 17 per cent of young people in this group spent time as hospital inpatients within the study period. There were significantly more hospital admissions among the two groups with challenging behaviour who did not have disabilities than among other groups, including those children and young people with severe health conditions and disabilities.[6] There was evidence from the case files that at least 13 of these young people were admitted to hospital because of self-harming behaviour and/or suicide attempts. Twenty-one (29%) of the young people with emotional or behavioural difficulties who were also offenders displayed self-harming behaviour during the course of the study. This is significantly more than amongst those who had only emotional or behavioural difficulties,[7] and an indicator of their extreme vulnerability. However, this same group were also least likely to access psychotherapeutic support: 43 (60%) of them saw a mental health professional within the timescale of the study, as compared with 91 (71%) of those with emotional or behavioural difficulties only and 33 (72%) of those who in addition had physical or learning disabilities.

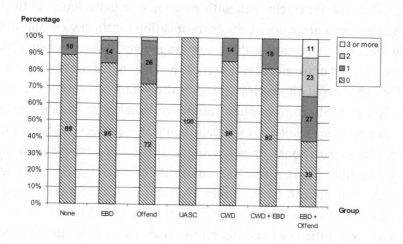

Figure 6.6: Unscheduled changes of school by group (n = 452)

As Figure 6.6 shows, young people with emotional or behavioural difficulties who also committed offences experienced substantially more
changes of school than those in other groups: just over a third of them
(28:39%) remained in the same school throughout the study period, and
all of those who experienced three or more unscheduled school changes
were in this group. The same group of young people also experienced
more school exclusions: 36 (50%) of them were excluded during the study
timeframe in comparison with only five (11%) of children who had disabilities in addition to emotional or behavioural difficulties and 31 (24%)
of those who had emotional or behavioural difficulties without showing
evidence of other additional needs. The difference between the exclusion
rates for the two groups with complex needs is statistically significant.[8]
Almost all the permanent exclusions involved young people with emotional or behavioural difficulties who also committed offences (29:78%);
there were none amongst the other complex needs group who also had
disabilities and eight (6%) in the group who displayed emotional or behavioural difficulties alone.

Young people with emotional or behavioural difficulties who were
also offenders were also the most likely to drop out of school before their
16th birthday (60%), to leave school with no qualifications (86%), and to

be unemployed (32%) at the end of the study. In comparison, some young people with emotional or behavioural difficulties who showed no evidence of other additional needs had successful school careers: four (10%) of them gained five or more GCSE passes at Grade C or above. However 12 (23%) of those young people in this latter group who had left school were unemployed at the end of the study.

Relationships between needs, costs and outcomes

Where children and young people showed no evidence of physical or learning disability, the data from the study appear to demonstrate an inverse relationship between costs and services for those with different levels of need. By and large young people who showed no evidence of additional support needs cost less, were more likely to find themselves in environments conducive to the development of secure attachments and had better opportunities for gaining maximum life chance benefits from child welfare services than those in other groups.

In contrast, many of the children and young people with emotional or behavioural difficulties who also committed offences displayed long-standing and complex problems that would require intensive and costly interventions in any setting. Even with substantial expert professional support there would have been a high risk of many of these difficulties persisting into adulthood. Other children and young people had less entrenched problems but, as Chapter 7 demonstrates, their unhappiness was reflected in a downward spiral of behavioural difficulties that jeopardized the stability of both their placements and their education. The question to resolve is how far the services offered to young people who are looked after by local authorities are able to meet their often extensive and varied needs.

The experiences of the group of young people with emotional or behavioural difficulties who were also offenders reflect a complex interrelationship between their own difficulties, the responses of professionals, and the transience of life in care or accommodation. Changes of placement were closely intertwined with changes of school, the one having a knock-on effect on the other, and each change reinforcing the impression of impermanence and instability. Many young people in this complex needs group had become alienated from the services that were supposed to support them. They were the group most likely to become looked after because their parents 'needed relief' (19:26%). They were also the group most likely to refuse health assessments (25:35%), dental care (13:18%) and mental health support (9:13%). They were the most likely to abscond from placements (51:71%) and to be absent from school for more than 25 days (16:22%). The response to their behaviour was often to reject them from yet another placement or to exclude them from another school.

While such responses are understandable, and perhaps inevitable, they increased both the costs of looking after these young people, and also the likelihood that they would fail to access the services necessary to support them. We have demonstrated elsewhere how the constant change experienced by some young people in care or accommodation is frequently accompanied by a loss of self-esteem and identity that follows the loss of cherished personal possessions (see Skuse and Ward 2003). There are also considerable practical implications: whenever young people move it takes time for health and school records to catch up. If they move area, they may be pushed to the back of CAMHS, orthodontists' or other specialists' waiting lists. Information about outpatients' appointments, dental appointments or ongoing programmes of psychotherapeutic support may not be passed on (see Ward *et al.* 2002). Young people who change schools have to establish themselves with a new peer group. They are likely to find that the new class has covered parts of the national curriculum that they have not encountered, and repeats parts that they have already completed. It is perhaps inevitable that constant movement will increase their alienation, and reduce their opportunities of accessing services intended to improve their life chances. As the interviews explored in detail in Chapter 7 show, while some of these services might take the form of intensive expert interventions, young people in care or accommodation also place great value on opportunities for informal discussions about their motivation and feelings with carers and mentors – opportunities that are unlikely to arise until relationships have been established (see Skuse and Ward 2003).

Young people with emotional or behavioural difficulties who also committed offences tended to cost nearly three times as much to look after as those who displayed no evidence of additional support needs, although their chances of accessing supportive services and achieving satisfactory outcomes were significantly less. The costs are related to their increasingly challenging behaviour. Any service designed to address the needs of some of these young people will be expensive, and it may be that effective interventions can only be provided for those with entrenched difficulties and/or damaging family situations if they are placed away from home. However, some of the findings from this study provide agencies with information that might be of help in making difficult choices concerning their care. First, there are differences in the ages at which children in each of the groups entered the care episode on which the study focused, and in the length of time that they had been continuously looked after, as Figure 6.7 demonstrates.

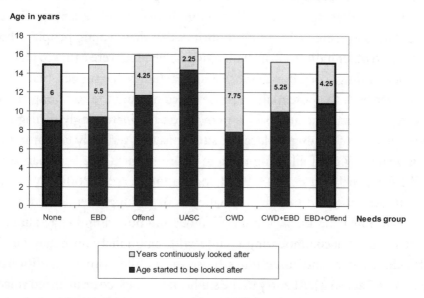

Figure 6.7: Average age at entry and length of time continuously looked after by group (n = 459)

These differences reach statistical significance when the two groups shown in bold outline at either end of the chart are compared. On average, young people with emotional or behavioural difficulties who also committed offences were nearly two years older when they started to be looked after than those who showed no evidence of additional support needs.[9] They had also spent on average nearly two years less in care or accommodation by the start of the study.[10] Other groups show a similar, though not so significant, trend: thus children with disabilities only (CWD) started to be looked after at an earlier age than those who also had emotional or behavioural difficulties (CWD + EBD). Those with emotional or behavioural difficulties alone (EBD) had entered at a later age than those with no evidence of additional support needs (None), though they were about 18 months younger at entry and had spent on average 15 months more in care or accommodation by the start of the study than those who were also committing offences (EBD + Offend). Apart from the asylum seekers, who had very different needs, the only group to buck the trend were the offenders, who, although entering care at an older age than those who also had emotional and behavioural difficulties, and spending about the same amount of time looked after, appeared to have more beneficial experiences. There were some suggestions from the authorities that these young people, who showed no other indicators of challenging behaviour, were easier to place.

Such findings corroborate those of other studies that suggest that concerns over both the potentially adverse outcomes and the spiralling costs of care have led some authorities to overlook the increasingly damaging consequences of leaving children in situations that seriously compromise their wellbeing or of allowing them to return to them (see Packman and Hall 1998; Sinclair et al. 2003; Ward, Munro and Dearden 2006). We have already demonstrated that the annual costs of looking after a child with both emotional and behavioural difficulties and offending behaviour are twice those of accommodating a child with emotional and behavioural difficulties alone, and three times those for a child with no additional needs (see Table 6.1). At entry to the study, the average costs incurred since the start of the care episode of looking after a child with emotional and behavioural difficulties who was also an offender (£423,504)[11] would still have been substantially higher than those for a child with no additional needs (£205,517), although the former would have been looked after for a considerably shorter period. Postponing entry in order to reduce costs may prove to be a false economy.

Second, greater transparency concerning the costs of looking after children with different needs makes it easier to compare different service options. The entrenched emotional or behavioural difficulties displayed by some young offenders are likely to have incurred substantial costs to a range of agencies wherever they were placed. Indications that, during the course of the study, a high proportion of these young people were admitted to hospital because of self-harming behaviour and/or suicide attempts demonstrates that their emotional difficulties are likely to have incurred continuing costs to health agencies; evidence that young people in this group also committed numerous and often serious offences indicates that they would have incurred substantial costs to the police, the courts and youth justice agencies.

We have already established that these young people also incurred high costs to children's social care, but appeared to gain few benefits: a number of them ran through the gamut of placements and eventually returned to their families as it became evident that they had little to gain from being looked after. Given that these young people are likely to incur continuing costs to a range of agencies throughout their adolescence and into adulthood, once the costs incurred by all agencies can be established, it should be possible to explore how they might be more effectively distributed. For instance, offering a package of multi-agency interventions, either within or outside the context of specialist foster care, might better meet the needs of these young people than the sequence of short-term residential placements with only sporadic access to specialist services that some of them now encounter. The emphasis on pooled budgets and greater integration of services introduced by the Children Act 2004 makes it clear that such negotiations are increasingly expected at both local and national level.

Differences between authorities

To some extent variations in both placement patterns and costs to local authorities can be explained by differences in the profile of their care populations. Expenditure is likely to relate to the proportion of children and young people in care with complex needs, as these will usually require the most expensive placements. Figure 6.8 shows the different proportions of children in each of the needs groups identified in this study in the samples from the participating authorities. For the purpose of this comparison the costs incurred by the small numbers of children with very complex needs are included in the calculation.

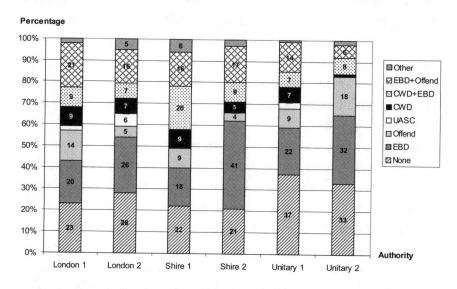

Figure 6.8: Percentage of children in cost-related groups by local authority. All groups included (n = 478)

As Figure 6.8 demonstrates, there were considerable differences between the authorities in the pattern of need displayed by the sample children. Unitary 2, for instance, had the lowest proportion of children with complex needs, a factor that may partly account for its consistently low costs (see Chapter 5). Both the shire authorities had low percentages of children and young people who showed no evidence of additional support needs, but the very high proportion of looked after children with complex needs in Shire 1 (42% of its sample) provides one reason for its higher expenditure. London 1 had the highest proportion (21%) of children with emotional or behavioural difficulties who also committed offences (EBD + Offend) but London 2 had a high proportion of children and young people with very complex needs (Other), which may be one reason why its costs were marginally higher than those of its pair.

However, differences in the pattern of need only provide a partial explanation for variations in expenditure between authorities. We have already noted that there were substantial disparities in the costs of looking after different children within each of the needs groups. Although to a certain extent these reflect the specific characteristics of individual children, they also reflect differences in service delivery between the authorities.

Figure 6.9 contrasts the mean estimated annual costs for each authority of looking after children and young people with no evidence of additional support needs and those with emotional or behavioural difficulties who were also offenders. In Shire 1 and Unitary 2, the estimated mean annual costs of looking after children and young people with no additional needs were both below £25,000. This is substantially lower than in the other authorities, where the mean costs were over £30,000, and more than £42,000 in London 2. The differences are largely accounted for by variations in the percentage of time spent in different placement types: no children and young people in this group in Shire 1 or Unitary 2 spent time in residential units, whereas these accounted for between 15 and 16 per cent

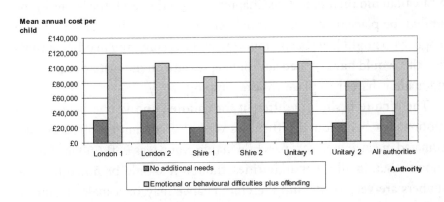

Figure 6.9: Costs for each authority of looking after children and young people in contrasting needs groups. Estimated mean annual costs per child updated to 2006–7 prices

of placement months in Shire 2 and Unitary 1, though somewhat less in the London authorities. This appears to have had a greater influence on costs than the percentage of time children and young people with no additional needs spent placed with parents or relatives, although this was substantially lower in Shire 1 (56%) and Unitary 2 (35%) than in their pairs (65%).

Shire 1 and Unitary 2 also showed very small variations in the costs of looking after individual children with no additional support needs, while there were substantial differences in costs per child in this group in Shire 2 and Unitary 1. It is possible that some children were wrongly categorized in these latter authorities, and that, in fact, they had additional support needs that were not apparent to researchers. Inadequate data might therefore account for the, apparently anomalous, higher costs they incurred. On the other hand, it is also possible that these authorities had a shortage of foster placements for children in this group, so some of those who could not be looked after by family members were placed in residential units, where they incurred high costs in settings that were unlikely to be geared to meet their relatively low support needs. In Shire 2 and Unitary 1, children with no additional needs only spent between 17 and 20 per cent of placement months in foster care. It is also evident that Shire 2 and Unitary 1 both had a substantially higher proportion of children and young people in care than did their pairs (see Chapter 2), with the result that some of the family type placements could have been taken up by children and young people who might have been supported in the community in other authorities; this would have created additional pressure on the system as a whole, and made it harder to place children appropriately.

The picture is slightly different for children and young people with emotional or behavioural difficulties who also committed offences. The estimated mean annual cost per child in this group was £80,668 in Unitary 2, lower than in all other authorities, though it should be noted that the numbers are very small, and therefore chance may be a major factor. In comparison with the other authorities, mean annual costs for young people in this complex needs group were also low in Shire 1 (£87,956), and high in Shire 2 (£126,262) and Unitary 1 (£106,985). In the latter two authorities these costs are similar to those in the inner London boroughs. However, the variations between the costs incurred by individual children in this group were highest in Shire 1 and Unitary 2.

Shire 1 and Unitary 2 both looked after very low percentages of their children in need (see Chapter 2). One could argue that these authorities were more efficient than Shire 2 and Unitary 1, supporting children in their families in the community, and placing minimum numbers in care or accommodation. One could also argue that when children were placed away from home, Shire 1 and Unitary 2 were better able to find placements that were suited to their needs. Children who have no additional needs are a more homogenous group and were most likely to be placed in family settings. Children with emotional or behavioural difficulties who also commit offences display a wider variety of additional support needs, and possibly require a more flexible service that is able to respond differently to different needs. In all authorities except for Shire 1 and Unitary 2, children and young people in this group spent over 50 per cent of their time in residential units. Unitary 2 had a clearly articulated policy to avoid residential care or out-of-authority placements. In this authority, children and young people in this group spent a high percentage of their time placed with relatives or friends (32%), placements that were barely used for young people with these complex needs in other authorities. A distinctive feature of Shire 1 is the high percentage of time this group spent placed with own parents (34%), more than double that in any other authority.

There are some indications that the greater efficiency shown by Shire 1 and Unitary 2 in providing placements is also reflected in some of the data on outcomes. As a whole, children in the sample from these authorities were most likely to gain at least one GCSE (Shire 1: 9/29 (31%); Unitary 2: 12/35 (34%)) and were least likely to be excluded from school (Shire 1: 9/55 (16%); Unitary 27/77 (9%)). All but three of the 36 children and young people in Unitary 2 who showed evidence of emotional or behavioural difficulties (92%) received psychotherapeutic support, significantly more than in Shire 2 or the two London authorities;[12] young people in Shire 1 were the next most likely to receive such support (23/30:77%). However, this trend is not consistent: young people in Shire 2 (27:68%) and Unitary 1 (19:61%) were more likely to complete their statutory schooling than those in Shire 1 (17:59%) or Unitary 2 (17:49%). There were also no significant differences in offending rates, which clustered between 24 and 29 per cent of all children, with Shire 1, at 29 per cent, the second highest.

Conclusion

This chapter has argued that in the sample as a whole, the experiences of the different groups of children showed an inverse relationship between costs and outcome. Children with the least evidence of additional support needs were likely to cost less than those in other groups, yet they had better opportunities of being placed in environments that were conducive to the development of secure attachments and of benefiting from the provision of health, education and social care services; conversely, those with emotional or behavioural difficulties who were also young offenders, the group that incurred the greatest costs, tended to benefit least.

Some young people have extensive and enduring needs that will require intensive, expert support from a range of agencies throughout their adolescence and into adulthood. In a study of this nature we cannot say whether those young people who receive intensive support services while remaining in the family home might have better opportunities for improving life chances than those placed in care or accommodation, though the spiralling costs and poor access to services of those young people who move swiftly through a sequence of placements would suggest that different configurations might be considered. Differences in average age at admission between the groups would also indicate that postponing admission for children with growing emotional or behavioural needs might prove to be a false economy. Differences in expenditure on different groups between the authorities could simply reflect substantial differences in the extent and complexity of need; however there is also evidence that some authorities were more able to provide placements appropriate to children's needs, and that this reduced costs without adversely affecting their life chances.

Summary of the key points from Chapter 6

- There were substantial differences in the average cost of looking after children in each of the different groups throughout the study period. Mean costs increased as children's needs became more complex. Moreover there were greater variations in costs for children with simple needs than for those with extensive support needs, suggesting that authorities were increasingly restricted in their choice of placements for the latter.

- Children who followed the least costly care pathways appeared to have the best opportunities for developing and sustaining secure relationships with adults and peers.

- Frequent changes of placement and sequences of short stays in residential units which had a high turnover of staff and residents, and which were often at a distance from home, were more likely to be experienced by children with complex needs, who followed more costly care pathways. Such experiences were least likely to help them develop and sustain attachments.

- The profile of most of the asylum-seeking children tended to follow most closely that of the young people who showed no evidence of additional support needs. That is, they tended to remain in stable placements, accept routine health care and have no unscheduled changes of school. Poor command of English after only a short time in this country may explain their relatively low academic achievements; there was also evidence that a number were continuing in further education post-16.

- Children with extensive additional support needs, particularly those who showed no evidence of disability but displayed emotional or behavioural difficulties and were also young offenders, were least likely to access routine health care, and most likely to be excluded from school, to leave without qualifications and to be unemployed at the end of the study. They were also least likely to access psychotherapeutic support.

- Some young people in this group had very extensive additional support needs that would require intensive, expert interventions from a range of agencies throughout their adolescence and early adulthood. They appeared to gain little benefit from being looked after. More transparent costing of services would make it easier to explore whether different packages of support could be identified that might more effectively meet their needs.

- Variations were found between authorities in the estimated average annual cost of looking after children with similar needs. The two authorities that appeared to provide the most cost-effective service on other criteria also appeared most efficient at finding placements appropriate to children's needs.

Notes

1 $\chi^2 = 875.14$, $df = 6$, $p < 0.001$.

2 Group A (none) to B (EBD only): $\chi^2 = 95.4$, $df = 1$, $p < 0.001$; A to C (Offend only): $\chi^2 = 86.67$, $df = 1$, $p < 0.001$; A to D (UASC only): $\chi^2 = 51.29$, $df = 1$, $p < 0.001$; A to E (CWD only): $\chi^2 = 281.07$, $df = 1$, $p < 0.001$; A to F (CWD+EBD): $\chi^2 = 788.16$, $df = 1$, $p < 0.001$; A to G (EBD + offend): $\chi^2 = 872.73$, $df = 1$, $p < 0.001$ (all continuity corrected).

3 $\chi^2 = 48.97$, $df = 1$, $p < 0.001$, continuity corrected.

4 $\chi^2 = 70.07$, $df = 1$, $p < 0.001$, continuity corrected.

5 In the year ending 30 September 2001, 68 per cent of looked after children had an annual health assessment (Department of Health 2002e).

6 $\chi^2 = 5.03$, $df = 1$, $p = 0.025$, continuity corrected.

7 $\chi^2 = 5.17$, $df = 1$, $p = 0.023$, continuity corrected.

8 $\chi^2 = 12.88$, $df = 1$, $p < 0.001$, continuity corrected.

9 $U = 3150.5$, $p < 0.001$.

10 $U = 3194.0$, $p < 0.001$.

11 Updated to 2006–7 prices.

12 Difference between London 1 (62%) and Unitary 2 (92%): $\chi^2 = 7.81$, $df = 1$, $p = 0.005$ (continuity corrected); difference between London 2 (60%) and Unitary 2 (92%): $\chi^2 = 8.84$, $df = 1$, $p = 0.003$ (continuity corrected); difference between Shire 2 (55%) and Unitary 2 (92%): $\chi^2 = 12.39$, $df = 1$, $p < 0.001$ (continuity corrected).

Chapter 7

The Relationship Between Cost and Value: Children's Views of the Value of Services

Introduction

So far this book has been concerned with the costs of different types of placement and service provision, and with the relationship between costs, access to services and 'hard' evidence of opportunities for improved life chances. In this chapter we introduce an important further dimension, namely the perspective of young people themselves on their experiences in care. A full picture of the value of services, as opposed to their cost, is not possible without the perspective of those whom they intend to benefit, and the insights that young people have can greatly help in the process of providing local authorities with the information they need to make informed choices about how resources should be deployed. How far the 'soft' and more nuanced evidence that reflects young people's views can or should be included in the development of the cost calculator model remains an important issue for debate.

This chapter uses some of the findings from the qualitative interviews carried out with 47 young people across the six local authorities as a basis for exploring their views of care and accommodation. The rationale for selecting children and young people for interview and the issues concerning access have been discussed in Chapter 2. The aim of this chapter is to provide additional information, given by the young people themselves, about their experience of being looked after by a local authority. In particular, we were interested in three areas: the factors which young people saw as important in making placements successful; the degree to which they were able to participate in decisions affecting them; and the particular issues facing disabled young people in care or accommodation. As we have seen in previous chapters, these issues play an important role in determining the cost both of placements and of social care processes; many of the young people's comments indicate additional factors that need to be taken into account in assessing the relationship between costs and outcomes of services.

There is not sufficient space to discuss every aspect of the views and experiences shared by the young people in the study; we have, therefore, sought to explore some of the most illuminating and interesting issues arising from our analysis of the data. Where appropriate, we indicate the number of young people expressing a particular viewpoint, as a way of illustrating whether that view was held by many, or few, of those interviewed.

Factors influencing placement success and failure

Distance

Earlier chapters have already discussed the high cost of out-of-authority placements. Cleaver (2000) demonstrated the excessive amount of time social workers devote to arranging and maintaining contact when young people are placed in care or accommodation, time that is multiplied if the placements are a long way from their homes. The young people had much to say about the distance that placements sometimes put between themselves and their birth families (or other significant members of their informal network).

The interviews generated a large number of comments, from almost half of the sample, about the link between the success of particular placements and the spatial, temporal and emotional distance from their friends and family. Typically, this involved young people making particularly positive comments about placements that brought them nearer to their family and friends, or which gave them easier access to visits either to or from members of their informal network. For instance, one young man, living with foster carers, said:

> I like everything about living here. There is nothing that I don't like. This is where I've been happiest. It's close to school, friends and family; it's just better here. (Young man, 14, foster care)

Correspondingly, another young man described his current placement as 'OK', but pointed to problems given the distance between him and his friends. This was an important issue as he approached independence.

> I want to be in my own flat. Near my dad. I picked a couple of places I'd like to live in and the social workers say they'll look for a flat for me... I've been treated fine by [authority]. There's nothing wrong about it. But it was a bit difficult to keep in touch with my family when I was younger. (Young man, 17, foster care)

These comments tally closely with other studies which have highlighted the importance of contact with birth families for looked after children. For instance, Shaw (1998), in a survey of over 2000 looked after children, found that over a third would have liked more frequent contact with birth family members, a finding particularly true for younger children.

While easier access to birth family, and to existing informal networks of friends (including boy/girlfriends), was generally seen as very valuable, two young people viewed the maintenance of an appropriate distance as important. These young people expressed an insight into the potential harm that excessive contact might bring. For instance, one young woman had spent many years in the same foster placement as her stepbrother, but now welcomed the fact that he no longer lived with her. She added that her only contact with him was an occasional visit, and that she preferred it that way. At the second interview, she described how her stepbrother had got into trouble with the police, and that this had made her question the wisdom of re-establishing contact with her mother.

An 18-year-old young woman expressed a similar viewpoint: she had recently moved closer to her mother and viewed this as a positive development, but also commented that she would not want to be any nearer. These views were only expressed by a small number of young people, and were substantially outweighed by the opinion that greater and easier access to birth families was desirable. However, they alert us to the fact that contact with birth families may not be preferred by some young people, a finding consistent with the survey carried out by Shaw (1998), which found that around 8 per cent of looked after young people would like less frequent contact. Skuse and Ward (2003) also found that a number of young people appreciated the extent to which care made it possible for them to distance themselves from family problems and renegotiate a difficult relationship with a birth parent:

> If I'd stayed at home I'd have ended up hating my mum and vice versa. And since I've moved into care, we've built a much better relationship. (Girl, looked after from age 12–13, quoted in Skuse and Ward 2003, p.194)

These contrasting perspectives on the appropriate distance that young people feel should exist between them and their birth family and friends illustrate the importance of establishing the views of young people them-selves when considering placements and access arrangements. However, the comments of one young man indicated that it is not simply a question of preferences about distance, but about recognising the other factors that contribute to the maintenance of appropriate and successful contacts. He talked about wanting to keep his distance from his birth mother, whose problem drinking continued to cause him some embarrassment in the town in which they lived:

> I was away from my family for so long we didn't know each other. You'd think when you come out of care you'd spend all your time down there – then you find you don't want to, I was so disappointed. I didn't want to go down there, I don't go down there much now. (Young man, 19, living independently)

Another young man had become looked after when the pressure of living with his mother and her often violent partner (both of whom were heroin users) became too much. He described many months of 'looking after' his mother before finally realizing that this often resulted in violence against him from her partner, and in him placing himself voluntarily in care. At second interview, he talked about how he had missed his mother, and about how he gradually increased his contact with her, partly because her life was now more stable as a result of the support she had received with her substance abuse problems.

These two cases illustrate how the problems young people can face in maintaining contact with birth families may be such that support for their parents is required – for instance, in managing drug problems, in dealing with domestic violence and in addressing the difficulties that parents can have in maintaining positive relationships with their children after many years of separation. The provision of support to parents (and other family members) in order to meet the needs of children and young people is enshrined in section 17 of the Children Act 1989, and reiterated in the current White Paper on looked after children (Department for Education and Skills 2007a, pp.32–3); these cases illustrate the importance of such services to young people.

Many of the points raised by the above discussion indicate variables that can be introduced into the development of the cost calculator model. It would, for instance, be possible to monitor frequency of contact with birth parents, or parents' access to adult support services and to quantify these and cost them as a component in the delivery of services. Indeed, the costs of maintaining contact, with all the different configurations of time, locality and supervision, would be a separate research project in itself. However the cost calculator model works on averages; because most children benefit from contact with their birth families and because the provision of services to adults tends to be valued, the assumption is that the costs in time and effort of providing such services are justifiable and likely to contribute to successful outcomes. It is not easy to see how the perspectives of individual young people, whose own experiences differ from the mainstream, can be routinely incorporated into what is, essentially, a broad brush approach.

Education

Education was an area of importance for all the young people we interviewed. Many appeared to be settled at school and reported themselves to be doing well and enjoying school life. A minority had experienced a range of problems at school, with some having been excluded at some point – eight young people talked about current problems at school, whether in terms of the threat of exclusion, or the need for extra support as a disabled student.

As Chapter 6 has indicated, there is a closely intertwined relationship between school and placement experiences. Specifically, young people with a particularly broken record of school attendance and exclusion were often those with a series of failed placements. One young woman said:

> I never felt settled at a school because I was moved so much, got into a lot of trouble at school, some of the things that were happening I took it out on other people, because I never had anyone to turn to. (Young woman, 16, living independently)

Such comments are consistent with other studies that have looked at how young people view the impact of being looked after on their education (see Skuse and Ward 2003). The survey conducted by Shaw (1998) also found that 47 per cent of looked after children reported doing better at school after coming into care, with 36 per cent reporting no change and only 8 per cent saying they had done worse. However, around a third of those who had experienced six or more placements reported having done worse since entry to care or accommodation. Brandon and colleagues (1999) also highlighted the particular difficulties for educational consistency when children experienced frequent changes of placement. Chapter 6 has explored the additional costs involved, both to local authorities and to young people themselves, when frequent changes of placement and schools occur; however, once again, the cost calculator model cannot capture children and young people's personal perceptions of frequent changes and the impact these have on their overall experience.

Educational support

We discuss later the key place of behavioural problems in disrupting place-ments, and the importance of support aimed at helping young people manage them. As the previous quote indicates, such difficulties play an important part in educational disruption; some of the young people reflected on the impact of their behaviour on their educational attendance and performance.

Specialist education centres / residential units

Three of the young people who had been excluded from school because of poor behaviour had experience, either at the time of interview or previously, of education in specialist centres or residential units. Chapter 6 has argued that many of those in care or accommodation require the type of specialist, expert support that such units can sometimes offer. On the whole, the young people in this study talked positively about their time in such units, and in particular the help provided in addressing their behavioural difficulties. One young man, who had been excluded from mainstream school and who attended a specialist educational unit some 30 miles from home, said:

> ...in a normal class there are, like, 30 people but in ours there's nine so it's easier, you get help with your work and all that. Only 60 in the whole school. I get more help, instead of the teacher running around the class and having your hand up for ages. (Young man, 12, foster care)

A young woman made a similar point, reflecting on her experience of being excluded from school and attending a specialist unit:

> Small classes means more attention, which means you get on with your work better. (Young woman, 18, living independently)

The generally positive light in which this more intensive educational support was reported is a significant factor to be weighed against the substantial costs incurred in offering this type of provision (see Holmes *et al.* forthcoming).

Support from all agencies

Young people also pointed to the complex interaction between placement and educational choices, which again serves to emphasize the importance of planning both in a sensitive and co-ordinated way. In some cases, young people were able to stay in a school of their choice only with the support provided by key workers or others not attached to the education service.

One young man, living in a residential placement, had struggled to get a place at the school closest to where he lived. In addition, in his first year at the school he had displayed some behavioural difficulties and there had been a possibility that he would be excluded. His key worker said:

> The school was talking about excluding him again, but we won't have that, and we'll do anything to avoid that. A support worker goes with him. The school welcome this; in fact, it's the only reason he's there 'cos they refused to have him before. We got no support at all trying to get him back in, we had to go in and sell ourselves really, and demonstrate the level of support, which is what we've done. (Residential key worker)

Similarly, another young man who had not yet been in trouble with the police, had been referred to a youth offending team because of school concerns about him slipping into truancy and possible criminal behaviour. This involved the YOT running sessions in school time looking at ways in which he, along with others in his school, could avoid engaging in criminal and anti-social activity. Again, this was described as a positive source of support, both by the young person and his grandfather, with whom he was living.

Previous research (Colton, Drury and Williams 1995; Skuse and Ward 2003) has shown that poor behaviour can often be related to insensitive responses from the school to the pressures faced by children in need. The interviews suggest that the kind of support described in the quotation above was welcomed by school and young person alike, and illustrates the importance of different agencies working together to underpin successful placements, and to prevent 'mutual disruption' between placements and schooling. The cost may be higher in the short term, but the value placed on such support by young people indicates possible longer-term benefits and hence, cost savings.

Lack of educational support

Support was generally valued by the young people interviewed; however, there were negative consequences for some when this was lacking. One important issue raised by young people in relation to their schooling included the apparent unfairness when rules about the receipt of benefits appeared to restrict the extent to which they could pursue preferred educational options post-16. One young man wanted to take just two A levels at his local college after dropping out of his secondary school. However, the rules concerning the amount of time students need to be studying each week to qualify for benefits had forced him to choose between taking three A levels or leaving education and looking for work. He chose the latter and was working in a call centre at the time of the interview.

Another young man had experienced a number of placement changes over the years, and had found himself in another unhappy foster placement despite being settled at the local school. He had been told that there was nowhere else for him to go given the lack of other available placements. His solution to the problems he had with his foster placement was therefore to artificially disrupt, or in his own words to 'sabotage' his schooling with the aim of precipitating another placement change via school exclusion, something he was successful in achieving. This is one of many findings from the interviews that demonstrate the importance of ascertaining young people's understanding of their experience. The costs of changes of placement and of school may be carefully calculated and accounted for, and frequent changes may, in general, be interpreted as indicative of poor outcomes. However a specific change may have a very different meaning to a particular individual, and this can only be identified by ascertaining young people's views of the experience (see also Skuse and Ward 2003).

Behaviour

We have discussed, in Chapters 5 and 6, the higher costs associated with providing placements and support for children and young people with emotional or behavioural difficulties. The long-term costs to public services of accommodating this group are extensive (Scott *et al.* 2001) and the importance of authorities finding ways to better understand, and better manage, children and young people with these difficulties cannot be overstated (Skuse and Ward 2003).

In this chapter, we have already touched on behaviour as a key issue raised by young people themselves when looking at their educational experience. It also, however, featured strongly in what they had to say about the success and failure of placements. This is important because, as we discussed in Chapter 6, children and young people with emotional or behavioural difficulties are more likely to experience disrupted placement histories, and therefore involve significantly greater costs to authorities in terms of more complex social care processes and more costly provision.

A total of 22 of the young people interviewed recognized that a key factor in previous failed placements had been their own poor behaviour, or what they saw as false accusations about how they had behaved. Sometimes, concern had been expressed by social workers and/or foster parents about inappropriate sexual behaviour. Sometimes, poor behaviour was linked to the young person's learning difficulties. However, the frequency with which young people reported behavioural issues as closely related to what they saw as the poor quality of care on offer was striking. This was true of children in foster as well as residential placements. One young man, now living in a residential unit and describing it in very positive terms, said:

> ...the last place I was in was terrible. I felt really unsafe and the supervision wasn't good enough. I needed protecting from other children but you would go to the staff room door, saying 'I'm going to get beat up' and they would do nothing about it, you ended up just standing around outside the staff room. (Young man, 14, residential placement)

He went on to say that this led directly to him getting caught up in the 'wrong crowd' and subsequently becoming involved in criminal and anti-social behaviour leading to placement breakdown and disrupted schooling. Indeed, several young people highlighted the importance of the poor behaviour of *other* young people they had encountered, particularly in residential placements, as having had a negative impact on their wellbeing and safety.

While acknowledging that their behaviour had been a contributory factor in the breakdown of previous foster homes, two other young people were keen to link this to their more general unhappiness in the placements:

> My previous foster mum and dad, they didn't give me no love, like. I know then I was a bitch. I was a bitch... (Young woman, 16, placed with friends)

Basically, if you don't want to be there, you're not going to be good. (Young man, 15, placed with parents)

Others talked about how a range of false allegations had been made about them, often by the birth children of foster parents; these had led to a deterioration of their behaviour, a reciprocal breakdown of trust with foster carers and the eventual breakdown of the placement. One young woman said:

> When I was younger I was with this family and I just didn't get on with the other children there. They used to accuse me of all sorts of things unfairly. In the end I ripped open all the Christmas presents and had to leave. They never liked me anyway, and I told them I didn't like them. (Young woman, 17, placed with parents)

The importance of matching children sensitively to the existing family structure, and in particular taking account of the age, gender and other characteristics of foster carers' own children, has been discussed in other research into the experiences of looked after children (Sinclair, Wilson and Gibbs 2001). Moreover, our interviews with the young people in this study lend weight to the argument that behaviour should be seen as an indicator of wellbeing, rather than simply as a problem requiring management (Aldgate and Statham 2001). Similarly, it is important to note that while disruptions are likely to entail both a financial cost to the authority and a wellbeing cost to the young people concerned, as well as, quite probably, to the carers and their families, this will not always be the case. In certain particular instances, a disruption may be viewed as a positive and inevitable outcome of an unsatisfactory placement; once again, the views of individual children are important in their own right and need to be specifically ascertained if they are not to be hidden by the weight of the general evidence.

Specialist support

A small number (five) of the young people we interviewed had been placed in specialist residential units after placement breakdowns linked to their behaviour, or had been put in touch with other specialist support services as a way of helping them manage behavioural difficulties. Again, there was generally a positive response to the extra support offered in this way, although the young people interviewed still had concerns about bullying, teachers not liking them or the environment being too strict. Extra support was not necessarily costly. One young woman talked about the problems she had had over several years in making and keeping friends, whether at school or among members of her foster family. In the time between interviews, she had been receiving help from her social worker, and her foster carer, on strategies for managing her mood swings:

> I still like living here and part of that is down to getting help with my moods. I used to be very moody and she [foster carer's own daughter] would get impatient with it, and we'd be stroppy with each other – not now! (Young woman, 15, foster care)

Similarly, a young man who had a long history of broken foster placements had been put in touch with a specialist youth work team for young people 'in crisis'. At the time of the second interview they were supporting him quite intensively, allowing him to sleep in their camper van by the beach until a new placement could be arranged. He said:

> To me they're like my brothers. They help me out in any way they can. Anything a family would do. (Young man, 15, currently unplaced)

One young woman, who had moved to a small residential placement, was keen to recognize the positive impact on her of the high staff/young person ratio. However, she was alarmed at the fact that her placement might end:

> …everybody wants me to move on because I've gone good now. (Young woman, 17, residential placement)

For her then, there was a perverse incentive to misbehave, given that her 'reward' for good behaviour was to be yet another placement change. As with the example discussed earlier, of the young man who felt he had to misbehave at school in order to secure a change of placement, there are indications that the behavioural difficulties of some young people are the product of a complex set of considerations including quality of placement, experience of schooling, an awareness of limited resources and the potential for poor behaviour to be seen as the way to access the latter.

More intensive support with behaviour is often very expensive; indeed, the boy quoted above went on to say that for a time his support from the youth service had been in jeopardy given possible cuts in funding. However, it is important to acknowledge the value placed on this support by young people themselves, who are often extremely perceptive about their need to receive help with behavioural difficulties. The longer-term gains in terms of encouraging pro-social behaviour in young people, and, as we discussed earlier, in keeping their education on track, may well justify the expense of such support.

Participation in decision-making

The participation of children and young people in decisions affecting them is a cornerstone of the Children Act 1989, the UN Convention on the Rights of the Child and the Every Child Matters agenda (Department for Education and Skills 2003). The principle that 'it is important that children have a chance to shape and influence the parenting they receive' is reinforced by the proposal in the current White Paper to require 'every local authority to put in place arrangements for a "Children in Care council", with direct links to the Director of Children's Services and Lead Member' (Department for Education and Skills 2007a, p.7). Participation in decision-making can be seen as of value not only to young people themselves, as both a basic right and a means of encouraging the development of their self-awareness and skills in taking increasing responsibility for themselves; it is also of value to authorities in improving their understanding of the needs of children they look after. However involving young people is also a costly social care activity; it is clearly also important therefore to appreciate the way in which they see their involvement so that the potential benefits can be maximized.

The picture emerging from our interviews is generally positive. Almost all of the young people reported that their views were listened to and that they felt able to participate both in the processes of being looked after, such as reviews, and in key decisions, such as where they lived and went to school. There was also a strong tendency in the interviews for young people to associate an absence of participation with the past. Many typically reported not really knowing why decisions had been made when they were younger, although this may partly be explained by poor recall of events, the improvement of social work practice in the intervening years, or as a reflection of the need for age-appropriate involvement in decision-making repeatedly emphasized as a key element in current policy (Department for Education and Skills 2003). Cleaver (2000), for instance, found that social workers were often more successful in seeking the views of older, as opposed to younger, children.

As other studies have also found (Grimshaw and Sinclair 1997; Skuse and Ward 2003), some young people talked about the process of participation in reviews in ambivalent terms. Typically, for these young people the review process was seen as something of a chore, or as a boring event that had to be endured, rather than as a key part of their involvement in the decision-making process. The following two quotations illustrate the feelings of many (though not all) of the young people interviewed:

> Reviews aren't particularly helpful – sitting in a room full of people you don't know, asking questions and gawping. (Young man, 17, living independently)

> I go to my reviews but find them boring – the same questions over and over again, such as which doctor you have, how school's going. (Young woman, 11, foster care)

However, this did not stop several young people pointing to ways in which the review process could be improved to make it more accessible for them, and to provide an environment where they would be able to make a bigger contribution. A common thread was the inhibiting presence of foster carers at reviews, which made honest and open comments about their happiness in a placement difficult to express. For example, one young woman, now placed with friends after having experienced unhappy foster placements, said:

> I always had this fear of being grounded in previous reviews when my foster carers were there. If I was asked about how I felt about living there, I would lie and say everything was OK, but inside I was crying. (Young woman, 16, placed with friends)

Others pointed to the importance of participation in decision-making being linked to action, with one young person saying that while she felt listened to, very often nothing would come of the discussions that took place at review. She cited in particular an unwillingness of professionals to address seriously the bullying she was experiencing. Another boy talked about the particularly off-putting practice of the chairperson of his reviews, who used a laptop throughout the meeting.

Clearly, then, we must be cautious in taking at face value the ambivalence that many young people feel about the processes designed to ensure their participation in decisions affecting them. Of course, some young people will not want to take too active a role, and for others in settled placements processes such as reviews may appear as events that interrupt them from getting on with their lives. However, we have also heard views about how participation in decision-making could be made more attractive, confirming what others have argued about the importance of friendly meetings, in appropriate settings, for the effective eliciting of children's views (Grimshaw and Sinclair 1997).

As part of current policy, data concerning the numbers of young people participating in their reviews are now collected on an annual basis. However, participation in this context is simply seen as counting the number of young people who were present and able to convey their views at a review meeting (Department for Children, Schools and Families 2007a). As the discussion above demonstrates, such data will not capture the extent to which participants regard themselves as genuinely involved or how far they value the opportunity to contribute. As their comments show, capturing young people's views is a more complex, nuanced process than quantitative data collection of the type required for government returns is likely to offer.

Empowering young people to express their views

The issue is brought into sharper focus when we consider the importance of providing the support and information necessary to make a reality of involvement. A number of young people said that while in theory they had been able to choose a course of action, their decisions had been made more difficult by the absence of information or guidance about how to make those choices. For example, one young man had been able to choose the courses he wanted to follow at his local college, but felt that he would have liked some help in arriving at his decision.

Five young people talked about the support they had received in order both to clarify to themselves their views on what were often very difficult, emotional decisions to take, such as choosing whether or not to return to live with a birth parent, as well as to assert those views. One young man had been placed with relatives, but had faced the prospect of returning to live with his father. He had mixed feelings about the wisdom of this move, eventually preferring to stay in his current placement. He described the process of deciding not to move back in with his birth father and was keen to point out his ownership of that decision. He felt in particular that the counselling support arranged by his social worker was critical in enabling him, over time, to assess the options open to him and to voice them in reviews, even when his birth father was present.

Another young man talked about the support he had received in speaking for himself and making the most of opportunities to participate in decision-making. This had also enabled him to reflect on the large number of failed foster placements he had experienced:

> Maybe if I'd talked to my carers, things would have been different… I felt that communication was the difficulty for me…it was partly because I didn't have the guts to talk to people about things. Now I realize I can talk about my problems. That is partly to do with the support I've had here [current youth service support]. They've helped me a lot to make my voice heard. I'm able to talk about anything and everything now. (Young man, 15, currently unplaced)

In addition, young people who had received support in developing and expressing their views highlighted the importance of the independence of those providing support, and of them not being identified too closely with children's social care themselves, a point also emphatically made by a similar group of young people who had recently left care, interviewed by Skuse and Ward (2003). Their accounts illustrate the importance of, and benefits to be gained from, taking a proactive and imaginative approach to empowering young people to speak out about things that concern them. They illustrate that galvanising young people to develop and express their opinions can involve hard work, and that asking for their views without understanding the difficulties they may face in clarifying them will often promote rather than challenge the ambivalence we, and others, have talked about. This reinforces the guidance accompanying the Children Act 1989 which states that: '...All children need to be given information and appropriate explanations so that they are in a position to develop views and make choices' (Department of Health 1991a, p.12).

Disabled looked after children: Additional barriers

One aim of carrying out in-depth interviews with young people was to explore the experiences of disabled children who are looked after. Chapter 2 explains how disabled children were identified and selected and discusses the decision we took to interview all children in the presence of 'a trusted adult', meaning that those with communication impairments could also be included.

The interviews with disabled young people shed further light on the value of including young people's views in attempting to relate costs to outcomes. They highlighted three sets of issues: first, the (in)visibility of some impairments and the importance of having one's disability status formally recognized as a route into receiving support; second, the need to acknowledge the fact that the range of difficult issues facing all looked after young people are frequently compounded by the additional barriers that disabled young people face, whether in terms of their access to services in the wider community or the availability of suitable, accessible placements and schools; third, the anxieties expressed by disabled young people and their carers about the transition to adulthood, and adult services.

Recognition and recording of impairments and the use of labels

The interviews highlighted the significance of the way in which disability is recognized and labelled. In selecting young people for interview in the original study we had specifically sought to identify a sample in which about 50 per cent were disabled (see above, Chapter 2). Data on disability were collected in all the Children in Need Censuses, and recorded on disability registers held on some (though not all) management information systems as well as on case files. However there was considerable dissonance between the recorded information about a particular young person's impairments and support needs, and what emerged in interviews with the young people themselves. For instance, one young man was described by his foster carer as having learning disabilities, and was in receipt of counselling support from the local child and adolescent mental health team. However, he was not recognized as disabled in the recorded information. Another young woman was included in the study as non-disabled, although a query was raised about her having learning disabilities in both interviews she took part in. Similarly, another young man was identified as non-disabled according to the children's social care management information system, yet his interview revealed that he had complex health care needs and had received a statement of special educational need. Finally, a young man who had been accommodated as an unaccompanied asylum seeker had not been identified to the research team as disabled, yet talked about the anxieties he had about finding employment with severe hand impairments caused by an exploding grenade some years ago, and indeed about his anxieties about losing his hand altogether.

The young people in these examples may well have been receiving appropriate support in relation to their impairments, and we are not arguing that the absence of accurate disability-related information on information systems necessarily means that these issues remain unaddressed. However, the cases discussed above indicate that the information kept by children's services departments about the impairments and support needs of looked after young people may often be inadequate. This is important given the role that diagnoses and disability labels play in allowing young people to access services and support. One young man described how he would like to get a formal diagnosis of his dyspraxia, given the difficulty he and his family had experienced in getting adequate support without the official sanction that such a label would provide. Similarly, one young woman, not identified as disabled in the information system, described a great deal of uncertainty about her status as having, or not having, learning disabilities and emotional or behavioural difficulties, and considered that this had led both to delays in finding the right placement for her and also to numerous failed placements. The extent to which emotional or behavioural difficulties were seen as related to, or indeed included within the definition of, a disability seemed to vary greatly among those who took part in interviews.

The definition of what counts as a disability is clearly subject to varied interpretation. Different formal and informal definitions in operation in different authorities will result in wide variations in the numbers of young people seen as disabled, and affect the accuracy with which information is gathered about their support needs. Chapters 4, 5 and 6 have demonstrated the high costs associated with finding placements, and providing support to, children with physical and learning disabilities and/or emotional or behavioural difficulties. Such findings make it particularly important that authorities share common and explicit definitions and find ways of recording and using information rationally about the needs and characteristics of young people. One of the issues that is currently being explored in the ongoing programme of research and development of the cost calculator model is the extent to which different types of impairment and support needs impact on the costs of children's services (see Chapter 9). Not only is it important to ensure that disability is accurately recorded, but that the information is sufficiently precise to allow for improved planning and distribution of resources.

The new Children in Need Census (2008–9) is likely to introduce a greater degree of consistency, for authorities will be required to record as disabled all children who come under the provisions of the Disability Discrimination Act 2005, and to specify different types of disability according to predetermined categories (Department for Children, Schools and Families 2007b). This will also provide an incentive for software houses to introduce improved facilities for recording disabilities on management information systems, an issue that has previously hampered the collection and retrieval of relevant data.

The compound effect of barriers on disabled looked after young people

Throughout the interviews, disabled young people, and their carers, described the additional barriers that they faced in accessing local facilities such as leisure centres, shops, employment and transport. For instance, one foster carer looking after a young woman with multiple and severe impairments talked about how restricted the young person's life was and how she spent much of the time sitting at a table because it was so hard to do anything else with her. She went on to elaborate on the nature of the difficulties her foster daughter faced, including the delays they had experienced in having adequate adaptations made to the family house and the absence of organizations able to take her daughter on holiday. Another young man had faced hostility from a small number of local residents in his village who had sought to stop the local authority from housing young people with learning disabilities close to their homes. Another family struggled to get their foster son into a local swimming club that had no experience of including disabled children. A young man with severe physical impairments had a weight problem which exacerbated the pressure placed on his legs and which required frequent monitoring. However, the only suitable equipment for weighing him was located in an acute hospital, requiring him to make frequent long journeys simply to be weighed.

These types of practical barriers faced by disabled young people may not surprise the reader. They are the product of a society that is focused largely on the needs of non-impaired children and adults. However, it is important in the context of this study to understand how such barriers can serve to compound the other issues facing looked after young people, many of which we have already discussed in other chapters. A key theme is the unavailability of suitable, nearby and adapted placements. Indeed, we highlighted in Chapter 6 how disabled young people are more likely to experience residential placements, and how those placements are often outside the area of the placing authority.

One young man had been placed at the other end of a large local authority because there was both a shortage of foster carers who felt able to accommodate disabled children, and no foster home nearer to his family that could meet his needs. Even in his current placement, his foster carer pointed to the problems he had faced:

> When he moved here we did get some adaptations done, such as the ramps and the extra stair rail, but we're still hopeful of having a bedroom and bathroom built downstairs for him, at the end of the house which would be more suitable. We can't get a wheelchair upstairs so he just has to make do at the moment, which is very difficult. (Foster carer of young man, 12)

In addition, the extra distance placed between him and the area of the authority where he had been living made keeping contact with family and friends more difficult. The lack of suitable placements had also led to more frequent changes, which had, in turn, led to his missing health appointments because of delays in transferring his health records when he moved. Moreover, the restricted choice of placements open to him meant that he was currently living in a very isolated rural area that was described as not really 'geared up' in terms of disability access. Clearly, in this case the absence of more local placements for disabled young people served to increase the wellbeing costs to the young person in terms of isolation and disrupted health care and the financial costs to the local authority in terms of additional social work time involved in managing changes of placement and supporting a young person in a remote foster home.

Similarly, at the time of the first interview one young disabled woman was attending a residential school several hundred miles from her family. While her parents were keen to point out the support they had received in travelling to the school to visit her, the young woman herself expressed a clear view that she would have preferred to attend a day school close to home. Again, costs were higher to local authority and young person alike. This is consistent with research carried out by Morris, Abbott and Ward (2002) in which they argue that the placement of disabled young people in residential schools may well reflect the needs of other family members more than those of the young people themselves (see also, Morris 1995). It is important, therefore, to reflect on the extent to which the additional costs associated with placing disabled young people in specialist residential accommodation reflect the higher value of the support provided. We have insufficient evidence to give a definitive answer: however, the comments of disabled young people and their carers suggest that while the support offered in these specialist placements may be valuable, it has to be offset against both the financial and the wellbeing costs of being placed at what is often a considerable distance from the family home.

Many of these costs, which spring from the shortage of placements and educational opportunities for disabled young people, have already been identified as significant factors in influencing the success of placements for young people in general, and include the extra difficulty of maintaining contact with birth families, or of attending an appropriate school. A project currently under way within the programme to develop the cost calculator model aims to introduce greater transparency into both the education and social care costs of such placements in order to explore whether resources might be justifiably deployed into developing alternative, local provision (see Chapter 9).

Transition to adult services

A final issue raised by disabled young people, their families, and professionals working with them, was anxiety about the quality of services likely to be available to them as they entered adulthood and adult services. One boy, living in a residential placement, had been allocated a transitions worker. However, there were concerns that the level of support that had been available to him as an adolescent would not be available when he left his current placement on reaching 19 years of age. Between her two interviews another young woman had left her residential school, moved back with her family, and was in the process of being transferred to adult services. She had yet to meet her adult social worker and felt that not only did she have less contact, but that the amount of support, particularly in maintaining social contacts with friends, had diminished since leaving children's services. Her concern about the availability of support as a disabled adult was expressed thus:

> No, I'm not impressed so far; they [the adult social work team] are useless as a bucket of worms. (Young woman, 18, living with parents)

Interviews with disabled young people in care reveal that they face many of the same difficulties as their non-disabled peers, but that these are exacerbated by an inadequate structure of specialist support. The result is an even greater shortage of appropriate, available placements and more restricted choice of schooling. Services to disabled children may provide valuable support, but the costs of that extra support may reflect the lack of alternatives as much as the quality of the placement itself. The problem is compounded by inconsistent labelling of disability and the limited recording facilities on some information systems, both of which may obstruct the strategic planning of services for disabled children and young people in care. Many disabled children and young people have needs which will persist into adulthood: one of the most important issues to be addressed is their transition from children's to adults' services. There is an increasing body of research on transitions to adulthood of non-disabled children from care (see Stein and Munro 2008), and the costs of such transitions are beginning to be explored (Dixon *et al.* 2006). Nevertheless, we need to know and understand more about the costs and outcomes of transitions of disabled children in care from children's to adult services, and how these might be improved.

Conclusion

Understanding the value that young people place on different placements and forms of support is an essential component in thinking about costs and outcomes in this area.

The process of working with young people to develop and express views and choices is one that can be lengthy and intensive. However, we were struck by how positively the young people responded to this support and the sense of empowerment and personal growth it had engendered in them. The young people we interviewed felt, on the whole, listened to, although participation in decision-making, especially in the formal settings of reviews, was often regarded as more of a chore than an opportunity.

The young people interviewed were keen to express the view that improvements can be achieved in their behaviour, in the success of placements and in their educational progress if investment is made in terms of intensive support in these areas. There also needs to be better awareness of how placement success is intricately linked to the factors we have identified, including appropriate physical and emotional distance from birth families, and the reciprocal relationship between placement problems and behaviour problems. They also identified the particular barriers faced by disabled children in care or accommodation. These young people will face the same range of issues as non-disabled children but the absence, for many, of appropriate and accessible placements, and the inaccessibility of the wider environment in which they live, serve to compound these difficulties. This forces us to question whether the higher costs of many placements for disabled young people may reflect the absence of alternatives rather than the presence of positive factors tailored to their needs.

However, while a series of focused interviews undertaken as part of a research study can identify a number of related factors, such as the above, that tell us much about how services for looked after children and young people can be more closely tailored to meet the needs of both the disabled and the non-disabled population in care and accommodation, it is not yet clear how users' views can routinely be brought into the cost calculator model that we are currently developing. It would, of course, be relatively simple to include routine data on, for instance, participation in reviews, among the outcomes variables that can be linked to the cost calculations. Such data are already required as part of a national return (Department for Children, Schools and Families 2007a). However quantitative responses will not tell us, as the interviews have done, that the presence of a young person at his or her review does not constitute participation, and that the opportunity for open and honest engagement in the discussion is what is valued.

More sophisticated methodologies for routinely obtaining users' views are currently being explored (see Chapter 9); however it seems clear that these will always remain relatively blunt tools. The cost calculator model that is currently under development builds on average costs and majority perceptions of outcome. It can show how the likely costs of looking after children with physical or learning disabilities differ from the costs incurred by children with no additional support needs. More focused development work may be able to tell us that these broad brush costs vary according to specific types of impairment and the services they require –

with the result that more refined cost calculations can be included in the model.

The model can also help us to explore relationships between costs and outcome, and this is another area that is currently being developed further. Certain outcomes, such as educational qualifications or improvements in behaviour, have positive connotations, and others, such as criminal behaviour and placement instability are considered negative. However such data can only demonstrate that young people have progressed in a certain direction, they cannot tell us why. Nor can they explain how users themselves rate their experiences or show where their evaluations differ from the normative view and why. A true understanding of users' views is difficult, if not impossible to obtain from questionnaires and surveys, and unlikely to be ascertained through the interpretation of quantitative data; such an understanding requires the time and effort that face-to-face interviews or focus groups demand – a point that needs to be taken into account in developing new technologies. It seems improbable that the cost calculator model can be developed to reflect the complexity of individual perspectives – nor is it likely that this would be a valuable new development. A different method must be sought for ensuring that users' views are included in assessing the outcomes of services and their relationship to costs.

Summary of the key points from Chapter 7

- The distance between placement and friends and family was a significant issue for many young people: close placements were generally perceived to be more successful.

- A link between being looked after and educational experiences was identified: often children did better at school when they became looked after, although frequent breakdowns at school were often associated with frequent placement disruptions.

- Educational support, whether in the form of specialist centres and/or residential units, or from a variety of agencies, was largely viewed positively, while a lack of support resulted in poor outcomes for some children and young people.

- Many children recognized that their poor behaviour was a key factor in failed placements. However, many reported that behavioural difficulties were linked to other placement problems, such as poor quality of care or their unhappiness with the behaviour of, or relationship with, other children they encountered – particularly in residential units. Some deliberately behaved badly in an attempt to change their circumstances.

- Despite being costly, support to help manage behaviour, sometimes within a residential setting, was also generally viewed positively by the young people and thought likely to provide long-term benefits.

- The majority of the children and young people felt listened to and involved in decision-making, but some expressed concern at the review process and felt their views were not acted upon. The provision of support, particularly if independent from children's social care, was remarked upon as empowering the young people to take a full role in decision-making.

- Many of the disabled young people and their carers considered that the barriers and difficulties which they faced were often not only problems in their own right, but also served to compound other issues encountered by all looked after children and young people, for example, finding appropriate placements.

- The inaccuracy and inconsistency of recorded information about disability is likely to have an adverse impact on the strategic planning of services.

- Obtaining users' views of care and accommodation is a complex exercise that produces valuable returns. Quantitative data that can be imported into the cost calculator model cannot take the place of the richly nuanced findings from face-to-face discussions.

Chapter 8

The Cost Calculator
for Children's Services

Introduction

Previous chapters have explored the development of unit costs for social care processes, and considered evidence on the differences between the policy and practices of local authorities, the profiles of their looked after populations and the placements they are offered, which are likely to account for the substantial variations in the costs of service delivery. This chapter describes the model that has been developed to utilize the data which we have so far explored – and which is held largely in the management information systems of the authorities themselves – to calculate the costs of different placements. The Cost Calculator for Children's Services described in this chapter has attracted widespread interest among local authorities and other childcare agencies. It is already implemented in several local authorities and is proving to be a valuable tool in helping to clarify the past, current and probable future costs of different patterns of placement provision and their associated outcomes. It should, however, be noted that the comparisons of estimated costs in different situations which it can produce should inform rather than direct policy decisions.

A demonstration version of the Cost Calculator (Soper 2007) is available from the website www.ccfcs.org.uk for trial use. Detailed information about its various functions as well as system requirements and installation instructions are given in the User Guide, also available from the website. This chapter outlines what the Cost Calculator does and examines some of the reports that it generates to show how it estimates costs.

Users who purchase the implementation version of the Cost Calculator can import their authority's own data into it and customize it in other ways. The free demonstration version of the Cost Calculator has all the functionality of the implementation version in terms of the analyses and reports that can be produced. However, it cannot be customized and it can only use the sample data with which it is supplied.

The Cost Calculator uses data on children and their placements to itemize the services that each child receives in a particular period of time. It combines this information with the unit costs of the different services and the allowances or fees paid for individual placements, which are also stored in the database. It thus separately costs each process that every child receives, and this cost information can be aggregated in various different ways. The User Guide explains the choices that users have about the calculations that are performed, and the reports that they can obtain.

The version of the Cost Calculator implemented at the time of writing (Version 6.5) calculates the social care costs incurred by children who are looked after by the local authority. It was initially constructed to perform the calculations for the study discussed in the earlier chapters of this book, and then later developed as a computer application that could be utilized by local authorities and other child welfare organisations to support their day-to-day activities. The flexibility of the model gives it considerable potential for future development. Further enhancements, to cover a wider range of children and a broader range of services, are now being planned and are discussed in Chapter 9.

Given that the research found that the cost of looking after a child depends on the child's characteristics, the type of placement and also its length, data on these items were selected for inclusion in the model, together with the allowances or fees paid for individual placements and the unit costs of the social care processes described in Chapter 3. The underlying concept of the Cost Calculator is that the cost of a placement can be calculated by taking into account its length, the frequencies of the social care processes that occur within it, the appropriate unit costs and the allowance or fee that is paid. Initially, therefore, the model was developed to calculate costs for whole placements. This allowed it to be used to calculate costs over all the available placement history data.

Modifications were needed, however, to make the model practically useful. Different children have placements that start and end on different dates. For meaningful cost comparisons a standard timeframe is required, which implies that for a placement that began before the start date or that continues after the end date of the calculation period, only that part of the placement cost that falls within the timeframe should be calculated. A facility has been provided to allow users to select start and end dates of their choice so that they can perform cost calculations for whatever time period they wish, for example for a financial year or for an individual month. The first standard timeframe used was the 20 months of the original study period. Calculations were carried out over this time period using the study data to generate the tables and charts shown in Chapters 4 to 6.

The cost calculations in the model are carried out for each individual child in the dataset for every placement that occurs at least partly within the user-specified time period. Costs can then be aggregated for a selected group of children, for a particular placement type, for a specified provider, or for the whole looked after population in an authority. The aggregated results are likely to be more meaningful than those for an individual child, because individual estimates are subject to random variation that the aggregation process averages out. The model is intended to be used for children who have one or more main placements sequentially. It can also be used for children who have both a main and a support placement, such as a residential school and foster care in school holidays and for children who have been adopted but continue to receive post adoption support.

Uses of the cost calculator model

The current version of the Cost Calculator calculates the cost of looking after a child or a particular group of children over a specified period of time, given their placement pathways. This cost is generated both by the allowances or fees paid for individual placements and by the eight social care processes which support the case management of looked after children (see Chapter 3). The cost calculations are directly linked to these processes because the model computes the separate cost of each service provided for every placement and builds these up to form totals. An advantage of this method is that the model can provide a cost breakdown for individual placements and processes. Individual process costs can be aggregated together with the allowance or fee that is paid to show the total cost of each placement during the specified time period; adding these gives the total cost for each child; and summing these totals for a particular group of children gives the total cost of providing them with care and accommodation. Multiplying by an appropriate ratio to express the total cost per 100 children allows the care costs for differently sized groups to be compared, as has been done in Chapter 4. Users can choose the cost calculations that are performed and the reports that are produced through the menu system, the main menu of which is shown in Figure 8.1.

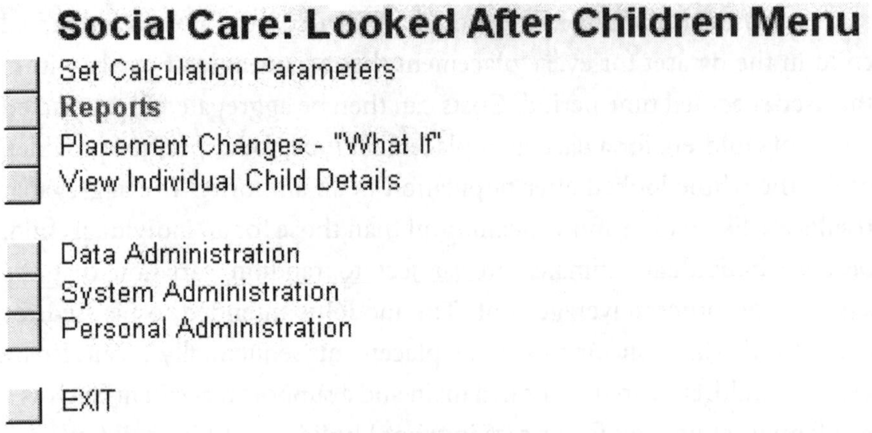

Social Care: Looked After Children Menu

Set Calculation Parameters
Reports
Placement Changes - "What If"
View Individual Child Details

Data Administration
System Administration
Personal Administration

EXIT

Figure 8.1: Main menu for looked after children

The cost calculations are carried out by bringing together data that are stored in child, placement and unit costs tables. This structure makes the model very flexible, because if different data are substituted in any of the tables, new cost calculations can immediately be carried out. The demonstration model includes an example dataset comprising anonymized placement information for 60 children, while users of the implementation version can substitute their own placement data, using the import mechanism provided. Users can switch between the unit cost tables that are available to them. Two sets of (average) unit costs are supplied, for London and out-of-London authorities, and additional customized unit cost tables can be created by users of the implementation version. Authorities using the implementation version can therefore either use the unit cost data produced by the research team or create their own unit costs tables based on specific information concerning activity and salaries (see Chapter 3).

Users are able to carry out cost calculations using each set of unit costs in turn and compare the results. In addition, they are able to make predictions, because the model can estimate the cost of continuing to look after a group of children until a specified future end date. The model is therefore potentially useful to planners, allowing them to estimate the likely continuing costs of placements for their current care population. At present it does this on the assumption that all children stay in their current placement until the end of the analysis period, and the approach can be used, for instance, to estimate the total cost of caring for a looked after population until the end of the current financial year. We anticipate that, if better historical data becomes available, it will eventually be possible to extend and improve on this predictive function, for instance to take account of the likely length of stay by children with different ages or needs.

The Cost Calculator also has an analytic function that allows users to compare costs for groups of children with different needs over different time periods and to gain a better understanding of why certain children (or groups of children) cost so much more than others. One of the strengths of the model is its use of longitudinal rather than snapshot data. This allows users to explore how costs accrue over time and vary when children follow different care pathways. The cost patterns for children with particular characteristics or who achieve specified outcomes can be compared. In addition, children can be selected according to their placement type, and by the name of their placement or its provider. This allows users to investigate the aggregate costs of placing children who have particular needs in specified groups of placements. Users can also explore alternative scenarios, for example, the impact on costs of substituting different placement types for those specified.

Although it is primarily designed to calculate costs, the model is also a tool that can collate the descriptive information that a local authority holds on its looked after population and relate this to cost-related activities. The Cost Calculator offers reports that show many different cross sections of the data, including some that analyse the number of days in each placement or the number of reviews or number of care plans that have occurred. These reports can be obtained for all looked after children, or only for those who have certain characteristics or who have been cared for in particular types of placement. For children who have exited care and returned, a report is available that provides information about the number of days spent in each placement and the number of days for which each child was out of care between placements.

Pilot study of practical issues for the model

The Cost Calculator was developed within the original study simply as a research instrument, but as the results were disseminated, it became evident that the model had potential as an analytical tool that might be used by practitioners and their managers in order to better understand the relationship between costs, quality of services and outcomes for children with a range of different needs. However before it could be made more widely available, further work was necessary to develop it to meet the needs of social care organizations and to identify those issues that would have to be addressed before it could be implemented in a practice setting. A short pilot study was therefore commissioned, testing out and developing a version of the Cost Calculator that could be utilized outside the research setting (see Ward, Holmes and Soper 2005).

The primary aim of the pilot study (2004–5) was to identify those modifications that would need to be made before the Cost Calculator could be viably implemented as a practical tool. A key consideration in selecting an authority to pilot the use of the Cost Calculator was therefore that it should have a sophisticated management information system, where the necessary data items about children's characteristics, placements and outcomes would be stored and kept up to date. We also needed an authority that was sufficiently advanced in its implementation of the Integrated Children's System, as one of the key questions to be asked in the pilot was how far the Cost Calculator could make use of data collected through this new recording system, designed to be used electronically. One of the four authorities selected for the first trial of the Integrated Children's System was therefore approached to participate in the Cost Calculator pilot.

The pilot study found that many of the data items the Cost Calculator required were available in electronic form because they were needed for government returns, and particularly by the SSDA 903 return on children looked after by local authorities (see Department for Children, Schools and Families 2007a). As a result, we decided to make minor changes to the way in which calculations were carried out in the Cost Calculator in order to take advantage of the general availability of these data. Advice from the pilot authority proved very useful in improving particular aspects of the calculation methodology. Certain other information was recognized as difficult to obtain in electronic form, in particular information on whether a child has emotional or behavioural difficulties, as well as data relating to offending and some other outcomes. Although some of these specific data items are likely to become more readily available following new requirements to produce more comprehensive child-level data, including SDQ scores on the national returns (Department for Children, Schools and Families 2007c) and the improved integration of children's services following the Children Act 2004, it was nevertheless evident that we should ensure that the Cost Calculator could perform, albeit in a more restricted way, without certain variables that might be difficult to obtain. The need for a robust but flexible piece of software became apparent and following the pilot study the decision was made to use Visual Basic for Applications programming to carry out the calculations rather than the Excel formulae that had been used hitherto.

The pilot study also demonstrated the usefulness of working with local authorities in developing the software to ensure that it is relevant to their needs and it utilizes the data they have available. Recognition of the value of developing a close working relationship with users has proved invaluable in the subsequent implementation programme.

Data about children and their placement characteristics required for the model

The model uses data on child characteristics, for example the child's date of birth and evidence of emotional or behavioural difficulties. The first of these is one of a number of mandatory variables without which the child cannot be included in the dataset, while the second exemplifies information which, if available, will improve the accuracy of the cost calculations. Information about the start and end dates of each placement, its type and the reason for the new placement episode is required by the model. The research study showed wide variations in the cost of specific placements within each placement type (see Chapter 3). Users can therefore improve their cost estimates by inputting the allowance or fee paid for each placement and indicating whether it is provided by the local authority or by an agency. Figure 8.2 shows the list of variables, and the # sign indicates which of them are mandatory. For the non-mandatory variables, the model substitutes default values for any missing values. Examples of the default values used are that the child does not have emotional or behavioural difficulties; that the fee or allowance is the average for that type of placement; and that the placement is provided by the local authority. In general, the default values are those that are likely to generate lower costs, so using them will tend to produce an underestimate. Use of the default settings therefore gives only rudimentary costings; the more accurate and comprehensive the data imported into the Cost Calculator, the better the cost estimates.

The model's import mechanism has been designed to accept the files which authorities have to submit for the national (SSDA 903) returns, so wherever possible, it uses identical terminology. These files provide key data for the model on placements and some child characteristics. Other data collections with which the model aims to be compatible are the Children in Need Census and the Integrated Children's System Placement Information Record. We also anticipate that, as integration of children's services continues, data collected for returns such as those related to youth justice and education may also become more accessible; these items will be included as we extend the model to cover a larger group of children accessing a broader range of services. The data collected in these various nationally implemented systems are likely to be held electronically in most authorities.

Since almost all the information concerning children's characteristics and placements that the model currently requires are included in the SSDA 903 return, the data are readily available to import into the implementation version using the Import Setup form provided. Further information about variable definitions is provided in the User Guide.

Variable Description
ITEMS INCLUDED IN SSDA 903 NATIONAL RETURNS
Unique identifier for each child #
Area Office
Gender
Date of Birth #
Ethnic origin code
Category of Need
Date episode (placement) commenced* #
Reason for new episode (placement)* #
Legal status* #
SSDA 903 Placement code* #
Date episode (placement) ceased*
Reason episode (placement) ceased*
Number of GCSE passes at A* to G
Number of GCSE passes at A* to C
Main Activity on 19th birthday
Dates of reviews
ITEMS RELATED TO THOSE IN SSDA 903 NATIONAL RETURNS
UASC?
Date when child first became LAC (looked after child)

Figure 8.2: Child and placement variables

continued on next page

Disabilities?
Sat GCSE?
Local Authority or Agency*
In or outside area of Local Authority*
Is the placement in support of an existing placement?
OTHER DATA THAT SHOULD BE INCLUDED
Emotional or behavioural difficulties?
Mental health support?
Is child an offender?
Does child have SEN Statement?
Is child excluded from school?
Surname
First name
Social work team
Placement name*
Placement provider*
Fees or allowances weekly*
Dates care plan updated
Date Youth Offending Team support started
Date Youth Offending Team support finished
Date of transfer to leaving care team
mandatory * separately for each placement

Figure 8.2: Child and placement variables continued

Importing data

The wide diversity of social care management information systems used by local authorities made it necessary to produce a flexible import mechanism, designed to make data transfer as seamless as possible. The Import

Setup form lists all the variables that can be imported into the Cost Calculator and allows the administrator to specify the format in which the data are available in the particular local authority. The import mechanism is designed so that minimal recoding of data is needed, and the data to be imported can be contained in a number of different files. Further details of how data can be imported and the validation checks carried out are given in the User Guide.

Reviewing and editing child data

The Cost Calculator menu includes an option which allows users to view the data held. A drop-down look up box is used to select a particular child, as shown in Figure 8.3, and case-specific information is then displayed. This form can be used by those with Data Administrator rights to edit the child's data. This mechanism provides a method of data entry that may be appropriate when computer based information is not available, or when the analysis is to be carried out for only a small number of children.

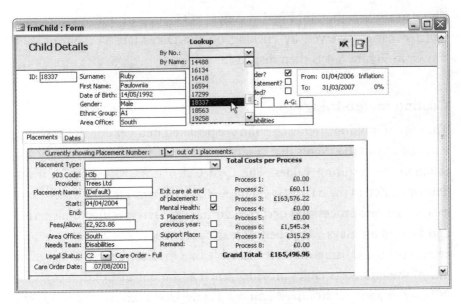

Figure 8.3: Form showing individual child details

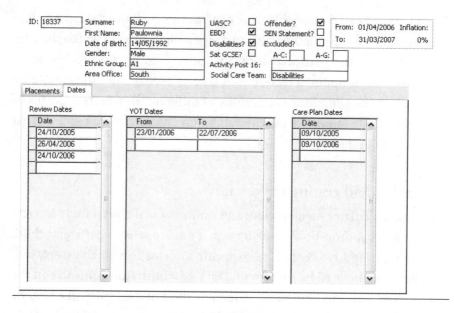

Figure 8.4: Form showing dates for individual child

The dates when the child had reviews, YOT support and his care plan updated can be viewed by clicking on the Dates tab. The information shown in Figure 8.4 is then displayed.

Costing methodology

The cost of looking after each child is calculated in the model by applying unit costs to all the events that comprise the child's placement history and totalling the resulting values. The Cost Calculator analyses the various dates included in the dataset (see Figure 8.2) to determine how many times each social care process has occurred during the user-specified time period and how many days were spent in each placement. The social care processes are costed using the unit cost table that the user selects. This can be one of the unit costs tables provided, such as the out-of-London costs for 2006–7 or a new customized unit costs table. Users can create customized unit cost tables in two different ways: they can copy one of those supplied and edit individual unit cost values in it, or they can use the Unit Costs Database supplied with the Cost Calculator to calculate customized unit costs from first principles by bringing in data on activity times and salaries in their local authority. The weekly fees or allowances used to calculate the cost of each placement are taken from the data read in for the individual placements where they are available; otherwise the average figure for the type of placement in the selected cost table is used as a default.

The Set Calculation Parameters option from the main menu (Figure 8.1) allows users both to choose the cost table to be used and specify the time period for the calculations. The demonstration data used for the cost calculations in this chapter relate to placements up to 31 March 2007, and the computations shown are all carried out for the financial year 2006–7. If the calculation time period were alternatively to be set as 1 April 2007 until 31 March 2008 using the same data, the model would then predict the impending costs of continuing to look after those children who were cared for on 31 March 2007 in their current placements for a further year.

Reports

Once the parameters have been set, the computations described in the following paragraphs are all performed automatically by the computer and any of the eight reports shown in the screenshot of the Reports menu in Figure 8.5 can be accessed to view the results. All the reports present the data in different ways, often with user options about which groups of

Figure 8.5: Reports menu

children or placements are included. Users of the Cost Calculator therefore have easy access to a myriad of different cross-section views of their data and they can also analyse patterns of costs and children's movements between placements over a time period of their choice. Some of the reports are discussed below; detailed descriptions of all of them are provided in the User Guide.

Cost calculation assumptions

The key assumptions made in the calculations are described below, with notes on the circumstances in which the different cost figures in the unit cost tables apply. The details of how the computer picks up the appropriate unit costs for the child and placement being costed, and of how the calculations are carried out are explained in the following section, using an example report. Each unit cost table is comprised of four cost sheets; parts of the sheets that form the out-of-London 2006–7 table are displayed in Figures 8.6 to 8.9. The columns of Figures 8.6 to 8.8 relate to the eight social care processes, and the rows show the various child and placement circumstances that cause the unit costs to differ. The figures on the Basic unit costs sheet shown in Figure 8.6 apply to all placements of the specified type. All values on the other sheets accessed by the tabs are additional unit costs that apply only in certain circumstances. The Conditional costs, Duration related costs and Age related costs are shown in Figures 8.7 to 8.9 respectively. Some conditional costs may apply for just part of a placement, for example, those that are related to the placement's duration or the child's age. The model takes account of this by calculating separate subtotals for some of the cost components, as described below. Placements coded as 'other' or 'unknown' have the same costs in the supplied cost tables as a local authority foster placement within the local authority area.

Processes 1 (Admit), 4 (Exit) and 5 (MoveP): Finding placements and exiting from care

Process 1, deciding to look after the child and finding the first placement, is assumed to take place at the start of each continuous period of care, unless the child is either an unaccompanied asylum seeker or is remanded

Basic Unit Costs | Conditional Costs | Duration Related Costs | Age Related Costs

Process

Description	Provider	Placement Names	1 Admin	2 CPlan	3 Mtn P	4 Exit	5 MoveP	6 Rview	7 Legal	8 16+	Avg Weekly Fees/Allow
Agency Independence out LA	(Default)	(Default)	772.82	119.89	27.04	263.38	462.55	815.61	2765.90	1164.27	438.69
LA Independence in LA	(Default)	(Default)	772.82	119.89	22.92	263.38	462.55	407.81	2765.90	1164.27	438.69
LA Independence out LA	(Default)	(Default)	772.82	119.89	27.04	263.38	462.55	815.61	2765.90	1164.27	438.69
Kinship Care in LA	(Default)	(Default)	639.40	119.89	37.98	263.38	204.53	407.81	2765.90	1164.27	136.86
Kinship Care out LA	(Default)	(Default)	639.40	119.89	42.13	263.38	204.53	407.81	2765.90	1164.27	136.86
Agency Mother & Baby in LA	(Default)	(Default)	772.82	119.89	27.04	263.38	462.55	407.81	2765.90	1164.27	752.04
Agency Mother & Baby out LA	(Default)	(Default)	772.82	119.89	27.04	263.38	462.55	815.61	2765.90	1164.27	752.04
LA Mother & Baby in LA	(Default)	(Default)	772.82	119.89	22.92	263.38	462.55	407.81	2765.90	1164.27	752.04
LA Mother & Baby out LA	(Default)	(Default)	772.82	119.89	27.04	263.38	462.55	815.61	2765.90	1164.27	752.04
Other	(Default)	(Default)	639.40	119.89	22.92	263.38	204.53	407.81	2765.90	1164.27	136.86
Parents in LA	(Default)	(Default)	390.18	119.89	22.92	263.38	79.92	815.61	2765.90	1164.27	0.00
Parents out LA	(Default)	(Default)	390.18	119.89	27.04	263.38	79.92	815.61	2765.90	1164.27	0.00
Post-Adoption Support	(Default)	(Default)	0.00	0.00	0.00	0.00	0.00	0.00	0.00	0.00	127.63
Ag Res + Ed + H in LA	(Default)	(Default)	772.82	119.89	22.92	263.38	462.55	407.81	2765.90	1164.27	2194.07
Ag Res + Ed + H out LA	(Default)	(Default)	964.13	119.89	27.04	263.38	653.87	815.61	2765.90	1164.27	2194.07
LA Res + Ed + H in LA	(Default)	(Default)	772.82	119.89	22.92	263.38	462.55	407.81	2765.90	1164.27	3013.22
LA Res + Ed + H out LA	(Default)	(Default)	964.13	119.89	27.04	263.38	653.87	815.61	2765.90	1164.27	3013.22
Agency Residential in LA	(Default)	(Default)	772.82	119.89	22.92	263.38	462.55	407.81	2765.90	1164.27	2104.70
Agency Residential out LA	(Default)	(Default)	964.13	119.89	27.04	263.38	653.87	407.81	2765.90	1164.27	2104.70
LA Residential in LA	(Default)	(Default)	772.82	119.89	22.92	263.38	462.55	407.81	2765.90	1164.27	3022.86

Values for the placement of the type *Agency Residential in LA* are in this row (see example below)

Figure 8.6: Average out-of-London basic unit costs (part of sheet, indicating values used in example report)

ID: 2 Description: Out of London 2006-7

Basic Unit Costs | Conditional Costs | Duration Related Costs | Age Related Costs

Process

Description	1 Admit	2 CPlan	3 Mtn P	4 Exit	5 MoveP	6 R view	7 Legal	8 16+
Care order	0.00	0.00	6.29	0.00	0.00	0.00	0.00	0.00
Remand, child on	0.00	0.00	0.00	0.00	0.00	0.00	0.00	0.00
UASC, unaccompanied asy	0.00	107.61	6.68	0.00	71.75	173.38	0.00	0.00
CWD, child with disabilities	161.11	-59.78	0.00	0.00	161.11	138.45	0.00	0.00
EBD, emotional and behvio	0.00	0.00	0.00	0.00	0.00	0.00	0.00	0.00
Mental health support	0.00	0.00	0.00	0.00	0.00	163.63	0.00	0.00
FCD, difficult to place in fos	430.46	0.00	0.00	0.00	430.46	0.00	0.00	0.00
RUD, difficult to place in re	573.95	0.00	0.00	0.00	573.95	0.00	0.00	0.00
ADD, difficult to place for A	0.00	0.00	0.00	0.00	24478.96	0.00	0.00	0.00
Age 16+	0.00	0.00	0.00	0.00	0.00	10.18	0.00	0.00
Started leaving care	0.00	0.00	0.00	0.00	0.00	125.53	0.00	0.00

Figure 8.7: Average out-of-London unit costs, conditional on child characteristics

ID: 2 Description: Out of London 2006-7

Basic Unit Costs | Conditional Costs | Duration Related Costs | Age Related Costs

Process

Description	1 Admit	2 CPlan	3 Mtn P	4 Exit	5 MoveP	6 Rview	7 Legal	8 16+
First 91 days	0.00	0.00	4.31	0.00	0.00	0.00	0.00	0.00
After 365 days in la	0.00	0.00	-0.80	0.00	0.00	0.00	0.00	0.00
After 365 days out la	0.00	0.00	-2.96	0.00	0.00	0.00	0.00	0.00
After 365 days, la fc, kinship	0.00	0.00	-12.64	0.00	0.00	0.00	0.00	0.00
Offending, YOT support	0.00	23.92	6.68	0.00	0.00	125.56	0.00	0.00

Figure 8.8: Average out-of-London unit costs, conditional on placement duration

la = local authority

fc = foster care

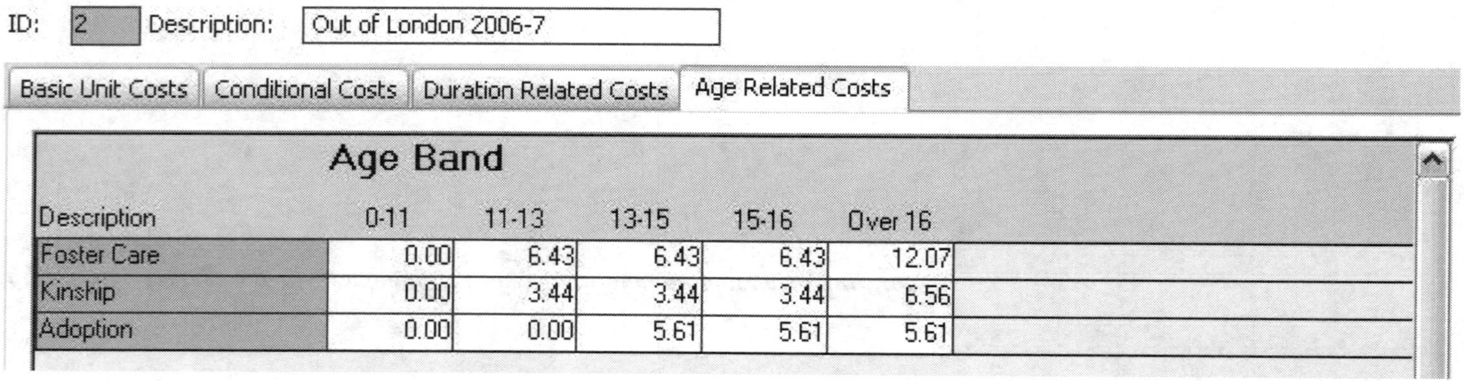

ID: 2 Description: Out of London 2006-7

Basic Unit Costs | Conditional Costs | Duration Related Costs | Age Related Costs

Age Band

Description	0-11	11-13	13-15	15-16	Over 16
Foster Care	0.00	6.43	6.43	6.43	12.07
Kinship	0.00	3.44	3.44	3.44	6.56
Adoption	0.00	0.00	5.61	5.61	5.61

Figure 8.9: Average out-of-London unit costs, conditional on child's age

into care. In these situations the authority does not have to decide to look after the child and Process 5, finding a placement without the decision to look after the child, is assumed to take place instead. Process 1 and Process 5 are mutually exclusive, with Process 5 being costed on the start date of all placements except those for which Process 1 occurs. If the child ceases to be looked after during the time period for which the model is being used, Process 4, exit care, is costed on the end date of the child's last placement. If a child leaves care and later returns, Process 1 is applied again at the start of the new care episode. Two of the variables collected for the SSDA 903 return are used to identify the start and end of care periods. The first shows whether the reason for a new placement, or episode, was that the child started to be looked after, and the second identifies whether the child left care at the end of a placement or moved to a new one.

As the first and fifth data columns of Figure 8.6 show, the basic unit costs of Processes 1 (Admit) and 5 (MoveP) may vary between types of placement. Additional costs that are incurred in particular circumstances are set out on the sheet shown in Figure 8.7. Costs for those processes that occur if the child is disabled are listed in the first and fifth columns of the CWD, child with disabilities row. Extra costs are also generated if a residential, foster or adoptive placement is used for a child who is difficult to place. These conditional costs are shown in the rows entitled RUD, difficult to place in res unit; FCD, difficult to place in foster care; and ADD, difficult to place for adoption. Practitioners consulted in the original study informed us that children are most likely to be considered difficult to place if they have emotional or behavioural difficulties and in addition either have disabilities or have had at least three placements in the previous year. As explained above, Process 5 is substituted for Process 1 in the case of unaccompanied asylum-seeking children. The additional cost incurred in placing these children is shown at the intersection of column 5 MoveP with the UASC, unaccompanied asylum-seeking child row in Figure 8.7.

Process 2 (CPlan): Care planning

The model requires care plan dates to be imported so that it can compute the number of times that the care planning process occurs during the time interval selected by the user. The authorities using the Cost Calculator do not all have sufficient information about these on their management information systems, but they do have the dates of reviews, since these are now required for the SSDA 903 data collection. The practitioners who contributed to the development of the unit costs advised us that care planning should take place after each review and therefore if the care plan dates are not available, the review dates can be imported as proxies. The figures in the second data column of Figure 8.6 (2 CPlan) show that the basic unit cost of care planning does not change with the type of placement. Additional costs shown in Figure 8.7 are incurred, however, if the child is an unaccompanied asylum seeker (UASC, unaccompanied asylum-seeking child row) while there is a reduction (CWD, child with disabilities row) if the child has disabilities (see Chapter 3). The Offending, YOT support row of Figure 8.8 shows that during the time period when an offender is receiving support from the youth offending team (YOT), there is a further additional cost in making care plans.

Process 3 (MtnP): Maintaining the placement

Process 3, maintaining the placement, continues while the child is being looked after. It is therefore costed on a daily basis. There are two facets to the basic costs, namely social care services and the placement fee or allowance paid to carers. Figure 8.6 lists the daily social care costs in column three. The fee or allowance figures used in computations are usually the values for individual placements, imported as part of the child and placement data. Since weekly fee figures are more readily available it is these that are imported and the Cost Calculator divides them by seven to get values on a daily basis. The column at the far right of Figure 8.6 contains average weekly fee or allowance figures for each placement type, but these are used in computations only if the individual placement value is not available. Both the basic unit cost elements vary considerably for different placement types.

As shown in the appropriate rows of Figure 8.7, extra daily unit costs of providing social care support apply if the child is an unaccompanied asylum seeker or has a care order. These extra costs are added to the two basic cost elements and the result is used to obtain a subtotal of Process 3 costs.

Separate subtotals are used for duration and age related Process 3 costs, as well as YOT support to offenders, since these may apply for just part of the placement. Duration related costs reflect additional activity in the first three months of each placement and a decrease in activity after a placement has lasted for twelve months. The initial increase is shown in the First 91 days row of Figure 8.8. The size of the later reduction depends on whether the placement is or is not in the local authority area and is shown in rows After 365 days in la and After 365 days out la respectively. There is a further reduction in costs for placements of at least a year's duration if they are with relatives or local authority foster carers (row After 365 days, la fc, kinship), reflecting a decrease in social work activity once the placement is well established.

Some authorities have difficulty in accessing the individual allowances paid for placements with foster carers, relatives or carers receiving post-adoption support and prefer to use the standard rates of remuneration in costing such placements. These rates usually rise with the child's age and therefore the Cost Calculator incorporates additional unit costs for different age groups in these three types of placement. The amounts of these Age related costs are shown in Figure 8.9.

Process 6 (Rview): Reviews

Reviews, which comprise Process 6, are costed on the dates on which they are completed. A list of such dates for each child forms a separate dataset that is imported into the Cost Calculator. Figure 8.6 shows that basic review costs are typically higher when the child is placed with parents or in a placement located outside the local authority area. Supplementary review costs (set out in Figures 8.7 and 8.8) are incurred for unaccompanied asylum seekers, children with disabilities and children who receive mental health support. For children who transfer to the leaving care team at about the age of 16 there is an additional one-off review cost that is added to the cost of the first review after the date when they transfer, and smaller additional costs at subsequent reviews. These are calculated as separate subtotals since they occur only at or after a particular point in time. Extra costs are also incurred for offenders if a review takes place during the period when the child is receiving YOT support.

Process 7: Legal

The legal process costed in Process 7 is the cost of obtaining a care order. If this is obtained, it is assumed to run until the child's 18th birthday, although the model could be adapted to reflect those that are rescinded earlier. The cost of the care order is therefore spread equally over the days from when the order is obtained until the child reaches the age of 18.

Process 8 (16+): Transition to leaving care services

If applicable, transition to leaving care services (Process 8) is costed on the date when the child transfers to the leaving care team. The child's 16th birthday can be used as a proxy for this. In most of the research authorities the files for unaccompanied asylum-seeking children and children with disabilities were not passed to a leaving care team; therefore the model offers users a choice as to whether Process 8 is costed for them.

Cost calculations – an example

The model calculates costs for each of a child's placements by identifying events and time periods along the care pathway and applying appropriate unit costs. An example of the detailed computations carried out for each placement is set out in the Individual Child ID and Placement Number report displayed in Figure 8.10. For every placement the model generates a total cost for each of the eight social care processes, as shown in the last column of the cost calculation section of the table. Using periods of time as a basis for cost calculations provides a flexible methodology that can be carried forwards as the model is adapted to include processes specific to education, health or juvenile justice as well as social care (see below). This section explains the calculations, using an example in our illustrative dataset. The following sections describe how the computer provides similar cost figures for every child, allowing users to analyse sequences of

	Cost Calculation for Child:	ID:	18337	Placement:	1
	calculation period:	from:	01/04/2006	to:	31/03/2007
	Weeks in placement before calculation period		103.9		
	Placement continues after calculation period				

Placement is	Residential	Agency	In LA Area		
Child is/ has	Ruby	Paulownia	Male	Age at start of:	Years
	A: White			selected	
				placement	11
	12: Disab+EBD+Offender			calculation	
	C2 Care Order - Full Care Order Date		07/08/2001	period	13
	Weeks from care order to age 18	457.4			

Process No	Process	Unit Cost	No of Times/ Days Incurred	Subtotal Cost	Process Cost
1	**Decide to Look After & Place**	£1,346.77	0	-	-
	of which: Basic	£772.82			
	Conditional extra	£573.95			
2	**Care Planning**	£60.11	1	£60.11	**£60.11**
	of which: Basic	£119.89			
	Conditional extra	(£59.78)			
	plus if YOT	£23.92	0	-	
3	**Maintain Placement (daily)**	£446.90	365	£163,120.06	**£163,576.22**
	Social work services	£22.92			
	Fees & Allowances per Day	£417.69			
	Conditional extra	£6.29			
	plus if YOT	£6.68	112	£748.16	
	11 - 12 Cost	-	0	-	
	13 - 14 Cost	-	365	-	
	15 - 15 Cost	-	0	-	
	16 - upwards Cost	-	0	-	
	plus during first 91 days	£4.31	0	-	
	less if over 1 year in LA	(£0.80)	365	(£292.00)	
	less if over 1 year out LA	(£2.96)	0	-	
	less if over 1 year (LAFC/kin)	(£12.64)	0	-	
4	**Exit Care (Return Home)**	£263.38	0	-	-
	of which: Basic	£263.38			
	Conditional extra	-			
5	**Find Later Placement**	£1,036.50	0	-	-
	of which: Basic	£462.55			
	Conditional extra	£573.95			
6	**Review**	£709.89	2	£1,419.78	**£1,545.34**
	of which: Basic	£407.81			
	Conditional extra	£302.08			
	plus if age group 16 or over	£10.18	0	-	
	plus if first for leaving care	£125.53	0	-	
	plus if YOT	£125.56	1	£125.56	
7	**Legal**	£2,765.90	0.114	£315.29	**£315.29**
	of which: Basic	£2,765.90			
	Conditional extra	-			
8	**Transition to Leaving Care**	£1,164.27	0	-	-
	of which: Basic	£1,164.27			
	Conditional extra	-			
				Total cost:	**£165,496.96**

Report printed on: 19/12/2007 Data imported on: 31/03/2007

Figure 8.10: Cost calculations[a]

a Figures in this table are rounded to the number of decimal places displayed. Calculations may therefore not reproduce exactly.

placements and their costs for different groups of children, and how users may utilize the different kinds of summary reports that are available to aggregate the costs in different ways for specified groups of children or placements.

The top section of the report shown in Figure 8.10 gives some summary information about the child and placement to which it relates; the lower section shows the detailed workings of the cost calculations for that placement over the specified time period. This report, then, relates to the child with ID number 18337 who is a boy of white ethnic origin called Paulownia Ruby (although children's names were not accessed in the research programme, and those in this illustrative dataset are fictitious, some authorities asked us to include the potential to import genuine names when they implemented the Cost Calculator). This is the same child whose details and dates are shown in Figures 8.3 and 8.4. The calculation time period that the user has selected (shown in the second row of Figure 8.10) is from 1 April 2006 until 31 March 2007. The report is for the child's first (and only) placement during that time period. He had been in the placement for almost two years before 1 April 2006 and he was still there on 31 March 2007. Paulownia was aged eleven when he started the placement and aged 13 on the date from which the cost calculations begin (1 April 2006). He has complex needs: disabilities together with emotional or behavioural difficulties and offending behaviour. He is looked after under a full care order which was obtained on 7 August 2001 and there are therefore 457.4 weeks from that date until his 18th birthday on 14 May 2010. Costs are for an out-of-London authority in 2006–7.

The details of the calculations are set out in the lower section of Figure 8.10. The eight social care processes are listed in the first two columns. The third column itemizes the unit costs with the basic and conditional extra unit costs for each process being shown in separate rows. For Process 3 there are two rows displaying the two basic unit costs elements: social care support and the fee or allowance paid for the placement. For each process the basic and conditional extra unit costs are totalled upwards so that they are shown alongside the process descriptions in the table. Multiplying these unit cost figures by the numbers of times or days that the processes occur gives cost subtotals for each process. These subtotals are also the total process costs except for Processes 2 (care planning), 3 (maintaining the placement) and 6 (review); separate subtotals are needed for these three processes because further conditional costs may apply for just part of the placement's duration. Adding the subtotals for each process gives the process cost and the sum of the process costs is the total cost of the placement in the calculation time period.

Values in the unit cost column

Since Paulownia is in a residential placement provided by an agency and located within the local authority area, figures from the Agency Residential in LA row indicated in Figure 8.6 have been picked up by the model and placed in the basic cost rows of the unit cost column in Figure 8.10. The values are – Process 1: £772.82; Process 2: £119.89; Process 3 (social work services): £22.92; Process 4: £263.38, and so on. The second basic cost element for Process 3, Fees and Allowances per Day (£417.69) has been obtained by dividing by seven the actual weekly fee (£2923.86) that has been read in. The default value for the average weekly fee or allowance (£2104.70) shown as the last figure in the unit costs row in Figure 8.6 is therefore not used in this calculation.

The costs shown in the Conditional extra rows of Figure 8.10 are those that are applicable to the particular child and placement. In this example, Paulownia has a care order; he is an offender, so he may have support from the youth offending team, but he is not on remand; he has both disabilities and emotional or behavioural difficulties and he has mental health support. His combination of complex needs imply that he is difficult to place. These child details determine which rows of Figure 8.7 are summed to obtain the conditional extra costs displayed in Figure 8.10. For each of the eight processes, the computer records the basic and conditional unit costs with their total in the line above, regardless of whether or not that process occurs for the particular placement being analysed.

For Processes 2, 3 and 6 further conditional costs may apply for part of the duration of the placement. The costs that would be relevant for the child and placement are picked up from Figures 8.8 and 8.9 and shown in the appropriate rows of the unit cost column of Figure 8.10. For example, during the time in which YOT support is provided to an offender there are additional unit costs of £23.92 for Process 2 (care planning), £6.68 per day for Process 3 (maintaining the placement) and £125.56 for Process 6 (review).[1] The additional costs that are related to the child's age are used only if the placement is in foster or kinship care or receiving post adoption support and if the individual placement allowances are not read in. These costs are therefore shown as blanks for the example placement since it is a residential one.

Values in the number of times/days incurred column

The number of days for which Process 3 is ongoing and the number of times that each of the other processes occurs during the calculation time period are calculated by the computer and set out as frequencies in the column of Figure 8.10 headed No of Times/Days Incurred. In this example, Paulownia was already in the placement before the start of the calculation period and he continued in the placement after the end of the timeframe. None of Processes 1, 4 and 5 therefore occurred during the time period to which the calculation relates. This implies that during the year under consideration he spent 365 days in the placement, as is shown for Process 3. The computer determines the number of times that Processes 2 and 6 occurred by examining the dates when the child's care plan was updated and when he had a review and checking which of these dates fall within the calculation timeframe. The computer identifies whether a transition to the leaving care team, Process 8, has occurred using the date of such a transfer or the date of the child's 16th birthday, together with the information provided by the user on whether this process takes place for children with disabilities or who are unaccompanied asylum seekers.

For the conditional costs that may apply for just part of the placement the computer uses the appropriate dates to compute the frequencies shown in the No of Times/Days Incurred column. For example, the start and end dates of YOT support are compared with the dates when the child's care plan was updated or a review occurred. Hence the example calculation shows that Paulownia was receiving YOT support at the time of just one of his two reviews, and he was not receiving it on the date when his care plan was updated. The number of placement days that are within 91 days of the start of the placement and the number that are more than 365 days from its start are each calculated by the computer by comparing the placement start date with the start and end dates of the calculation period. In this example Paulownia had been in this placement for more than a year for all 365 days of the calculation period.

The frequency for Process 7 is determined differently from all the other values in the column. The frequency figure for a care order represents the proportion of its cost that is allocated to this calculation. The computer calculates this fraction as the 'number of days in this placement during the calculation time period' divided by the 'number of days between the care order being obtained and the child's eighteenth birthday'. In the example, this is: $365/(457.4 \times 7) = 0.114$.

Cost calculations

The cost calculation set out in Figure 8.10 shows that for Process 1 (decision to look after and finding first placement) the basic unit cost would be £772.82 while the conditional cost for a child with disabilities and who is hard to place would be £573.95. These are totalled in the top row, giving the Process 1 unit cost of £1346.77. Given that the child was already in this placement before the start of the calculation period, the computer determines that Process 1 does not occur and so the value 0 is shown as the number of occurrences. The unit cost is then multiplied by the number of occurrences, giving a nil cost for this process during the calculation time period. Similarly, since the placement neither commenced nor ended during the calculation period Processes 5 and 4 did not occur and nor did Process 8, since he did not attain the age of 16 years. The frequency in the No of Times/Days Incurred column of Figure 8.10 is 0 for each of these processes and each of them has a nil total cost.

The top row of Care Planning in Figure 8.10 shows that, apart from a possible additional cost for YOT support, the total unit cost of Process 2 in this placement is £60.11, the sum of the figures £119.89 and -£59.78. The number of times that care planning occurs, shown as 1, has been found by the computer examining the dates when child's care plan was updated (see Figure 8.4) and determining that only 9 October 2006 falls within the calculation timeframe. Multiplying the number of occurrences, 1, by the unit cost gives a subtotal of £60.11 for the cost of care planning. Since Paulownia received YOT support only from 23 January 2006 until 22 July 2006 (see Figure 8.4) he was not receiving it when his care plan was updated and the frequency for it is therefore shown as 0, giving a YOT care planning subtotal of £0. The total cost for Process 2, obtained by adding the two subtotals, is therefore £60.11.

Figure 8.10 lists a plethora of unit cost figures for Process 3 (maintaining the placement). The computer has to calculate separately many of the cost elements for this process because the category determining a conditional cost may be applicable for only part of the time the child spends in the placement. The different values in the No of Times/Days Incurred column are the relevant number of days for each sub-process. Using the child's date of birth, the start and end dates of the placement and the calculation timeframe, the computer has determined that Paulownia spent the complete year of the calculation period in this placement; for all of that time he was in the age 13 to 14 age group; and also for all of that time span he had been in the placement for more than one year. The time interval when Paulownia received YOT support (23 January 2006 to 22 July 2006) overlaps with the calculation timeframe of 1 April 2006 to 31 March 2007 and the computer has determined that the number of days between 1 April 2006 and 22 July 2006 is 112. The YOT cost subtotal is therefore shown as £748.16. The only pertinent item relating to placement duration is the cost reduction for placements within the local authority area when they have lasted for more than a year. The reduction of £0.80 per day applies for the whole 365 days calculation period, giving a subtotal of -£292.00. Summing all the subtotals for the process gives the total cost of maintaining the placement during the calculation timeframe of £163,576.22.

Given that the placement is within the local authority area, the basic unit cost of a review (Process 6) is £407.81 and there is an additional conditional cost of £302.08 because the child has both disabilities and mental health support. These values apply throughout the placement and are totalled to show a unit cost of £709.89 in the Review row of Figure 8.10.

The computer identifies the number of reviews (two) from the two review dates, 26 April 2006 and 24 October 2006, that lie within the calculation timeframe. Multiplying this frequency by the unit cost gives a subtotal of £1419.78. The calculations use subtotals because YOT costs and extra costs after age 16 might apply. In this case there is one review date (26 April 2006) that lies within the period for which the boy had YOT support (23 January 2006 to 22 July 2006) and so a frequency of 1 is shown in the plus if YOT row. Since the unit cost for this is £125.56, a subtotal of £125.56 is formed. Adding all the review subtotals gives the total cost of Process 6 as £1545.34.

The basic unit cost of obtaining a care order (Process 7) is £2765.90 to the local authority. An additional cost of £5370 to the courts could be added to this, but has not been included in our calculations. No conditional unit costs have yet been identified for this process. The sum of £2765.90 is a relatively large unit cost and relates to the whole period for which a child is continuously looked after rather than to the particular placement in which the care order was obtained. This cost is therefore apportioned from the date of the care order until the boy's 18th birthday. The calculation of the fraction 0.114 as the frequency value for this year is explained above. Implicitly, the other part of the care order cost will be allocated to other time periods both before and after the current calculation timeframe. The total cost of Process 7 is the product of £2765.90 and 0.114, namely £315.29.

Now that all the separate process costs are calculated the computer adds them together to find the total cost of the placement during the year 1 April 2006 to 31 March 2007 which is £165,496.96.

Displaying cost and placement patterns for selected individual children

The cost calculations that have just been described are carried out by the computer for each placement of every child in the dataset. Key totals from these calculations can be viewed in a Separate Placements report. An example of such a report is shown in Figure 8.11. The table in the lower part of the screen shot displays the key variable that the user has selected (in this case total costs) for all children in the dataset who meet the criteria which the user has set in the filters above the table. Note that the filters allow the user to select children by variables such as needs, time looked after, placement types and so on. This includes the possibility of selecting all the placements that have a particular name or are with a particular named provider, which allows analysis of the cost and duration of the selected named placements.

A number of outcomes variables can also be used as filters in this report. This means that users can select all children who have a particular outcome (for example, they have sat a GCSE) and compare their placement costs over the calculation time period. The pilot authority held very little outcome data on its management information system, and we know from other sources that these items are not always available at child-level (see Gatehouse and Ward 2003). The new requirements to include outcomes data in the SSDA 903 return is likely to result in greater accessibility of these data items; we intend to improve and extend this function in line with these developments.

Separate Placements – total costs report

In Figure 8.11 the table shows the total costs in the year 2006–7 only for the ten children in the dataset who have both emotional or behavioural difficulties and disabilities, as these are the filters that have been set to Yes. The values in each row of the table are the total costs of looking after the child with the ID number shown, during the year 2006–7, separately for each placement in which they were incurred. Each child's placements during the calculation timeframe are numbered sequentially and determine the size of the table that is produced; the placement numbers form column headings with the last data column always corresponding to the highest placement number of any child in the table. The first and last cost figures for each child may relate to only part of a placement, the remainder of it having occurred outside the calculation period. The last column in the table shows the total of the values in each row and therefore gives the estimated total cost of looking after each of the ten children between 1 April 2006 and 31 March 2007. Note that one child who meets the selection criteria and therefore appears in the table is Paulownia Ruby (ID number 18337) whose detailed cost calculations were examined in the previous section.

The children whose costs are shown in Figure 8.11 all have the same combination of complex needs, yet the total costs incurred in looking after them during the year 2006–7 range from £34,535 to £235,251. The Cost Calculator offers various ways of investigating the reasons for the differences, for example by using the View Individual Child Details option and by accessing the Individual Child ID and Placement Number reports for the separate placements, as described above for Paulownia Ruby.

Summary of Total Costs
From 01/04/2006 to 31/03/2007 Out of London 2006-7

Gender	(All)	
Ethnicity Group	(All)	
Time Looked After	(All)	
Age at start of Calc period	(All)	
EBD?	Yes	
Disabilities?	Yes	
Offender?	(All)	
UASC?	(All)	
Area Office	(All)	
Socal Care Team	(All)	
Placement Type	(All)	
Placement Name (Actual)	(All)	
Provider Type	(All)	
Provider Name (Actual)	(All)	
Local Authority Area?	(All)	
Support Placement?	(All)	
Three plus Placements in Yr?	(All)	
Excluded from School?	(All)	
SEN Statement?	(All)	
Sat GCSE?	(All)	
GCSEs A to G	(All)	
GCSEs A to C	(All)	
Activity Post 16	(All)	

Click on one or more arrows to the left and select the categories to be shown in the table

10 Children in the table

Total Costs	PINo				
Child	1	2	3	4	Grand Total
01200	£124,463				£124,463
01225	£5,493	£42,800	£3,285		£51,578
01280	£34,535				£34,535
01700	£112,050				£112,050
18337	£165,497				£165,497
18563	£43,208	£123,702			£166,910
19258	£54,241	£4,721	£8,247		£67,209
21286	£12,457	£141,500	£30,969		£184,926
21486	£1,639	£233,612			£235,251
26378	£1,600	£83,633	£44,308	£88,637	£218,179

Figure 8.11: Separate Placements report for children with disabilities and emotional or behavioural difficulties – total costs

Separate Placements – placement days report

One reason for the cost variations may be that the children were not all looked after throughout the year. Information about this can be obtained by running another Separate Placements report and this time requesting that it shows placement days rather than total costs. The results are shown in Figure 8.12. The table is laid out in the same way as the one in Figure 8.11, but the values in the cells are now the number of days that each of the children spent in their separate placements, and the last column displays the number of days for which each child was looked after during the calculation timeframe. This shows there were two of the ten children who were not looked after for the entire year, and one of them is the one for whom the total costs were lowest, child 01280.

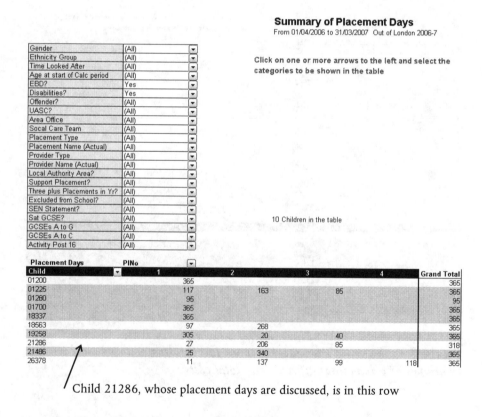

Summary of Placement Days
From 01/04/2006 to 31/03/2007 Out of London 2006-7

Gender	(All)
Ethnicity Group	(All)
Time Looked After	(All)
Age at start of Calc period	(All)
EBD?	Yes
Disabilities?	Yes
Offender?	(All)
UASC?	(All)
Area Office	(All)
Socal Care Team	(All)
Placement Type	(All)
Placement Name (Actual)	(All)
Provider Type	(All)
Provider Name (Actual)	(All)
Local Authority Area?	(All)
Support Placement?	(All)
Three plus Placements in Yr?	(All)
Excluded from School?	(All)
SEN Statement?	(All)
Sat GCSE?	(All)
GCSEs A to G	(All)
GCSEs A to C	(All)
Activity Post 16	(All)

Click on one or more arrows to the left and select the categories to be shown in the table

10 Children in the table

Placement Days	PINo				
Child	1	2	3	4	Grand Total
01200	365				365
01225	117	163	85		365
01280	95				95
01700	365				365
18337	365				365
18563	97	268			365
19258	305	20	40		365
21286	27	206	85		318
21486	25	340			365
26378	11	137	99	118	365

Child 21286, whose placement days are discussed, is in this row

Figure 8.12: Separate Placements report for children with disabilities and emotional or behavioural difficulties – placement days

The availability of reports on the values of different variables is useful for comparison purposes. For example, using the two tables shown in Figures 8.11 and 8.12 users can create another Excel table of cost per day for each placement of every child. In fact the Separate Placements report can be produced showing the values of other variables too. As well as total costs and placement days (shown in Figures 8.11 and 8.12) the report can show the costs for any of the eight social care processes, or the number of reviews, or the number of times the care plan was updated. There is also an option at the report specification stage to create it not for all children in the dataset (as was done for the reports shown) but for those children that have the ten highest values of the variable being analysed. This facility helps users to pinpoint the children with the highest costs so that they can then identify the reasons for them.

Children Who Have Exited Care and Returned Report

The report shown in Figure 8.12 allows users to see which children were not looked after throughout the calculation timeframe but it does not reveal whether or not their placements were continuous. The pilot authority was concerned about children who had required readmission soon after they had left care and they suggested it would be useful to have a report that identified them. A report on all children in the dataset who have exited care and been readmitted during the calculation period has been developed to provide this information (see Figure 8.13). The Out of Care columns show the number of days out of care that preceded each placement within the calculation timeframe. Child 21286 appears in both the reports shown in Figures 8.12 and 8.13. The days he spent in each of his three placements are shown in both, but in Figure 8.13 it is also possible to see that he spent 28 days out of care between his first and second placements, and that he moved directly from his second placement to his third. Using View Individual Child Details to discover more about this young man reveals that his first placement was to a residential unit while after his 28 days out of care he was placed in secure accommodation, probably because he had absconded in the interim.

Data Admin Children Who Have Exited Care and Returned.xls

Children Who Have Exited Care and Returned
From 01/04/2006 to 31/03/2007   Out of London 2006-7
Showing Number of Days in each Placement Preceded by Days Out of Care

TotalDay (All)

PINo   Data

	1		2		3		4		5		6		Total Out Of Care	Total In Care
Child	Out Of Care	In Care	Out Of Care	In Care	Out Of Care	In Care	Out Of Care	In Care	Out Of Care	In Care	Out Of Care	In Care		
01640	0	16	27	45	118	24							145	85
16594	0	41	39	118	0	19	87	11	0	34	0	16	126	239
17299	0	30	65	270									65	300
21286	0	27	28	206	0	85							28	318
21294	0	39	0	27	27	100	0	51	0	82	0	39	27	338

Report printed on: 08/0?/2008 Data imported on: 31/03/2007

Summary -

Days in and out of placements for child 21286 are in this row

Figure 8.13: Children Who Have Exited Care and Returned report

Summarizing costs for different groups of children

Costs by Needs Group report

Once the individual costs for each placement of every child have been computed, the data can be aggregated in various ways. Given that the original research study identified children's needs as a factor that impacts on the cost of service provision (see Chapters 5 and 6) a Costs by Needs Group report was designed to analyse the costs incurred over the calculation time period for groups of children with different needs. The cost-related needs factors identified by the research are: disabilities, emotional or behavioural difficulties, unaccompanied asylum-seeking child and offending behaviour. The research showed that children with any one of these needs tended to be more expensive to look after than children with no additional needs, while children with complex needs combining two or more of these attributes on average generated even greater costs. The report shown in Figure 8.14 therefore has a row for each possible needs combination, ranging from no additional needs to all four of them.

The 60 children included in the report shown in Figure 8.14 form the demonstration dataset that is supplied with the Cost Calculator. Their personal characteristics and placement histories are based on those of real children, but they have been selected to provide illustrations of different situations that occur rather than as a representative sample of the actual care population. Accordingly, the average costs per week shown for the

Data Admin Analysis of Costs by Needs Group.xls

Analysis of Costs by Needs Group
From 01/04/2006 to 31/03/2007 Out of London 2006-7

Needs	Number of Children	% of Total Children	Total Cost	% of Total Cost	Total Weeks	Average Cost per Week	Average Cost as % of Overall Average Cost	Weeks per Child
00: None	11	18%	£258,550	6%	457.3	£565	33%	41.6
01: Disabilities only	5	8%	£246,239	5%	179.6	£1,371	81%	35.9
02: EBD only	9	15%	£519,968	12%	453.0	£1,148	67%	50.3
03: UASC only	3	5%	£63,395	1%	119.6	£530	31%	39.9
04: Offender only	5	8%	£406,533	9%	260.7	£1,559	92%	52.1
05: Disabilities+EBD	4	7%	£322,626	7%	170.0	£1,898	111%	42.5
06: Disabilities+UASC	1	2%	£122,494	3%	52.1	£2,349	138%	52.1
07: Disabilities+Offender	2	3%	£98,174	2%	104.3	£941	55%	52.1
08: EBD+UASC	1	2%	£47,048	1%	52.1	£902	53%	52.1
09: EBD+Offender	9	15%	£959,372	21%	310.4	£3,090	182%	34.5
10: UASC+Offender	2	3%	£120,453	3%	77.7	£1,550	91%	38.9
11: Disab+EBD+UASC	1	2%	£67,209	1%	52.1	£1,289	76%	52.1
12: Disab+EBD+Offender	4	7%	£752,584	17%	201.9	£3,728	219%	50.5
13: Disab+UASC+Offender	1	2%	£182,680	4%	52.1	£3,503	206%	52.1
14: EBD+UASC+Offender	1	2%	£121,707	3%	52.1	£2,334	137%	52.1
15: Disab+EBD+UASC +Offender	1	2%	£218,179	5%	52.1	£4,184	246%	52.1
All Needs Groups	**60**	**100%**	**£4,507,210**	**100%**	**2647.3**	**£1,703**		**44.1**

Report printed on: 08/01/2008 Data imported on: 31/03/2007

Summary

Figure 8.14: Analysis of Costs by Needs Group report

different needs groups in Figure 8.14 should not be used as robust estimates of weekly costs for children who have the specified characteristics. It will be observed, however, that the children in Figure 8.14 who have more complex needs do tend to cost more to look after, although there are exceptions to this general rule.

Costs by Placements report

The original research study found that the type of placement used was a key factor in determining its cost (see Chapter 4). Given their significance in cost calculations and the wide variations between them, the Cost Calculator distinguishes a large number of placement types. The Costs by Placements report (Figure 8.15) gives information on the costs each placement type incurs. The computer generates this report by aggregating the costs during the calculation period for all the different individual placements or part-placements that are of each of the specified types. Since a child may have several different types of placement during the calculation period, costs attributable to one child may be included in different rows of this table as appropriate. The final column of this table shows the average

Analysis of Costs by Placement Type
From 01/04/2006 to 31/03/2007   Out of London 2006-7

Description	Type	Provided By	Location	Costs	Weeks Looked After	Average Weekly Cost
Adoption in LA	Adoption	Local Authority	In LA Area	£35,499	70.1	£506
Adoption out LA	Adoption	Local Authority	Outside LA	£62,779	66.7	£941
Agency Foster Care in LA	Foster care	Agency	In LA Area	£90,986	70.0	£1,300
Agency Foster Care out LA	Foster care	Agency	Outside LA	£208,218	167.6	£1,243
LA Foster Care in LA	Foster care	Local Authority	In LA Area	£87,675	193.3	£454
LA Foster Care out LA	Foster care	Local Authority	Outside LA	£92,020	206.4	£446
Hospital in LA	Hospital	Local Authority	in LA Area			
Hospital out LA	Hospital	Local Authority	Outside LA			
Agency Independence in LA	Independence	Agency	In LA Area	£13,013	14.6	£893
Agency Independence out LA	Independence	Agency	Outside LA	£119,902	98.4	£1,218
LA Independence in LA	Independence	Local Authority	In LA Area	£11,682	16.4	£711
LA Independence out LA	Independence	Local Authority	Outside LA	£18,660	16.9	£1,107
Kinship Care in LA	Kinship care	Family	In LA Area	£52,495	121.1	£433
Kinship Care out LA	Kinship care	Family	Outside LA	£37,230	83.4	£446
Agency Mother & Baby in LA	Mother And Baby	Agency	In LA Area	£93,630	49.6	£1,889
Agency Mother & Baby out LA	Mother And Baby	Agency	Outside LA	£3,900	3.1	£1,241
LA Mother & Baby in LA	Mother And Baby	Local Authority	In LA Area	£39,237	41.4	£947
LA Mother & Baby out LA	Mother And Baby	Local Authority	Outside LA	£25,650	19.6	£1,311
Other	Other					
Parents in LA	Placed with parents	Family	In LA Area	£33,838	138.3	£245
Parents out LA	Placed with parents	Family	Outside LA	£15,925	52.1	£305
Post-Adoption Support	Post adoption	Local Authority				
Ag Res + Ed + H in LA	Res+Education+Health	Agency	In LA Area	£122,494	52.1	£2,349
Ag Res + Ed + H out LA	Res+Education+Health	Agency	Outside LA	£292,575	124.7	£2,346
LA Res + Ed + H in LA	Res+Education+Health	Local Authority	In LA Area	£123,702	38.3	£3,231
LA Res + Ed + H out LA	Res+Education+Health	Local Authority	Outside LA	£68,487	21.0	£3,261
Agency Residential in LA	Residential	Agency	In LA Area	£430,208	136.9	£3,143
Agency Residential out LA	Residential	Agency	Outside LA	£145,340	62.1	£2,339
LA Residential in LA	Residential	Local Authority	In LA Area	£6,169	2.0	£3,084
LA Residential out LA	Residential	Local Authority	Outside LA	£308,241	127.1	£2,424

Figure 8.15: Costs by Placement Type report

weekly cost of each type of placement. For the placement types shown in Figure 8.15 the minimum average weekly cost is £245, incurred when children are placed with their parents within the local authority area; the maximum figure is £3261 for residential placements offering both education and health care facilities that are provided by another local authority. The rows indicated by arrows are discussed in the What If? analysis.

Flexible placement mapping

In view of the large deviations around the mean cost within placement types, a flexible placement mapping facility has recently been added. This allows users to define their own subsets of placement types within the major categories of placements used in the SSDA 903 returns. For example, users can define different payment bands for different categories of foster carers.

What If? analysis

The reports that the model produces are based on the current set of data with which it has been provided. If any of the child, placement or unit cost data are changed, all subsequent reports are based on the new dataset. Comparison of the 'before' and 'after' reports allows the impact of the changes to be studied. The model therefore has the facility to investigate the impact of implementing policy changes, as well as the effects of variations in unit costs.

Although alterations to the cost values in customized cost tables and edits of the information relating to individual children can only be made by those who have Data Administrator privileges, all users may explore how changing the services provided to looked after children would impact on total costs by using the What If? function available from the main menu shown in Figure 8.1.

For instance, the current White Paper on looked after children proposes to introduce measures to prevent local authorities from placing children outside their local area unless they are satisfied that such placements are in the child's best interests (Department for Education and Skills 2007a, p.59). In view of such measures, an authority may be interested in exploring the cost consequences of replacing out-of-authority placements with those that might be provided locally. As an example of the type of What If? analysis that may be useful to carry out, we begin by examining the Placement Type report in Figure 8.15. This shows that £208,218 is being spent on placing children in agency foster care outside the local authority area at an average cost of £1243 per week for 167.6 weeks, while the average cost for children placed in local authority foster care within the local authority area is £454 per week for 193.3 weeks.

We decide therefore to investigate the impact on costs if all children who were placed in agency foster care outside the local authority area during the calculation period had instead been placed in local authority foster care within the local authority area. We use the What If? mechanism to make the hypothetical change and then run the Placement Type report again. This yields a new report, part of which is shown in Figure 8.16. There are now blanks in the row for agency foster care outside the local authority area since the children who were in this type of placement are now treated as if they were placed elsewhere.

Analysis of Costs by Placement Type
From 01/04/2006 to 31/03/2007   Out of London 2006-7

Description	Type	Provided By	Location	Costs	Weeks Looked After	Average Weekly Cost
Adoption in LA	Adoption	Local Authority	In LA Area	£35,499	70.1	£506
Adoption out LA	Adoption	Local Authority	Outside LA	£62,779	66.7	£941
Agency Foster Care in LA	Foster care	Agency	In LA Area	£90,986	70.0	£1,300
Agency Foster Care out LA	Foster care	Agency	Outside LA			
LA Foster Care in LA	Foster care	Local Authority	In LA Area	£156,285	360.9	£433
LA Foster Care out LA	Foster care	Local Authority	Outside LA	£92,020	206.4	£446

Figure 8.16: Costs by Placement Type report after placement change

Their 167.6 weeks of care are now added to the 193.3 weeks of care that had already been used for local authority foster care within the local authority area so that the total number of weeks of this provision is now shown as 360.9. The hypothetical total cost of this care is £156,285 and this can be compared with the sum of the actual costs for the two types of placement: £208,218 + £87,675 = £295,893. The result of the What If? analysis is therefore that if the children in agency foster care outside the local authority area had all instead been placed in local authority foster care within the local authority area there would have been a reduction in total costs of £295,893 - £156,285 = £139,608.

It should be noted that while the Cost Calculator can provide information on what the total cost would be if particular placement changes were made, it takes no account of whether it would be practically possible to make such changes, nor does it include additional costs that might be generated by the process of making the changes. Moreover, it must be evident from the discussion in preceding chapters that, even if adequate numbers of local authority foster carers were available, they would not necessarily have the skills to care for the high needs children who tend to be placed in agency, out-of-authority placements. Nevertheless, one of the strengths of the What If? analysis is that it can show the amount of funding that a change of direction might release that could be used to fund the development of a highly skilled service.

Within our current research programme we are undertaking a short study similar to the example used as an illustration of the What If? analysis function described above: to compare the costs of Multi-Dimensional

Treatment Foster Care (MTFC) with the existing provision for children with high levels of need who are eligible for this specialist pilot programme (Holmes, Westlake and Ward forthcoming b). Once the unit costs have been calculated (and these would need to include the set-up costs of the new programme), the What If? analysis function could be utilized to calculate and compare the costs of the two types of provision. The Separate Placements reports function will already allow comparisons of placement lengths. At a later stage of development it should be possible to compare items such as frequency of disruptions and outcomes such as school exclusions and offending behaviour for children in the two types of service provision.

User input to model development

The benefits of working with local authorities in developing the model were demonstrated in the pilot study. Since then the research team has sought to facilitate collaboration in its further development. Prospective users have been encouraged to become research partners and Knowledge Transfer Partnerships have been set up with two local authorities to extend the Cost Calculator as described in Chapter 9. Contact between users is fostered by the provision of discussion forums on the web site.

One of the most interesting models for establishing a partnership between users and the research team has been developed by a consortium of all 12 local authorities in the North East region. These authorities are undertaking a formal implementation programme across the region, with the support of a liaison officer employed specifically for that purpose. The project will not only be able to inform all potential participants about key issues concerning implementation and the ways in which the various reports can be utilized to support cost-analysis and planning at both strategic and individual levels. It also offers joint opportunities to discuss pertinent issues to be raised with the research team; for example, the North East partnership is advising about future reports and their potential. Questions about customization have led to an expert seminar from the cost calculator developer; concerns about the accuracy of average unit costs calculated for both local authority residential placements and foster care have led to the introduction of flexible placement mapping (see above) and to further work on the calculation of overheads. Working on these methodologies in conjunction with local authorities ensures that the development of the model is aligned with the needs of users.

Conclusion

The cost calculations and different analyses provided by the cost calculator model are proving invaluable to local authorities in assessing the relative costs of care for children with different types of needs, looked after in different kinds of placements. The many different factors that the calculations take into account, together with the variety of reports and the different ways in which they can be focused, provide users with new insights into patterns of care provision, its costs and its outcomes. Key data for the model were already available in electronic form in local authorities because they are required for government returns. The Cost Calculator provides authorities with a way of analysing these data and using them to inform their decision-making.

The pilot study proved the benefits of working with local authorities and their advice has been utilized for improving the calculation methodology, developing additional reports and improving unit cost estimates. A User Group is now in operation and contact between users is fostered by web site discussion forums.

Summary of the key points from Chapter 8

- The cost calculator model that was originally produced for research purposes has now been developed into a practical computer application. It has been implemented in several local authorities and is proving to be a valuable tool in analysing the costs of different patterns of placement provision and their associated outcomes.

- Almost all the child and placement data utilized by the model are already required by government returns and are therefore likely to be already held electronically on management information systems in most authorities. Other data should be similarly available following changes to current data collections and the implementation of the Integrated Children's System. The unit costs are those calculated for the research studies, updated to 2006–7.

- Calculations are performed automatically by a computer and take account of all the many child and placement circumstances that cause unit costs to differ. The model is sufficiently flexible to accommodate additional customized or updated unit costs tables.

- The model carries out calculations for a user-specified time period. For every placement or part-placement within that period it calculates the cost of each social care process and adds these together with the fee or allowance paid to form the cost of that placement within the calculation timeframe. Costs of sequential placements for individual children can be produced along with aggregate costs for selected groups of children or placements.

- Because it uses a 'bottom-up' approach to calculate the costs of social care processes over a period of time, the model is flexible enough to be developed further, as is described in Chapter 9.

- The various Cost Calculator reports that are described in this chapter are available in the demonstration version of the model which can be downloaded from the website www.ccfcs.org.uk.

- The model has some predictive power in that it can estimate the impending costs of continuing to look after a group of children in their current placements until a specified future end date. The model is therefore potentially useful to planners, allowing them to estimate the likely continuing costs of placements for their current care population.

- It is possible to select all children who have a particular outcome in combination with particular needs and compare the costs and patterns of their placements. This is an area to be developed further as outcome data improve.

- Costs and placement length can be analysed by placement type and by the name of the provider.

- A What If? function allows users to investigate the impact on costs of using an alternative type of placement.

Notes

1   YOT costs currently included in the Cost Calculator are the basic costs of providing support to the child. They do not yet include variations according to items such as types of criminal order or reflect additional activity such as preparations for court appearances.

Chapter 9

Conclusion: Cost Calculations and their Implications for Policy and Practice

Introduction

This book describes a methodology for costing services accessed by children in need over specific time periods and assessing their effectiveness, together with a computer application that has been developed to assist in doing these things. The basis of the work is a specific study designed to calculate the social care costs of placing children in care or accommodation and explore the relationship between costs and outcomes. The developments that have ensued are based not only on the research results of that initial study but also on the recognition that the concepts underpinning its methodology and the computer model it developed for calculating how costs accrue over time have a wider application. A subsequent programme of work is now seeking to extend further both the conceptual framework and the software application developed for the original study to cover a wider group of children and a broader range of services. The ultimate objective is to make it possible for agencies to calculate and compare the full costs of providing services to children with different levels of need, and explore their relationship to outcomes. This programme for extension is grounded in the empirical findings from a number of research studies as well as extensive development work. This chapter first draws together the key findings from the original study, links them with the Cost Calculator software tool and examines their implications for policy and practice before going on to discuss the current and potential extensions to the programme.

Key findings from the initial study

Costing methodology

The costs of providing social care to looked after children are made up of two elements: the eight case management processes that underpin the delivery of care and the day-to-day costs of providing placements and other services. Once the unit costs have been calculated, it is possible to multiply them by the number of times each process occurs, or the number of hours or days for which a service is provided, over a specific time period. By totalling the costs of all the processes the social care costs of periods spent in care or accommodation can be calculated. The methodology can be extended to include the unit costs of both case management processes and service delivery from numerous agencies for wider groups of children and may cover time spent in or out of placement.

There are, however, extensive variations to each unit cost which need to be reflected in cost calculations when a 'bottom-up' method, such as the one we have developed, is utilized. Variations in the social care costs of placing children in care or accommodation are engendered by differences in local policies and practices, types of placement used and the needs of the children concerned. The cost calculator model that has been developed uses data to represent all these variations and takes them into account in calculating cost estimates.

Factors identified as generating cost variations

Our initial study calculated unit costs in the manner described above, using data on the needs, experiences and outcomes of a sample of 478 children looked after by six local authorities over a 20-month period. The findings were used to explore variations both between authorities and between children with different needs, together with their experiences, including the placements they received, in care.

The study was able to trace how differences between authorities in both the needs of their care population and the patterns of response can substantially affect the costs of service provision for both individual children and groups at any one time and over a particular period.

Costs and children's needs

While age and length of stay have an obvious impact on the cost of care episodes, a number of other characteristics displayed by looked after children influence the cost dynamics of placements. Indicators of additional support needs that increased costs for children and young people in this study were: asylum-seeking status, physical and learning disabilities, emotional and/or behavioural difficulties and offending behaviour. Groups of young people displaying different combinations of these factors were identified. This included a sizeable group of children and young people who displayed none of these cost-related attributes; they cost substantially less to look after than those who displayed one of them, and children and young people who displayed combinations of two or more cost substantially more than those who displayed just one.

Looking after a child who showed evidence of emotional or behavioural difficulties *or* who committed offences cost the authorities over 50 per cent more than providing care or accommodation for children who showed no evidence of additional support needs. However when young people displayed *both* emotional or behavioural difficulties *and* committed offences the cost was three times that of those with no additional support needs. Unaccompanied asylum-seeking children showed patterns of need that were similar to those of the children who displayed no evidence of additional support needs, although there were additional costs that related to their specific circumstances. It was also evident that a very small number of children with exceptionally high needs could skew the costs of the care population in a whole authority over a number of years. The impact of different groups of children with different configurations of need moving through the care system may be a major reason for fluctuations in costs over time.

Additional support for children's particular needs may be provided from services outside social care, such as CAMHS or special education services. There was, however, a paucity of data on the extent to which looked after children received such services. Until these are more readily available, it will not be possible to link the provision of such services to particular placements. However such data as were accessible showed that, when costs were calculated over a period in care or accommodation, there appeared to be an inverse relationship between the costs of provision and children and young people's opportunities for improving their life chances and developing or sustaining stable relationships with adults and peers. By and large children with the least extensive needs appeared to cost least and benefit most from care or accommodation.

The group who appeared least likely to benefit were those with the most extensive needs, particularly young people with no evidence of physical or learning disability, but who displayed emotional or behavioural difficulties and also committed offences. Many of these young people had extensive and entrenched needs; they would have been likely to require intensive expert services wherever they were placed. Once they became looked after they tended, eventually, to be offered the most costly placements, though often only after they had run the gamut of other, cheaper options. There is insufficient evidence to determine whether the more expensive placements provided a better quality of care. However the experiences of this group over the 20 months of the study suggest that they were least likely to access routine health services or psychotherapeutic support, and the most likely to be excluded from school. The only service for which they gained disproportionate access was treatment as hospital inpatients in response to overdoses or other self-harming behaviour. Poor access to other services was partly related to their increased alienation and refusal to accept help, but it was also related to the frequency with which they moved. Frequent moves from one placement to another were also likely to further damage the fragile wellbeing of these vulnerable young people and may, in the long term, have increased the costs of meeting their needs.

The Cost Calculator utilizes whatever information on children's needs is available. Data on each of the indicators of additional support needs can be read in. Alternatively, the Cost Calculator is able to infer that children have disabilities if the social care team that has responsibility for them is designated a 'disabilities team', and also that children with a youth justice legal status display offending behaviour.

Costs and placement types

Variations in costs between the authorities were related to different configurations of need in their sample care populations, and to the proportion of time children and young people spent in different placement types. The average unit cost for maintaining a child for a week in a residential placement was 4.5 times that of an independent living arrangement, eight times that of the cost for foster care, 9.5 times that of a placement with family and friends and more than 12.5 times that of a placement with own parents. As an illustration, eight children could be placed in foster care for every child placed in a residential unit, though the latter placements tended to be shorter.

There were, therefore, wide variations between the costs of different placement types: residential care was almost always more costly than foster care, although some other placements, such as independent living, turned out to be surprisingly expensive when all accompanying support costs were included. There were also substantial differences within placement types: for instance, data from one local authority showed that some agency residential placements could cost three times as much per week as others.

Agency foster placements tended to be more costly both to procure and to maintain than those provided in house. Our study was unable to identify how far additional costs of such placements related to the complex needs of the children they received, although this is an obvious area for further research. Agency residential placements were more costly to arrange than those provided by the authorities, but the fees were sometimes less than the day-to-day costs of in-house provision.

Placements outside the area of the authority tended to be more costly both in terms of expenditure and children's wellbeing than those nearer to home, largely because of the long distances from home and neighbourhood and the travelling time necessary to maintain contact. However this was not necessarily true in small authorities such as London boroughs where such placements could sometimes be nearer the child's home than those made within the boundaries of large authorities.

Variations between local authorities

While in general children and young people with the most extensive needs received the most costly placements, this was not always the case, and indeed the costs of looking after children with similar needs varied between the authorities. One authority, that had invested heavily in procedures designed to ensure that only those children whose needs could not be met in other ways were placed in care or accommodation, had reduced its care population to a minimum, but was left with a group with extensive and complex needs who cost more per head, though less overall, than more mixed care populations. The two authorities that appeared to provide the most cost-effective service on other criteria also appeared most efficient at finding placements appropriate to children's needs and to have a smaller group with little evidence of additional support needs in their care populations.

Cost Calculator analyses and reports

Alongside the more conventional research findings, our initial study also produced a computer application that enabled us to link unit costs to data about children in care or accommodation. Chapter 8 has given a detailed description of the Cost Calculator and discussed its evolution from research instrument to practice tool. Both the pilot phase and the subsequent implementation show that it can help local authorities and other child welfare agencies utilize the child-level data they routinely collect, generating cost estimates and informing their decision-making.

The analyses and reports that the Cost Calculator generates are based on the research findings. Users can obtain separate costs for each of a sequence of placements for a particular child and they can request summary reports showing total and average costs for different groups of children according to their needs or the types of placements they have experienced. The facility to predict the impending costs of continuing to look after the current care population during a future time period allows users to estimate future costs for children moving through the care system, taking account of the extent of their needs. If authorities have children with exceptionally high needs who are particularly expensive to care for, this ability to predict the costs that they will generate in future is especially useful.

The accuracy of the cost estimates depend on the quality of the data used for the calculations. For example, if information about children's needs is missing default values are used that are likely to generate lower costs and thus produce underestimates. Given the importance of the fees and allowances paid to carers and residential units, in that they accounted for well over 90 per cent of all social care costs for looked after children in the initial study and show extensive deviations from the means, a facility has been provided that allows users to input specific placement fees at individual child level. Using the actual amount paid for each placement rather than the average for that type of placement (which is the default value) is an important step towards achieving accurate cost calculations.

Implications for policy and practice

Some of the findings from the study have considerable implications for the development of policy and practice at both national and local levels, and for the strategic planning of services.

Analysis of need

First, there is much evidence that a thorough analysis of children's needs at entry to care is fundamental to the efficient planning of services. The implementation of the Framework for the Assessment of Children in Need and their Families (Department of Health, Department for Education and Employment and Home Office 2000) appears to have improved assessment of needs at an individual level (Cleaver, Walker and Meadows 2004); however there is less evidence that aggregate data on the prevalence of cost-related needs, such as those identified in earlier chapters, are routinely collated and used in the planning of social care services for children and young people (see Gatehouse, Ward and Holmes 2008). Understanding how many children and young people who enter care have missed out on their education or failed to access adequate health care is an important component in setting baselines, monitoring progress and assessing outcomes (see Ward 2004). Findings from our study demonstrate that knowing how many children and young people enter the care system each year showing evidence of emotional or behavioural difficulties, offending behaviour and/or physical or learning disabilities, how long they stay and what services they access, is necessary for planning appropriate services and managing budgets.

Routine monitoring of the prevalence of these attributes in a care population might also demonstrate, as this and other studies have done (Skuse and Ward 2003; Ward and Wynn forthcoming), that, while those with extensive needs are over-represented, a sizeable group of children and young people entering care and accommodation show no evidence of additional support needs. Many of this group appear to have a relatively satisfactory experience of care, with stable placements and reasonable outcomes. The children and young people who fell into this group in our study had entered at an earlier age and spent a longer period in care than all but one other group, a finding that supports a more positive view of the benefits of care than is sometimes advanced (e.g. Sergeant 2006). Their presence in the care system often goes unacknowledged, amidst the numerous and justifiable concerns about the adverse experiences and poor outcomes of others. In fact, as our study demonstrates, the population of children and young people who come into care are a heterogeneous group; there are wide variations in both their needs and their experiences of care, reflected in significant differences in costs and outcomes. Increased awareness of this diversity would make it easier to tailor services to need and increase their effectiveness. If data on individual children's needs are imported into the Cost Calculator, reports are available that aggregate the data in different ways. Users can select groups of children according to their needs, outcomes or length of stay so that information on children's needs in relation to costs and placement types can be made available to policy makers.

Potential for regularly reviewing placement costs

The Cost Calculator utilizes data that are already collected on a regular basis by all local authorities. Importing these data into the Cost Calculator allows authorities to obtain a myriad of different cross-section views of their data, thus informing their policy decisions. Data on children and their placements can be updated regularly and reports obtained on costs and on the pattern of placement changes. The Cost Calculator also provides a facility for What If? analysis that allows users to investigate the impact on costs of using an alternative type of placement.

Potential to make false economies

The findings also identified areas where the need to reduce costs in the immediate term led to a risk of producing false economies in the long run. Authorities that appeared to use resources efficiently tended to place a high proportion of children and young people who showed only simple additional support needs in placements with relatives and friends or non-related foster carers, or indeed with own parents, leaving the more expensive residential placements for children with more extensive and complex needs.

Family-based placements were clearly most appropriate to this relatively low needs group, but there sometimes appeared to be a tendency to regard placements, particularly with family or friends, as potentially cost free. The data collected for developing unit costs showed that some authorities offered only minimal allowances to aunts, uncles and grandparents caring for looked after children, and some only provided financial support when requested to do so. While there has since been a legal judgement requiring authorities to pay family and friends the same rate of fostering allowance as non-related carers (R v. Manchester City Council 2001), financial discrimination remains a concern, and there is evidence that kinship carers are sometimes denied additional allowances and skills fees if they are approved foster carers, or receive sketchy and unpredictable remuneration if they have a different legal status (Fostering Network 2007). Such strategies may prove to be false economies, for ignoring the needs of carers can exacerbate difficulties in the placement and jeopardize its stability (see Ward, Munro and Dearden 2006). There is evidence from this and other studies (see Ward, Munro and Dearden 2006; Farmer and Moyers 2008) that many placements with birth family members, as well as those with local authority carers, will require intensive support services from a range of agencies if children's needs are to be adequately met.

Furthermore, authorities might also explore how closely reductions in costs represent true efficiencies and how far they reflect a lack of responsiveness to children's needs. Young people with extensive emotional and behavioural difficulties who also committed offences during the course of the study were on average nearly two years older at admission to care or accommodation than those with less evident needs, suggesting that concerns over spiralling costs may sometimes have led agencies to overlook the consequences of leaving children in damaging family situations that seriously compromise their wellbeing. These were the children who ricocheted around the care system, experiencing frequent disruptions as they moved to ever more costly placements. Although these children and young people spent significantly fewer months in care or accommodation, the costs of their care episodes tended to be higher and their outcomes less satisfactory than those for children with less extensive needs who were looked after for longer periods. Deferring the decision to place these young people may also have proved a false economy, incurring greater costs, to less effect, than earlier admission might have done.

The Cost Calculator allows users to select children with particular needs and view the number of days they have spent in each of their placements, so that children who have changed placement frequently can be easily identified. The sequence of placement types that a child has experienced can be examined, together with their costs. It is therefore possible to identify those children who move frequently and establish how their costs escalate.

Towards a systems approach

The findings also demonstrate the importance of taking a systems approach in analysing the costs of looking after children. The costs incurred by placing children in care or accommodation should be considered within the context of the costs of providing targeted services to all children in need – and against the wider background of providing universal services to all children within an authority. Those authorities that place only minimal numbers of children in care or accommodation may be offering placements largely to children with extensive support needs and thereby incurring high average costs per child for their looked after population. Costs per head of care or accommodation are usually higher than those for providing support in the community; even if these authorities are spending more on providing family support services, they may nevertheless be reducing their overall costs.

There was evidence that the authority in our study that had succeeded in reducing its care population to a minimum was indeed spending proportionately more on supporting other children in the community. Nevertheless, there is an obvious risk that, without a systems approach that explores the relationship between needs, services, costs and outcomes for all children in need, costs may simply be reduced by retracting services and leaving vulnerable groups of children unsupported.

A comprehensive systems approach should also show how costs are spread across agencies. Young people who are excluded from school are more likely to offend (Social Exclusion Unit 1998), so reducing costs to education may increase the costs to youth offending teams and the police. Increasing the level of provision from child and adolescent mental health services, and therefore the costs to the health authority, may reduce the costs to children's social care if young people with emotional or behavioural difficulties can be better supported at home or in the less expensive placements with relatives or foster carers. Current policies, introduced and/or strengthened by the Children Act 2004, to promote better integration of both services and budgets, should lead to the adoption of such a systems approach to costing services and also to greater transparency concerning the costs incurred by both individual children and groups. Some children with exceptionally high support needs will require intensive and costly services from a range of agencies for many years. Once agencies are able to calculate both the current and the probable future costs of such services it then becomes possible to consider whether different configurations might offer more efficient and effective use of resources and produce better outcomes.

The Cost Calculator for Children's Services and the ongoing research and development programme

The Cost Calculator is now being implemented by a number of local authorities. Almost all of these have chosen to collaborate with us in the ongoing research and development programme, not only as members of the user group which advises the team on potential enhancements to the software and issues concerning implementation, but also as partners in specific development projects, or as active participants in the research that underpins the overall initiative. These three strands, of research, development and implementation, are closely intertwined. The evolving programme of work is designed both to engage with some of the findings from the original study and to inform and be informed by the concerns and the needs of users.

Implementation issues

Authorities that are implementing the Cost Calculator for Children's Services have commended the ease with which it will import their data and welcomed the different analyses that are then available to them. Three questions raised by them are: How far do 'bottom-up' costs relate to 'top-down' expenditure? How can cost calculations be improved? And how can they ensure that children's views of the value of services are not overlooked in assessments of costs and outcome? The first two questions are discussed below; the final, and perhaps most important, question is explored in the concluding paragraphs of this chapter.

Shortfall in aggregate cost estimates

We discussed in Chapter 1 how 'bottom-up' costs that itemize activities involved in supporting each service user reflect a more complex picture of the way in which costs accrue in the delivery of children's services than do 'top-down' calculations. In theory, providing all items that contribute to costs are included in a 'bottom-up' approach, and so aggregating all such costs should produce totals that are similar to the expenditure values used in top-down calculations. However, the first total cost estimates that have been obtained in authorities that have implemented the Cost Calculator show a considerable shortfall between the two methodologies, with 'bottom-up' calculations accounting for only a proportion of total expenditure.

There are several possible reasons for these discrepancies. First, there are some conceptual differences in the methodologies, in that the Cost Calculator sometimes takes a longer view of costs than the timeframe in which expenditures occur, but aggregating values over the whole population of looked after children reduces the impact of these differences. Some parts of the underestimates relate to gaps in data held on local authority management information systems. Chapter 8 showed how our cost calculations take as a default position a child with no additional support needs, placed with local authority foster carers, which is one of the least costly scenarios. We also noted that extensive variations around the mean meant that too much reliance on the average fee or allowance for the placement type would produce insufficiently valid calculations. Social care users of the Cost Calculator are now working to procure better data on children's needs from their colleagues in education and youth justice, and on the fees for individual placements from their finance departments. It is expected that importing improved data into the Cost Calculator will do much to close the gap between aggregate 'bottom-up' costs and expenditure.

Planned enhancements

Ongoing work includes projects both to refine the methodology for calculating unit costs and to improve the available data, for deficits in both are widely regarded as responsible for much of the shortfall. There are plans to introduce additional variations relating to the distance at which children are placed from their home authority. These will take account of the additional costs incurred in visiting children placed at long distances from their homes. New requirements for national returns provide opportunities to calculate and introduce further variations related to children's needs, such as the severity of emotional or behavioural difficulties (through the introduction of Strengths and Difficulties Questionnaire [SDQ] scores) and the impact of different types of disability (through more precise definitions held in education databases). Such issues are currently being explored not only within the implementing authorities, but also throughout the research and development programme.

Planned improvements to methodology and unit cost estimates

The discrepancy between aggregate costs and expenditure is thought to reflect much wider issues than the implementation of the software application, highlighting concerns about the overall costing of children's services; its discovery has led to a number of initiatives to try to improve general cost calculations in this area. Cost calculation methodology should be greatly improved by a joint initiative between participating authorities to explore and refine the elements included in calculations of overheads and the way in which they are applied. The current formula is thought to produce a substantial underestimate by omitting some elements such as the cost of recruiting and training foster carers and the costs of top level management services. These omissions may help to explain why in-house placements for looked after children often appear less costly than those provided by the voluntary or independent sector. In addition, within the current research programme (see below) we intend to triangulate the activity data collected through focus groups with event records completed by practitioners, detailing the amount of time spent on supporting children who show different profiles of need. We also plan to obtain more detailed estimates of adoption costs.

At present the cost predictions that the Cost Calculator can produce are based on the assumption that all children who are currently looked after remain in their existing placements until the end of the calculation time period. As better data on placement histories becomes available, it may be possible to predict the mean length of stay in a placement for children with different needs and to predict costs only for the length of time that the placement is expected to continue. Such a facility might be very valuable in allocating budgets, but it would be important to recognize that every child is an individual, and some will not follow the general pattern.

Moreover, the mean length of stay is not necessarily the desirable length: for instance the findings have shown that the average lengths of placements for children with complex needs such as emotional or behavioural difficulties plus offending behaviour, are shorter than those for other children, probably because so many disrupt. Users would need to take action to ensure that predictions based on such patterns do not become a self-fulfilling prophecy.

Adopting a systems approach: extending the Cost Calculator to include education and health

As we have seen, the findings from the original study demonstrate the importance of taking a systems approach in analysing the costs and consequences of services for children in need. Focusing solely on social care ignores the costs and contributions of other children's services such as health, education and youth justice; it also means that analyses of changes in service delivery ignore the impact on other agencies. Moreover a separate approach is becoming increasingly inappropriate following closer integration of children's services and more extensive opportunities for joint funding. It was evident at an early stage that our cost calculations would need to reflect a wider range of service provision.

Two local authorities have entered into Knowledge Transfer Partnerships with the research team to help develop the cost calculator model more widely; one partnership is extending it to take account of education, and the other to incorporate the costs of health provision. Both focus specifically on services for children in need, with a particular interest in processes and services for children placed away from home, either in social care, education, health or jointly funded placements.

The health project encompasses both physical and mental health and focuses on joint commissioning of services and placements. At the time of writing it is at a relatively early stage. The findings will be used to develop the Cost Calculator further in 2009. However the education project is now well established. A wide variety of education services have been mapped, together with seven case management processes that support their delivery; variations to both processes and services have been identified and comprehensive unit costs developed, reflecting the complexity of providing education to children with a wide range of needs. Key variables concerning children's needs, experience and outcomes incorporate child-level data items already collected for national returns on education as well as social care (see Holmes *et al.* forthcoming). While the focus is on services for children with special educational needs, the education costs are intended to cover the delivery of services to any child. The Cost Calculator is now being extended; a new version, currently being trialled in the partner authority and due for release in 2008, will be able to calculate education and/or social care costs incurred by two overlapping groups of children and young people: those with special educational needs and those placed in care or accommodation.

As indicated above, we are using a consistent methodology, drawn from the original research programme, to extend cost calculations within each service type. First, case management processes and specific services are mapped; unit costs are then developed for each process or time unit of service delivery; variations are identified and linked to cost-related variables such as children's needs, frequency of process or type of service; costs are then calculated over specific time periods and linked to evidence about child welfare outcomes. Key variables are restricted to routinely collected data such as those required for statutory returns. Following the extension of the Cost Calculator to cover all children in need (see below) and to include case management and services from education, health and social care, we plan to incorporate youth justice and socio-legal services, should funding become available.

The programme to broaden the cost calculations to include services delivered by more than one agency has raised important issues. A recurring theme touches on the ongoing debate about the extent to which, whatever the ethical arguments, there is technical capacity for data on services for children in need to be shared between agencies that are sometimes more closely integrated in theory than in practice (see Cleaver *et al.* 2007a). There are also questions about which services should be included in calculations of cost and outcome. Should cost calculations be restricted to those services funded by the local authority implementing the Cost Calculator? Should they include extensive, and largely hidden, opportunity costs to carers? Should they include 'cost-neutral' services funded by central government – a particular issue following devolved budgets and local management of schools? The answers depend on the perceived purpose of cost calculations: to better understand how the budget is spent, or to explore the cost-effectiveness of services designed to support better outcomes. Issues raised by the partner authorities are discussed in the wider user group and form part of the context for the evolving research and development programme.

Adopting a systems approach: extending the cost calculations to include services to all children in need

The original study was restricted to exploring relationships between costs and outcomes for children in care or accommodation. From the start the boundary was perceived as somewhat arbitrary: the factors that precipitate children into the care system are many and complex, and care is best understood as part of a continuum of services offered to children with a range of needs rather than as a separate specialist intervention provided to a group whose characteristics are clearly distinguishable from those of their peers. Our overall costing project has, however, benefited from this initial focus, for data of the type and quality necessary for developing the cost calculator model has, for many years, been more readily available for children in care than for other children in need. A standardized recording system for children in the care system was launched in England and Wales in 1995 (Department of Health 1995b) and, as we have seen (Chapter 8), the national returns require the collection of extensive child-level data items on their needs, placements, processes and outcomes that can be linked to unit costs (Department of Children, Schools and Families 2007a).

However, as the findings from the original study demonstrate, we need to adopt a systems approach to analysing the costs and outcomes of social care. The costs of care may be reduced by raising thresholds and cutting numbers, but the consequences of such a strategy need to be assessed within the context of costing and evaluating services and assessing outcomes for the wider range of social care provision. Our ongoing programme therefore includes a major research and development project to explore how both the conceptual framework and the practical application of the cost calculator model can be extended to include services for all children in need. The study should increase understanding of the comparative costs and consequences of placing children in care or accommodation or providing family support services under Section 17 of the Children Act 1989. More specifically, we are identifying and costing the processes of social care management for children in need, mapping those services provided or commissioned to support this group, and developing unit costs and identifying variations for a selection of those most commonly available. Many of the unit costs will build on the work of other research teams in the original Costs and Outcomes Research Initiative (see Berridge *et al.* 2002; Carpenter *et al.* 2003; Cleaver, Walker and Meadows 2004). Additional unit costs will be incorporated into the Cost Calculator, as will new variables relevant to this wider population. The study will include the construction of a new dataset, designed to help us model relationships between needs, experiences, outcomes and costs, with all their complex variations, for a new sample of 240 children receiving a range of services in four local authorities. This dataset will furnish the empirical basis for extending the Cost Calculator further and trialling prototypes.

The potential for extending the Cost Calculator to include a wider group of children in need is greatly enhanced by recent initiatives to improve the quality of data collected for this group. Implementation of the Framework for the Assessment of Children in Need and their Families (Department of Health, Department for Education and Employment and Home Office 2000) and the Integrated Children's System (2006–7; see Department of Health 2002b), as well as the introduction of the Children in Need Census (2000–5; to be reintroduced in 2009) (see Department of Health 2001a), has increased the likelihood that appropriate data will be recorded. The new requirements for the national returns, currently under discussion, should improve the quality of child-level data available (Gatehouse, Ward and Holmes 2008). Improved integration of children's services means that the enhanced Cost Calculator should be able to utilize data and calculate costs for a wider spectrum of children's services and not be restricted to social care.

Although the research programme focuses on extending the Cost Calculator for children in need, it will also produce empirical findings that underpin initiatives introduced by the wider group of users and partners to develop the Cost Calculator to include the costs of education and health and to improve the accuracy of cost calculations.

Conclusion

This book has explored a number of issues concerning the development of methodologies to better understand the relationship between costs and consequences of children's social care. The original research project, conceptualized as a single academic exercise to calculate the relationship between costs and outcomes for children in care or accommodation, has led to the development of a computer application that can be used routinely by local authorities. Implementation of the software has raised further questions about deeper issues concerning the general accuracy of costs for children's services and how they might be improved. The findings from the original study have led to initiatives to develop the cost calculator model further to cover a broader range of services accessed by a wider group of children in need.

The calculations produced by the Cost Calculator are fascinating in themselves, reflecting, as they appear to do, the varied outcomes achieved by groups of children with dissimilar needs who may have very different experiences of services. The spectrum of reports that the Cost Calculator offers make a valuable contribution to improving the quality of decision-making. It is salutary, however, that the implementing authorities should have emphasized the importance of ensuring that children's views of the value of services are an essential component in assessments of costs and outcome, for it is dangerously easy to overlook them in the midst of more abstract calculations. As Chapter 7 has shown, this is a difficult issue, for collecting factual data on issues such as attendance at reviews cannot reflect the nuances of lived experiences, while qualitative data gained from lengthy interviews are difficult to include in formal cost calculations. Consulting young people about their experiences and seeking their comments on how calculations might be interpreted may prove a more effective method of including them than seeking quantifiable data in response to questionnaires. We should also constantly try to ensure that an initiative such as this one does not focus on cutting costs and reducing support to our most vulnerable children, but on ensuring that public money is effectively deployed in the provision of services that have a proven value in promoting their wellbeing.

Summary of the key points from Chapter 9

- A 'bottom-up' approach to calculating the costs of looking after children provides a methodology that can be extended to other groups of children and the services with which they are provided. Extensive variations to each unit cost need to be included in the calculations, and the cost calculator model developed as a spin off from the initial research study takes these into account.

- Factors identified as generating cost variations include the different combinations of additional support needs that children have and the types of placement that they experience.

- The analyses and reports available from the Cost Calculator collate data on children's needs and placements; show the separate costs of a sequence of placements for each child; and provide information on the total and average costs for different groups of children. The software provides a practical tool that can inform decision-making.

- At present the Cost Calculator makes predictions on the assumption that children remain in their current placements. In future a different methodology may be used, based on both evidence of need and expected placement length.

- The quality of data imported into the Cost Calculator has an important impact on the accuracy of its calculations. Improvements in unit cost estimates and methodology are planned that are expected to reduce the current discrepancy between aggregate cost estimates and expenditure.

- The research findings demonstrate the importance of adopting a systems approach to analysing the costs of looking after children. Authorities that place only a small number of children away from home may be restricting placements to those with high support needs and thereby incurring high average costs per child looked after. They may also need to increase expenditure on family support to meet the needs of children who otherwise have been placed in care or accommodation. Nevertheless their overall costs are likely to be reduced. Further research is now under way to extend the cost calculator model to include services to all children in need.

- Children placed with parents or relatives often require intensive support in meeting their needs. It is a false economy to pay relatives minimal allowances or to consider such placements as relatively cost free.

- A systems approach should also demonstrate how costs are spread across agencies so that reducing the costs to one may increase the costs to another. Policies which promote better integration of both services and budgets should introduce greater transparency concerning how costs are divided, and make it possible to consider how different configurations could improve the effective deployment of resources. Studies are currently being undertaken to include education and health services in the cost calculator model.

- The removal of obstacles to the sharing of data about vulnerable children and a comprehensive information strategy suggest that the necessary data for calculating variations in costs are increasingly likely to be held on management information systems.

- Authorities need to monitor how far reductions in costs represent true savings and how far they simply represent a failure to offer an appropriate and timely response to need. Consulting children about their experiences may help to ensure that the services with which they are provided are effective in promoting their wellbeing.

References

Aldgate, J. and Statham, J. (2001) *The Children Act Now: Messages from Research*. London: The Stationery Office.

Ayres, M. (1997) *Report on the Review of Children's Agency Placements Conducted during July and August 1997*. Suffolk: Suffolk Social Services Department.

Barlow, J., Davis, H., McIntosh, E., Jarrett, P., Mockford, C. and Stewart-Brown, S. (2007) 'Role of home visiting in improving parenting and health in families at risk of abuse and neglect: Results of a multicentre randomised controlled trial and economic evaluation.' *Archives of Diseases in Childhood 92*, 229–33.

Bebbington, A. and Miles, J. (1989) 'The background of children who enter local authority care.' *British Journal of Social Work 19*, 349–68.

Beecham, J. (2000) *Unit Costs – Not Exactly Child's Play. A Guide to Estimating Unit Costs for Children's Social Care*. University of Kent: Department of Health, Dartington Social Research Unit and the Personal Social Services Research Unit.

Beecham, J. and Knapp, M. (2001) 'Costing psychiatric interventions.' In: G. Thornicroft (ed.) *Measuring Mental Health Needs*. London: Royal College of Psychiatrists.

Beecham, J. and Sinclair, I. (2007) *Costs and Outcomes in Children's Social Care: Messages from Research*. London: Jessica Kingsley Publishers.

Berridge, D., Beecham, J., Brodie, I., Cole, T., Daniels, H., Knapp, M. and MacNeill, V. (2002) *Costs and Consequences of Services for Troubled Adolescents: An Exploratory, Analytic Study for the Department of Health*. Luton: University of Luton.

Biehal, N. (2005) *Working with Adolescents. Supporting Families, Preventing Breakdown*. London: British Association of Adoption and Fostering.

Bradshaw, J., Kemp, P., Baldwin, S. and Rowe, A. (2004) *The Drivers of Social Exclusion: A Review of the Literature for the Social Exclusion Unit in the Breaking the Cycle Series*. London: Office for the Deputy Prime Minister.

Brandon, M., Thoburn, J., Lewis, A. and Way, A. (1999) *Safeguarding Children with the Children Act 1989*. London: The Stationery Office.

Broad, B. (ed.) (2001) *Kinship Care: The Placement Choice for Children and Young People*. Dorset: Russell House Publishing.

Bullock, R., Courtney, M.E., Parker, R., Sinclair, I. and Thoburn, J. (2006) 'Can the corporate state parent?' *Child and Youth Services Review 28*, 11, 1344–58.

Bullock, R., Gooch, D. and Little, M. (1998) *Children Going Home: The Reunification of Families*. Aldershot: Ashgate.

Bullock, R., Little, M. and Millham, S. (1993) *Going Home: The Return of Children Separated from their Families*. Aldershot: Dartmouth Publishing Company.

Butler, I. and Payne, H. (1997) 'The health of children looked after by the local authority.' *Adoption and Fostering 21*, 28–35.

Carpenter, J., Tidmarsh, J., Slade, J., Schneider, J., Coolen-Schrijner, P. and Wooff, D. (2003) *Outcomes and Costs of Therapeutic Family Support Services for Vulnerable Families with Young Children. Report to Department of Health.* Durham: Centre for Applied Social Studies, University of Durham.

Carr-Hill, R.A., Dixon, P., Mannion, R., Rice, N., Rudat, K., Sinclair, R. and Smith, P. (1997) *A Model of the Determinants of Expenditure on Children's Personal Social Services.* York: University of York.

Cleaver, H. (2000) *Fostering Family Contact: A Study of Children, Parents and Foster Carers.* London: The Stationery Office.

Cleaver, H., Nicholson, D., Tarr, S. and Cleaver, D. (2007b) *Child Protection, Domestic Violence and Parental Substance Misuse: Family Experiences and Effective Practices.* London: Jessica Kingsley Publishers.

Cleaver, H., Unell, I. and Aldgate, J. (1999) *Children's Needs – Parenting Capacity: The Impact of Parental Mental Illness, Problem Alcohol and Drug Use and Domestic Violence on Children's Development.* London: The Stationery Office.

Cleaver, H. and Walker, S. with Meadows, P. (2004) *Assessing Children's Needs and Circumstances: The Impact of the Assessment Framework.* London: Jessica Kingsley Publishers.

Cleaver, H., Walker, S., Scott, J., Cleaver, D., Rose, W., Ward, H. and Pithouse, A. (2007a) *An Evaluation of the Impact of the Integrated Children's System on Social Work Practice, Inter-Agency Cooperation, Collaboration, and Information Sharing – Final Report.* London: Department for Children, Schools and Families.

Colton, M., Drury, C. and Williams, M. (1995) *Children in Need: Family Support Under the Children Act 1989.* Aldershot: Gower.

Cooper, P. (2002) *Delivering Quality Children's Services: Inspection of Children's Services.* London: Department of Health.

Curtis, L. (2007) *Unit Costs of Health and Social Care 2007.* Kent: Personal Social Services Research Unit, University of Kent.

Darker, I., Ward, H. and Caulfield, L. (2008) 'An Analysis of Offending by Young People Looked After by Local Authorities.' *Youth Justice 8,* 2.

Department for Children, Schools and Families (2007a) *Children Looked After in England (including Adoption and Care Leavers). Year Ending 31 March 2007.* London: Department for Children, Schools and Families. Accessed 31/07/07 at www.dfes.gov.uk/rsgateway/DB/SFR/s000741/index.shtml

Department for Children, Schools and Families (2007b) *Children in Need Census 2008–9, Technical Specification.* London: Department for Children, Families and Schools. Accessed 12/12/07 at www.dfes.gov.uk/datastats1/guidelines/children/2008-09%20CIN%20Census%20Specification%20v1-1.doc

Department for Children, Schools and Families (2007c) *Guidance on Data Collection on the Mental and Emotional Health of Children and Young People in Care.* London: Department for Children, Families and Schools. Accessed 01/08/07 at www.dfes.gov.uk/datastats1/guidelines/children/pdf/SDQ%20guidance.pdf

Department for Education and Employment and Department of Health (2000) *Education Protects: Guidance on the Education of Children and Young People in Public Care.* London: Department for Education and Employment and Department of Health.

Department for Education and Skills (2003) *Every Child Matters. cm 5860.* The Stationery Office: London.

Department for Education and Skills (2004) *Children in Need in England: Results of a Survey of Activity and Expenditure as Reported by Local Authority Social Services Children and Families Teams for a Survey Week in February 2003.* London: Department for Education and Skills.

Department for Education and Skills (2006) *Children in Need in England: Results of a Survey of Activity and Expenditure as Reported by Local Authority Social Services Children and Families Teams for a Survey Week in February 2005.* London: Department for Education and Skills.

Department for Education and Skills (2007a) *Care Matters: Time for Change. cm7137.* The Stationery Office: London.

Department for Education and Skills (2007b) *Children Looked After by Local Authorities: Year Ending 31 March 2006.* London: Department for Education and Skills.

Department of Communities and Local Government (2007) *2008–09 National Performance Indicator Set.* London: Department of Communities and Local Government.

Department of Health (1991a) *Children Act 1989: Guidance and Regulations, Volume 4, Residential Care.* London: HMSO.

Department of Health (1991b) *The Children Act 1989; Guidance and Regulations; Volume 3, Family Placements.* London: HMSO.

Department of Health (1995a) *Child Protection: Messages from Research.* London: HMSO.

Department of Health (1995b) *Looking After Children: Assessment and Action Records for Children Aged Under 1; 1–2; 3–4; 5–9; 10–14; 15; plus Essential Information Records, Care Plans, Placement Plans and Review Forms.* London: Stationery Office.

Department of Health (1998) *Research Briefing: Costs and Effectiveness Research Initiative.* London: Department of Health.

Department of Health (1999) *The Government Objectives for Children's Services.* London: Department of Health.

Department of Health (2000a) *The Children Act Report 1995–1999.* London: Department of Health.

Department of Health (2000b) *The Children (Leaving Care) Act 2000: Regulations and Guidance.* London: Department of Health.

Department of Health (2001a) *Children in Need in England: Results of a Survey of Activity and Expenditure as Reported by Local Authority Social Services Children and Families Teams for a Survey Week in February 2000.* London: Department of Health.

Department of Health (2001b) *Personal Social Services Statistics: Finance.* Department of Health. Accessed 01/08/07 at www.dh.gov.uk/en/Publicationsandstatistics/Statistics/StatisticalWorkAreas/Statisticalexpenditure/DH_4000111

Department of Health (2001c) *Children's Social Services Core Information Requirements Data Model.* London: Department of Health.

Department of Health (2002a) *CiN 2001: Local Authority Tables.* London: Department of Health.

Department of Health (2002b) *The Integrated Children's System: Version 1.* London: Department of Health.

Department of Health (2002c) *Key Indicators Graphical System 2002.* London: Department of Health.

Department of Health (2002d) *Children Looked After by Local Authorities: Year Ending 31 March 2001 England. Volume 1: Commentary and National Tables.* London: Department of Health.

Department of Health (2002e) *Outcome Indicators for Looked After Children. Twelve Months to 30 September 2001, England.* London: Department of Health.

Department of Health (2003a) *Children's Social Services Core Information Requirements Process Model.* London: Department of Health.

Department of Health (2003b) *Social Services Performance Assessment Framework Indicators.* London: Department of Health.

Department of Health (2003c) *Guidance for the Children in Need National Collection 2003.* London: Department of Health.

Department of Health (2003d) *Key Indicators Graphical System 2003.* London: Department of Health.

Department of Health, Department for Education and Employment and Home Office (2000) *Framework for the Assessment of Children in Need and Their Families.* London: The Stationery Office.

Dixon, J., Wade, J., Byford, S., Weatherly, H. and Lee, J. (2006) *Young People Leaving Care: A Study of Outcomes and Costs. Final Report to the Department for Education and Skills.* York: Social Work Research and Development Unit, University of York.

Farmer, E. and Moyers, S. (2008) *Kinship Care: Fostering Effective Family and Friends Placements (Quality Matters in Children's Services).* London: Jessica Kingsley Publishers.

Fostering Network (2007) *The Role of the State in Supporting Relatives Raising Children Who Cannot Live with their Parents.* London: Fostering Network.

Friedman, M., Garnett, L. and Pinnock, M. (2005) 'Dude, where are my outcomes? Partnership working and outcome-based accountability in the United Kingdom.' In: J. Scott and H. Ward (eds). *Safeguarding and Promoting the Well-Being of Children, Families and Communities.* London: Jessica Kingsley Publishers.

Gatehouse, M., Statham, J. and Ward, H. (2004) *The Knowledge: How to get the information you need out of your computer and information systems. A practical guide for children's social services.* London: Thomas Coram Research Unit, Institute of Education, University of London.

Gatehouse, M. and Ward, H. (2003) *Information and Information Systems for Looked After Children: Final Report to the National Assembly for Wales on the Data Analysis Network.* Loughborough: Centre for Child and Family Research, Loughborough University.

Gatehouse, M., Ward, H. and Holmes, L. (2008) *Developing Definitions of Local Authority Services and Guidance for the new Children in Need Census Report to the Department for Children, Schools and Families.* Loughborough: Centre for Child and Family Research, Loughborough University.

Gordon, D., Parker, R. and Loughran, F. (2000) *Disabled Children in Britain: A Re-analysis of the OPCS Disability Surveys.* London: Stationery Office.

Grimshaw, R. and Sinclair, R. (1997) *Planning to Care: Regulation, Procedure and Practice under the Children Act 1989.* London: National Children's Bureau.

Heptinstall, E. (2000) 'Gaining access to looked after children for research purposes: Lessons learned.' *British Journal of Social Work 30,* 6, 867–72.

Hicks, L., Gibbs, I., Byford, S. and Weatherly, H. (2007) *Managing Children's Homes: Developing Effective Leadership in Small Organisations.* London: Jessica Kingsley Publishers.

Holmes, L., Beecham, J. and Ward, H. (in press) 'Measuring social work: Time and costs.' *Child and Family Social Work.*

Holmes, L., Lam, S.C., Ward, H. and Simpson, M. (forthcoming) *Special Educational Needs Processes: Their Costs and Variations.* Loughborough: Centre for Child and Family Research, Loughborough University.

Holmes, L., Westlake, D. and Ward, H. (forthcoming a) *The Costs of Multi-Dimensional Treatment Foster Care: Report to the Department of Children, Schools and Families.* Loughborough: Centre for Child and Family Research, Loughborough University.

Holmes, L., Westlake, D. and Ward, H. (forthcoming b) *Variations in the Costs of Adoption: A Study of Practice in Four Local Authorities.* Loughborough: Centre for Child and Family Research, Loughborough University.

Jackson, S. (ed.) (2001) *Nobody Ever Told Us School Mattered: Raising the Educational Attainments of Children in Care.* London: BAAF.

Jackson, S. and Thomas, N. (1999) *On the Move Again? What Works in Creating Stability for Looked After Children.* Essex: Barnardo's.

Knapp, M. (1984) *Children in Care: Planning Without Costs.* York: Nuffield Provincial Hospital Trust.

Kufeldt, K. and Stein, M. (2005) 'The voice of young people: Reflections on the care experience and the process of leaving care.' In: J. Scott and H. Ward (eds). *Safeguarding and Promoting the Wellbeing of Children, Families and Communities.* London: Jessica Kingsley Publishers.

Liddle, M. (1998) *Wasted Lives: Counting the Costs of Juvenile Offending.* London: NACRO.

Little, M. and Gibbons, J. (1993) 'Predicting the rate of children on the child protection register.' *Research, Policy and Planning 10,* 15–18.

Local Government Data Unit – Wales (2003) *Child Personal Social Service Indicators 2001–02.* Local Government Data Unit – Wales. Accessed 05/06/08 at www.dataunitwales.gov.uk/Documents/Publications/lgd01000_Stats_Wales_2001_02_bi.pdf

McCann, J., James, A., Wilson, S. and Dunn, G. (1996) 'Prevalence of psychiatric disorders in young people in the care system.' *British Medical Journal 313,* 1529–30.

McCrone, P., Weeramanthri, T., Knapp, M., Rushton, A., Trowell, T., Miles, G. and Kolvin, I. (2005) 'Cost effectiveness of individual versus group psychotherapy for sexually abused girls.' *Child and Adolescent Mental Health 10,* 1, 26–31.

Meltzer, H., Gatward, R., Corbin, T., Goodman, R. and Ford, T. (2003) *The Mental Health of Young People Looked After by Local Authorities in England.* London: TSO.

Millham, S., Bullock, R., Hosie, K. and Haak, M. (1986) *Lost in Care: The Problems of Maintaining Links Between Children in Care and their Families.* Aldershot: Gower.

Morris, J. (1995) *Gone Missing? A Research and Policy Review of Disabled Children Living Away from their Families.* London: The Who Cares? Trust.

Morris, J., Abbott, D. and Ward, L. (2002) 'At home or away? An exploration of policy and practice in the placement of disabled children at residential schools.' *Children and Society 16,* 3–16.

Munro, E.R., Holmes, L. and Ward, H. (2005) 'Researching vulnerable groups: ethical issues and the effective conduct of research in local authorities.' *British Journal of Social Work 35,* 1023–38.

National Assembly for Wales (2002) *Social Service Statistics for Wales.* National Assembly for Wales. Accessed 01.08.2007 at www.wales.gov.uk/topics/statistics/publications/publication-archive/ssw2002/?lang=en

Netten, A. and Curtis, L. (2002) *Unit Costs of Health and Social Care 2002.* Kent: Personal Social Services Research Unit, University of Kent.

Office for National Statistics (2003) *Census 2001: Key Statistics for Local Authorities in England and Wales.* London: The Stationery Office.

Packman, J. and Hall, C. (1998) *From Care to Accommodation: Support, Protection and Control in Child Care Services.* London: The Stationery Office.

Parsons, C. and Castle, F. (1998) 'The cost of social exclusion in England.' *International Journal of Inclusive Education 2,* 4, 277–94.

Phillips, R. (1998) 'Disabled children in permanent substitute families.' In: C. Robinson and K. Stalker (eds). *Growing Up with Disability*. London: Jessica Kingsley Publishers.

Pinnock, M. and Garnett, L. (2002) 'Needs-led or needs must? The use of needs-based information in planning children's services.' In: H. Ward and W. Rose (eds). *Approaches to Needs Assessment in Children's Services*. London: Jessica Kingsley Publishers.

Poirier, M-A, Chamberland, C. and Ward, H. (2006) 'Les interactions entre les adultes qui prennent soins d'un enfant placé en famille d'accueil: une étude sur les pratiques quotidiennes de collaboration.' *La Revue Internationale de l'Education Familiale: Recherches et Interventions 20*, 51–86.

Quinton, D. and Murray, C. (2002) 'Assessing emotional and behavioural development in children looked after away from home.' In: H. Ward and W. Rose (eds). *Approaches to Needs Assessment in Children's Services*. London: Jessica Kingsley Publishers.

R (on the application of L and others) v. Manchester City Council; R (on the application of R and another) v. Same [2001] EWHC Admin 707, CO/3954/2000, CO/965/2001.

Robinson, C., Weston, C. and Minkes, J. (1995) *Making Progress: Change and Development in Services to Disabled Children under the Children Act 1989*. Bristol: Norah Fry Research Centre, University of Bristol.

Scott, S., Knapp, M., Henderson, J. and Maughan, B. (2001) 'Financial cost of social exclusion: Follow up study of antisocial children into adulthood.' *British Medical Journal 323*, 191–6.

Sellick, C. (2006) 'Opportunities and risks: Models of good practice in commissioning foster care.' *British Journal of Social Work 36*, 8, 1345–59.

Sellick, C. and Connolly, J. (2002) 'Independent fostering agencies uncovered: The findings of a national study.' *Child and Family Social Work 7*, 2, 107–20.

Sellick, C. and Howell, D. (2004) 'A description and analysis of multi-sectorial fostering practice in the UK.' *British Journal of Social Work 34*, 481–99.

Selwyn, J., Sturgess, W., Quinton, D. and Baxter, C. (2006) *Costs and Outcomes of Non-Infant Adoptions*. London: BAAF.

Sempik, J., Ward, H. and Darker, I. (2008) 'Emotional and behavioural difficulties of children and young people at entry into care.' *Clinical Child Psychology and Psychiatry 13*, 2, 221–233.

Sergeant, H. (2006) *Handle with Care*. London: Centre for Policy Studies.

Shaw, C. (1998) *Remember My Messages: The Experiences and Views of 2000 Children in Public Care in the UK*. London: The Who Cares? Trust.

Sinclair, I., Baker, C., Wilson, K. and Gibbs, I. (2003) *Foster Children: Where They Go and How They Get On*. London: Jessica Kingsley Publishers.

Sinclair, I. and Gibbs, I. (1998) *Children's Homes: A Study in Diversity*. Chichester: Wiley.

Sinclair, I., Wilson, K. and Gibbs, I. (2001) 'A life more ordinary: What children want from foster placements.' *Adoption and Fostering 25*, 4, 17–26.

Sinclair, R. (1984) *Decision Making in Statutory Reviews on Children in Care*. Aldershot: Gower.

Skuse, T., Macdonald, I. and Ward, H. (2001) *Looking After Children: Transforming Data into Management Information: Third Interim Report to the Department of Health*. Loughborough: Centre for Child and Family Research, Loughborough University.

Skuse, T. and Ward, H. (2003) *Outcomes for Looked After Children: Children's Views of Care and Accommodation. An interim draft report for the Department of Health*. Loughborough: Centre for Child and Family Research, Loughborough University.

Social and Health Care Workforce Group (2000) *Social Services Recruitment and Retention Survey 2000*. London: Social and Health Care Workforce Group.

Social Exclusion Unit (1998) *Report on Truancy and School Exclusion.* London: Social Exclusion Unit.

Social Exclusion Unit (2003) *A Better Education for Children in Care.* London: Social Exclusion Unit.

Soper, J. (2007) *Cost Calculator for Children Services, V6.0 Demonstration Version.* Loughborough: Centre for Child and Family Research. Available at www.ccfcs.org.uk.

Statham, J. (2000) *Outcomes and Effectiveness of Family Support Services: A Research Review.* London: Institute of Education, University of London.

Statham, J., Candappa, M., Simon, A. and Owen, C. (2002) *Trends in Care.* London: Institute of Education, University of London.

Stein, M. (2004) *What Works for Young People Leaving Care?* Barkingside: Barnardos.

Stein, M. and Munro, E.R. (eds). (2008) *Young People's Transitions from Care to Adulthood: International Research and Practice.* London: Jessica Kingsley Publishers.

Taussig, H. (2003) *Kinship Care.* Paper presented at IXth IPSCAN Regional European Conference on Child Abuse and Neglect, August 2003.

The Children Act 1989. London: HMSO.

The Information Centre for Health and Social Care (2007) *Personal Social Services Key Indicators Graphical System, Years 2000–1 to 2005–6; Detailed Unit Cost Indicators by Council 2005–2006.* London: ICS.

Utting, S.W. (1997) *People Like Us: The Report of the Review of the Safeguards for Children Living Away from Home.* London: The Stationery Office.

Ward, H. (2002) 'Current initiatives in the development of outcome-based evaluation of children's services in England and Wales.' In: A.N. Maluccio, C. Canali and T. Vecchiato (eds). *Outcome Based Evaluation in Child and Family Services: Cross-National Perspectives.* New York: Aldine de Gruyter.

Ward, H. (2004) 'Working with managers to improve services: Changes in the role of research in social care.' *Child and Family Social Work 9,* 1, 13–25.

Ward, H. (forthcoming a) *Separating Families: How the Origins of Current Child Welfare Policy and Practice can be Traced to the Nineteenth Century Child Rescue Movement.* London: Jessica Kingsley Publishers.

Ward, H. (forthcoming b) 'Who moves and why? Placement stability for looked after children.'

Ward, H., Holmes, L., Dyson, P. and McDermid, S. (2008) *The Costs and Outcomes of Child Welfare Interventions: Extending the Cost Calculator to include cost calculations for all children in need. Interim Report to the Department of Children, Schools and Families.* Loughborough: Centre for Child and Family Research, Loughborough University.

Ward, H., Holmes, L. and Soper, J. (2005) *CCFR Cost Calculator for Children's Services: The Pilot Phase. Report to Department for Education and Skills.* Loughborough: Centre for Child and Family Research, Loughborough University.

Ward, H., Jones, H., Lynch, M. and Skuse, T. (2002) 'Issues concerning the health of looked after children.' *Adoption and Fostering 26,* 4, 8–18.

Ward, H., Munro, E.R. and Dearden, C. (2006) *Babies and Young Children in Care: Life Pathways, Decision-making and Practice.* London: Jessica Kingsley Publishers.

Ward, H. and Wynn, A. (forthcoming) *Clusters of Need in Children Entering Care.* Loughborough: Centre for Child and Family Research, Loughborough University.

Waterhouse, R. (2000) *Lost in Care: Report of the Tribunal of Inquiry into the Abuse of Children in Care in the Former County Council Areas of Gwynedd and Clwyd since 1974.* London: The Stationery Office.

Subject Index

Author Index